The Color of Freedom

Laura Coppo

Edited with an Introduction and Notes by
David H. Albert

Common Courage Press Monroe, Maine

Cover design by Erica Bjerning

ISBN 1-56751-276-3 paper
ISBN 1-56751-277-1 cloth

Library of Congress Cataloging-in-Publication Data is available on request from the publisher

Common Courage Press
121 Red Barn Road
Monroe, ME 04951
800-497-3207

FAX (207) 525-3068
orders-info@commoncouragepress.com

See our website for e versions of this book.
www.commoncouragepress.com

Printed in Canada
First Printing

All royalties from the sale of this book go to further the work of Land for the Tillers' Freedom (LAFTI) in Tamil Nadu, India (See Chapter 7: Towards Village Republics).

Arut Perum Jothi
Thani Perum Karunai
Arut Perum Jothi

Boundless benevolent shining light

God in-dwelling in that shining light

The light of compassion coming to rule the world.

Tamil Prayer by Sri Ramalinga Swami (aka Vallalar)

Contents

Acknowledgments

A special thanks goes to Elena Camino and Nanni Salio for believing in me and encouraging me to undertake this project, Bhoomikumar Jagannathan for his support, help, valuable suggestions, and precious personal contributions this book. David Albert, for flying all the way to Italy to help translate the book, and making the American edition possible, and Dr. Vandana Shiva, for writing a foreword to this edition (sometimes dreams come true!).

In India, of course many thanks to Jagannathan and Krishnammal for all the time, care, and attention they gave to me. Thanks to all my friends in the Gandhigram and Kuthur *ashrams*: in particular to Vallarmati for her constant help, Karti for the daily coconut milk, Muttikumar for driving me from place to place, the Kuthur cooks for their delicious food and to all the children of the *ashrams* for their smiles. Thanks to Veerasami's wife for the best fish I have ever eaten.

Thanks to K. M. Natarajan of *Gram Swaraj Movement*, to M. Mariappan, to Lila, A. R. Chandran ,and C. Veerasamy from LAFTI, to Rajendra Nattar, M. K. Arumugam, Subramanya, Mr and Mrs Vijayakumar, Armanikam and the lawyer Natarajan for their contributions and the time they dedicated to me—may you always have the strength to continue your extraordinary work.

Thanks to dearest Sathya for treating me like a sister and for being such a source of inspiration. Also thanks to Satish Kumar for his input for the book and for the inspiration he has provided in my life.

Finally thanks to Adam for his love and never-ending patience, and to Maya and Jasmin for being so full of light.

To the memory of George Thozhuthumkavayalil Dharmarama

—Laura Coppo

And my thanks to Laura Coppo for allowing me the privilege of assisting on a project I have dreamt about for almost 25 years, and to Greg Bates at Common Courage Press for believing in it enough to make it see the light of day.

—David H. Albert

A Note from the Gandhian Foundation

The Gandhian Foundation, established in the late 1960s to encourage and support projects in nonviolent action, is proud to provide fiscal sponsorship to enable this book to be written and published. I believe it is an important contribution to the growing library of books detailing the lives and struggle of pioneers in non-violent social change.

The Color of Freedom is the story of two good people of India, one born an "untouchable", the other of the higher castes, both turned Gandhian. This book opens a door into an India seldom entered by the hurried traveler from the West.

Together, Krishnammal and Jagannathan have sought to further the Gandhian vision of a village-based new India. They have walked miles and miles across the subcontinent, begging for land for the landless from the rich landlords, and even persuading some of them to sell it to them. They have often prevailed upon government banking institutions to provide low-cost loans to the new peasant owners. But as they do so, they have continued to urge and assist the untouchables to take control of their lives. They have helped build their own homes. In recent years they have mounted a serious challenge to multinational corporations invading India and appropriating large areas of coastal farmland for industrial prawn fisheries, depriving the villagers of land and the means of earning a living.

I first met Krishnammal and Jagannathan 40 years ago, and on several return trips have walked with them and shared their food, and supported their calling. Patiently, cheerfully, and with open hearts they continue their work. They are the salt of the earth. I invite you to taste this salt.

George Willoughby, Secretary
The Gandhian Foundation
Deptford, New Jersey

A Tribute to the Jagannathans

Over the past decade, I have had many occasions to serve S. Jagannathan and his wife Krishnammal in their struggles for justice, sustainability, and real democracy. I first worked with them when they commenced their *satyagraha* ("truth force" or "truth grasping", Gandhi's form of active nonviolent action) against industrial shrimp farming on the coast of Tamil Nadu. In fact, if it were not for their direct actions, India and the world would not know that the tiger prawn that arrives on our dinner plate has a footprint of acute ecological violence and social devastation behind it. The Jagannathans had filed public interest litigation in the Indian Supreme Court to halt the destruction caused by industrial aquaculture. Their lawyer asked me to help with the evidence and arguments. So I went down to visit Tamil Nadu and Andhra Pradesh and Orissa, and see things with my own eyes. What I witnessed was unbelievable—agriculture and fisheries destroyed by an industry that used 15 times more fish as feed than it produced, an industry that left ten dollars of destruction in the local economy and ecosystem for every dollar of profits for the shrimp trade, an industry that wiped out 200 acres of mangroves and coastal ecosystems for every acre of a shrimp farm.

But the violence was not just ecological—it was also political. Jagannathanji was ruthlessly assaulted again and again during his nonviolent struggles. People's huts were burnt if they joined the protest. The shrimp industry had given rise to a prawn mafia that had no respect for law or human rights. In the midst of this violence, the Jagannathans continued their nonviolence struggle, which was recognized as just by the Supreme Court on December 11, 1995. The Government has tried to undo the court order through an Aquaculture Bill. But together we formed an alliance against industrial shrimp farming and have prevented the Bill from becoming law. In the coastal villages, the Jagannathans have continued to struggle as the prawn mafia subverts the court order through collusion with corrupt officials. Despite their advanced ages, the Jagannathan's tireless fight has been a constant inspiration for me. They carry a century of Gandhian thought and action in their lives. They are India's soul. They are the spirit of freedom for her dispossessed and disenfranchised.

In 2000 in Meerut, the place where in 1857 India's first freedom struggle was initiated, we invited Jagannathanji to launch a renewal of our freedom movement in the context of globalization. We pledged collectively to defend our freedoms and sovereignties on which our lives depend:

- Seed Sovereignty (Bija Swaraj)
- Land Sovereignty (Bhu Swaraj)
- Water Sovereignty (Jal Swaraj)
- Forest Sovereignty (Van Swaraj)
- Food Sovereignty (Anna Swaraj)

We are blessed that Amma and Appa have been our guides and inspiration to create a movement for real democracy, a living democracy, an earth democracy in which no being is excluded, crushed, or exterminated. Readers are blessed that the life story of this amazing Gandhian couple will reach them through *The Color of Freedom.*

—Dr. Vandana Shiva,
Research Foundation for Science,
Technology and Ecology,
Dehra Dun, India

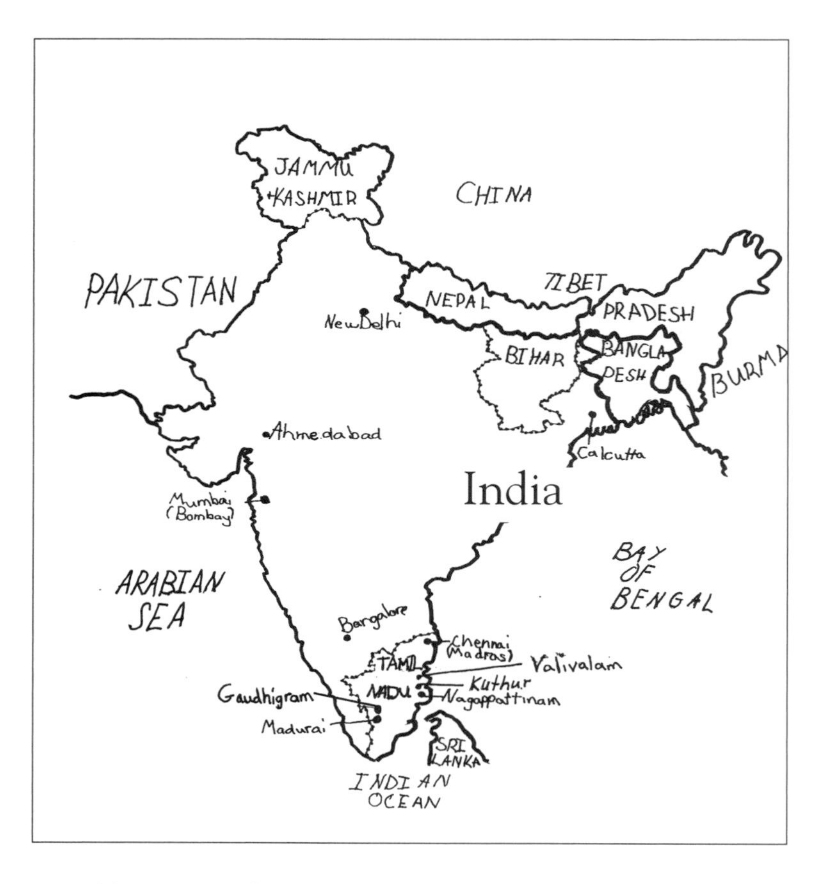

Map courtesy of Lauren McCann.

Introduction

David H. Albert

It is stifling, but not unusually so, in a courtroom that is always stiflingly hot. Around the defense side of the courtroom, there are 112 lawyers, all in suits. The suits were tailored in light, elegant tropical worsted wool in the finest tailoring establishments in New Delhi, Mumbai (Bombay), Chennai (Madras), Hong Kong, Singapore, Los Angeles, New York. Seated around and in back of them are their assistants, usually younger, with tailoring not quite so formidable. Most of the rest of the courtroom is filled with representatives of their employers—more than 100 Indian, other Asian, and multinational corporations—in suits of the more expensive variety, and observers from the state and national governments and, more than likely, the World Bank, which has much at stake here. The trial hearing before the Supreme Court of India will go on for 20 days, for six hours each day, from 10:30 in the morning until 4:30 in the afternoon. There will be many changes of suits, the combined value of which, taken together—and including the cost of the uncomfortable shoes and ties which accompany them—would likely feed the village of the petitioner for several years.

Among the hundreds of people in the courtroom, there are only four around the petitioner's table, including a relatively young lawyer plus his two legal assistants. The fourth, the petitioner, is there, an old man, seemingly taller than he actually is on account of a perfectly straight back and an almost aristocratic bearing. His face bears virtually no wrinkles other than some rather deep laugh lines around his mouth and his eyes, surprising perhaps, given that the petitioner can no longer count the number of times he has been imprisoned in his close-to-85 years. His limbs are strong and sinewy, betraying a former grace, but he moves more slowly now, as he suffers from a cataract in one eye, and glaucoma in both. He hears the proceedings with difficulty, as he has become deaf in one ear.

The petitioner may be the only comfortably dressed individual in the courtroom. He is not wearing a suit, but is dressed all in white. A *dhoti,* a piece of cloth one meter long and one-and-a-half meters wide, is slung around his waist. His lightweight short-sleeve shirt, open at the neck, hangs loosely from his shoulders. Both the dhoti and shirt are made from cotton thread the petitioner spun himself and gave to the village weaver, as he has every piece of clothing he was worn on his body—when not traveling in colder climes—for more than 50 years. On his feet are backless leather sandals, with wooden soles.

The petitioner is asking for something extraordinary. He is demanding the closure of virtually every intensive prawn[1] farming operation on the coast of southern India, and unspecified damages for the suffering they have caused. In doing so, he is essentially asking for an indictment of the United Nations Food and Agriculture Organization, which recommended the projects; the World Bank that partially funded and promoted them; the Government of India that backed them; and the politicians and investors seeking a quick killing who got caught up in this latest 'development' craze. He is indicting the engines of multinational capitalism that have despoiled coastal lands from the Philippines to Ecuador, destroyed entire fisheries, and left millions of people without any means of earning a living. And he has indicted the consumers of Japan, Europe, and North America, who go into their supermarkets and purchase human misery, without any clue or interest really in what they are buying. He has a knack, by simply being who he is, of raising embarrassing question, the kinds most of us what would like to leave unasked, such as "What is the true cost of unbridled greed?"

The petitioner is engaged in a radical experiment with truth that has been, and will continue to be, his life, He has the strong beginnings of an answer to the questions he raises, whether there is someone listening or not. In the meantime, anyone who has followed the story of this old—or maybe not so old—man, and that of his wife, also knows that this is an unfair fight.

The suits will lose.

* * * * *

The challenge facing any biographer or oral historian is locating his or her subjects in time and space. In this particular case, the challenge of placing S. Jagannathan (the petitioner) and Krishnammal Jagannathan[2] (whom I, the author Laura Coppo, and probably several hundred thousand other people know affectionately as "Appa" and "Amma", "father" and "mother" in Tamil, their native language) is especially daunting. For anyone who confronts India at the beginning of the 21st Century, the first impression is of time and space that is almost totally fluid.

An image provided to me by an Indian friend I think encapsulates it best. There is an Indian nuclear power plant (one of 14), modeled, it is said, closely on the same Soviet design as the one that exploded in Chernobyl. It operates almost error-free, the result of the efforts of some of the brightest and best-trained (as well as best-dressed) nuclear scientists and engineers in the world. During the day, barefoot *chai wallahs* in khaki shorts and shirts and wearing security badges go from room to room, dispensing overly sweet tea through a rubber hose from large metal samovars strapped to their backs. Lunch is brought in on bicycles, carried in *tiffin pots* (an especially ingenious piece of engineering, consisting of three stainless steel bowls, form-fitting, stacked one on top of the other and held together by a metal brace that doubles as a handle) on bicycle handlebars and racks, thousands of them, without a single error being made by the bicycle transporters, wearing plastic sandals and towels around their heads, regarding who gets what. Mistakes would be cause for great consternation, as more than half the staff is *veg*.[3] All of a sudden, the monitors indicate a major incident is about to occur, and the sirens go off. But after hours of checking, no one can find anything wrong. Finally, workers, without any protective clothing—which would be too hot to wear in any case—are dispatched to enter the cooling vessel. They poke and prod at the reactor core with bamboo poles. It works! The gauges return to their normal settings. It seems that an unrestrained lizard was chewing through some of the gauge wires.[4]

The reality one confronts in thinking or writing about contemporary India is that virtually everything that can be said is true, but so is its opposite. It is a primarily rural country, but with some of the largest, most overcrowded, fastest-growing, and most polluted cities in the world. It is home to great poverty, as the shacks and shanties near the major railway stations attest, and also home to the world's largest middle class—with perhaps the largest agglomeration of TV satellite dishes to be found anywhere on the planet. Modern buses and automobiles vie for position on major motorways with wooden carts, affixed with massive rubber truck tires, and pulled by highly decorated camels, if not lumbering water buffaloes, large flocks of sheep and goats crossing the roads at irregular intervals, and contentedly chewing cows lying down elbows akimbo in the middle of the black-top and acting as natural speed controls. It is a land filled with temples, holy sites, pilgrims, and more than its share of religious fanatics, and the first democratically elected avowedly atheist (Tamil Nadu, 1948) and Communist (Kerala, 1957) governments in the world. It is by far the world's largest democracy, with some of the highest voter participation rates to be found anywhere, but with a single family ruling the country for most of its 50-year post-colonial history. It is self-sufficient in, and an exporter of, food grains, and has been for decades, but tens of millions of people are malnourished. It exports brainpower, trained at its best universities—it is hard to imagine either Silicon Valley or hospitals in American cities without Indian-trained professionals—but 600 million people are without clean drinking water. Major computer manufacturing facilities and international call centers grow up beside rice paddies; ten-year-olds rent out cell phones to illiterate villagers from within little straw huts especially constructed for that purpose. There is fertile land, and land that has been so covered with toxic chemicals leaching from rayon or chemical manufacturing plants—equipped with World Bank-financed effluent treatment devices—that even the crows disdain it (but people continue to live there.)[5] Internet cafes are located next to restaurants serving "Meals Ready" on banana leaves. *Sadhus* and sages and devotees with ten-inch needles passing through holes in both cheeks, untreated human waste flowing into holy rivers, auto rickshaws careening down overpasses, blue parrots sitting undisturbed in coconut palms, centuries-old music and dance forms competing, sometimes successfully, with the world's largest movie industry, sacred cows, beef rendering plants, and a booming frogs-legs exporting business—this is the testing ground for the new modernity, the natural (or not-so natural) and human landscape where our 77- and 90-year-old heroine and hero find themselves and call home.

* * * * *

If this description of present space-time is dizzying rather than orienting, the very longevity of our heroes' lives, and the changes they have witnessed, is almost as difficult to hold in mind. Jagannathan was born in what is now Tamil Nadu, India's southernmost state, in 1914, a year before Gandhi returned to India from South Africa. We think of Gandhi's association with the spinning wheel, but when he began his struggles for Indian independence, British dominance of the country was so complete—and so brutal—that he couldn't find a single working spinning wheel in the entire country. They had all been destroyed by the British to ensure a market for the English cloth-manufacturing industry. A vast land that had been completely self-sufficient in village-based cloth-making for centuries couldn't supply a single one of its residents with a pair of home-made underwear, even if he could afford to wear any. British rule marked for India a descent into a new medievalism, marked by the fueling of religious divisions that plague India to this day. Prior to British rule, there hadn't been a religious war in India for more than a thousand years. And so Jagannathan is born into a time when, as if in some primordial tale, his grandfather is killed by thieves, stuffed into a bag of salt, and pulled home by a team of bullocks that have never known another route.

The prime decades of struggle against British colonialism were also the formative years for our couple, and once having freed themselves from the shackles of family expectations, for them these were especially heady times. It was as if everything had become possible—freedom from British rule, yes, but also freedom from centuries of superstition, ignorance, discrimination, poverty. The omnipotence of youth, coupled with the attainment of independence from British rule without firing a shot, gave them and thousands like them the sense that absolutely anything was possible!

Nation-building was to begin at the bottom, not at the top, in the slums and villages, rather than in the capitals. Rooted in the example of Gandhi, but also in the long tradition of Indian and, specifically, Jain religious practice (from which Gandhi, though a Hindu, drew many of his principles and orientation[6]), the independence of the new nation was to be built upon the awakening and complete moral self-examination and scrupulousness of *new* and renewed men and women in the process of making and remaking themselves.

This nation-building, for Gandhi and, as we shall see, for our couple, was to draw upon many traditional Indian forms. First among these is the ashram, an intentional community where (at least in theory) people live and work together in harmony. Much in decline during the British years, the *ashram* was traditionally a place where a sage or scholar lived with his disciples to study the spiritual nature of being, to learn and share knowledge. Perhaps we in the west can best think of it as a cross between a medieval university and a religious retreat. But, as revivified by Gandhi, the *ashram* became a place where people could support themselves collectively by their own labor, take part in spiritual and religious practices, recollect themselves for social and political struggle, plot strategy, and ensure care for their children while they themselves engaged in other activities. They were, as the founder of *Resurgence* magazine Satish Kumar notes, "models of sustainable, convivial, frugal, ecological, self-reliant, and spiritual society."[7] The *ashram* provided a way for individuals to be *in* the world, but not *of* it. There is virtually no period during their adult lifetimes that Krishnammal and Jagannathan were not closely associated with *ashram* communities, often ones they physically built themselves.

A second traditional form, elevated to a high political art, was the *padayatra*, or consciousness-raising footmarch. Its greatest political manifestation during the pre-Independence period was of course Gandhi's Salt March of 1930. The British greatly miscalculated in allowing the Salt March to go forward because of their failure to appreciate the role of the *padayatra* in Indian life (as well as their lack of the understanding of its potential impact on newly emerging world media.) For millennia, Hindu, Jain, and Buddhist holy men and novitiates would walk from village to village with begging bowls, gathering under a tree or on a verandah in the mornings and evenings to share their wisdom, retelling the stories of the traditional Indian epics the *Ramayana* and *Mahabharata*, and dispensing advice to the common folk on all aspects of village life. The *padayatra* also served as the main conduit by which the various religious sects communicated with their followers, and recruited to fill the ranks of their religious orders. Finally, the *padayatra* was one of the key methods by which a mendicant reinforces his or her commitment to non-attachment. When Krishnammal and Jagannathan engage in a *padayatra*, as they have done on scores of occasions, it would be a mistake to understand it as amounting to little more than a protest march, for it is understood by all to be so much more.

With Independence came both optimism, and a reality check. The country was now free, and the politicians took their homespun and Gandhi caps into government, but, for the vast majority of the population, little had changed, except there was no foreign ruler to blame. The traditional mal-distribution of land, later to be exacerbated by the U.S.-backed so-called 'Green Revolution', left hundreds of millions of people on the brink of starvation, open to political exploitation, but also to the quite sincere efforts of those who looked to the Maoist revolution in China as a model.

Into this breach stepped Vinoba Bhave and the *Bhoodan* (land-gift) and *Gramdan* (village-gift) movements of the 1950s and 1960s. Looking back at a global century of hate, war, and mass destruction on a scale unparalleled at any other time in human history (and, hopefully, never to be witnessed again), it seems difficult to believe that such movements ever happened, and our hero and heroine still look back upon this period of their lives with very real astonishment. Over the course of a decade, a small band of Gandhian adherents fanned out over the country, and, in a kind of religious enthusiasm, collected four million acres of land for redistribution to the poorest of the poor. They had gone forth without a plan, other than walking, and, in places where their work was consolidated, brought forth changes in both village economic and social structures that were astounding.

Here again, we see the use of traditional forms being used for revolutionary purposes, in this case, 'begging'. Only it was not begging as we know it in the West. The followers of traditional monastic sects for centuries had gone about with their begging bowls, but there were rules to be strictly observed. One goes where the doors are open, not closed. One accepts gifts only from those who give happily. The food to be accepted should not be specially prepared, but come out of that which is prepared for the family. And one is to fill one's bowls from many places, never accepting more than a single person is able to be without.

Vinoba's movement, in which Krishnammal and Jagannathan were intimately involved, built on these long-standing traditions. The idea was not to alienate the landlord from his gift of land, but to bring him into the larger embrace of the village community. The movement depended first and foremost upon a transformation of the heart, a harnessing of the 'divine spark', so that the poor would simply be seen as members of the same extended family, as the Hindu proverbial sixth son with whom one's belongings had to be shared. And often, much more often than the western rational mind would have cause to expect, it worked!

The *Bhoodan* movement was at once short-sighted and yet ahead of its time. It was forward-thinking in its notion of government as a mediator of interests and enforcer of social consensus, rather than as a leading institution of change. In the newly independent India of the 1950s, in the heady development of Five-Year Plans, and the proclamation of a new force of active neutrality in world affairs by Jawarharlal Nehru, this was a quite startling idea. As Vinoba was to say when he first heard the plea for land, "I have no land in my pockets, and I can't bring land from Delhi." The community itself, rather than the national government, had to be the locus of social and economic transformation, an understanding that was to stay with Krishnammal and Jagannathan throughout the rest of their lives.

However, the shortcomings of *Bhoodan-Gramdan* are just as apparent. While it was remarkably successful in organizing landlords to give of their lands, it was on the whole much less successful in organizing and empowering the poor in such a way as to make good use of it. This should not be seen as surprising. Virtually all of the followers of Vinoba—Krishnammal Jagannathan being a very notable exception, and with implications that will be discussed later—came from the upper castes, and were perhaps often more comfortable visiting with the wealthy and simply preaching to the poor as they walked on, rather than digging deep roots into the communities. Maybe even more salient, and with Jagannathan as a critical exception, the *Bhoodan* adherents neglected one of the key psychological lessons of the Independence movement itself: namely, that their own self-confidence was a result of personal transformations and empowerment which occurred for them as individuals as a result of the struggle itself. This route for the building of personal and political self-esteem, of new men and women—a crucial element in the entire lifetime of struggles waged by our hero and heroine—was almost entirely absent among the recipients of the land-gifts. This was only partially offset in the communal experiments of *Gramdan* that succeeded the land-gift phase, (Tamil Nadu being again a key exception).

Virtually unique among the post-Independence Gandhians, Krishnammal and Jagannathan continued the use of *satyagraha* through the 1960s. But they too might have veered off into confining themselves to the constructive program or Gandhian institution-building if it was not for an event that was to utterly transform their lives.

Krishnammal recollects her own dark forebodings, even as the event was transpiring: "On Christmas night in 1968, I was sitting by myself in Gandhigram. The moon was shining high in the sky. I could not sleep, and I kept on thinking about how humanity seems not to have understood the importance of Christ and his teachings." That night, though as yet unknown to her, 44 women, children, and infants were being murdered by landlords and their henchmen in the village of Kilvenmani, the scene of a labor struggle, some 200 kilometers from where Krishnammal and Jaganathan lived, a place where they had never been and knew no one, and which would transform what little remained of something bordering on a normal home life for the rest of their lives. Forty-three of them were burned alive; the forty-fourth—a newborn—was stabbed through the heart and was found pinioned to a tree by the knifeblade.

For Krishnammal, perhaps, this new phase was peculiarly one in which she was to take the lead. It was "a call from God", she recalls, and although Jaganathan disapproved, his absence allowed her to move her (and, eventually, his) entire base of operations. To this day, Krishnammal says she remains committed to her struggles by the reality that the souls of these murdered women and children now live inside her.

Those burned alive were *dalits*—variously called "untouchables", "*harijans*" ("children of God", a term coined by Gandhi, but now thought by many to be patronizing), pariahs. It is easy for an outsider to forget, or to not even notice, that India today is as divided by something akin to race as the United States would have been prior to 1950,and with roots even deeper. When westerners learn about India, they are almost always taught about the caste system, consisting of the *brahmin* or priestly caste, a warrior caste, a merchant caste, and a laboring class, conceived of in classical Hindu thought as the head, arms, torso, and feet of the body politic. What we are not taught is that the largest group of people has no caste at all, but are simply the mud upon which the other four castes heavily trod. When one speaks of the lack of safe drinking water, or electricity, or sanitation, or primary school enrollment, or illiteracy, or hunger and malnutrition, or lack of access to justice in India, one is primarily addressing the conditions of the more than 200 million *dalits*, the backbone of the nation's unskilled workforce and, especially, its agrarian economy.

Krishnammal, herself born into a *dalit* family, and of whose hardships she speaks so eloquently in the text, illustrated this to me personally in 1990. She took me to a celebration in a village not far from Kilvenmani, where land had just been purchased from a landlord and distributed to the landless. She told of purchasing the land at a fair price, but insisting that the landlord throw in all the improvements to the land and, especially, his house, as part of the sale. That day, the formerly landless were taking possession of the house and turning it into a community center. What I never would have learned from a newspaper account of this event was the symbolic nature of the changeover. For centuries, the *dalits* had never been allowed even to walk on the road in front of this house, and the mere touch of a *dalit's* shadow on the walls and fences surrounding the house compound could result in his being killed. In this context, the celebration that took place on that day was somewhat akin to what the Israelites might have felt if they had been redeemed from Egypt, and then given the palace!

By the time Krishnammal moved to Thanjavur (now Nagai-e-Millath) District in 1969, sides were already chosen up. The landless were to find no other real allies. There were to be no appeals to the landlords' magnanimity, no direct building of community across caste divides. The landless *dalits* were to learn to rely on their own resources, aroused to action by one of their own—and a woman yet!—and their capacity to provoke the government into action on their behalf.

It was an historically important moment, too, though one of which Krishnammal and Jagannathan were probably only dimly aware at the time. Soon, the new dams erected well upriver from the Cauvery Delta were to irrigate much of the arid lands of Tamil Nadu and Karnataka, the neighboring state to the north, but were to leave this traditional granary of Tamil Nadu with less water for intensive agriculture. The land was now well-suited for subsistence farming (though heavily affected by cycles of flood and drought). At the same time, it was less fit for the continuing but less than liquid investment of the upper castes, whose sons and daughters were increasingly making their way to European and American shores (and many of whom became extraordinarily wealthy in the emerging computer-related industries.) Being tied to the land was no longer so desirable for the newly mobile rich.

Having watched as the Communists and others organized the landless laborers for better wages through strikes and other forms of work stoppages, Krishnammal became more keenly aware of a reality that Gandhi himself had recognized, but that the government-run

Krishnammal Jagannathan at Thanjavur Temple after receiving land for 550 families, December 1990. Child is the editor's daughter Aliyah Meena Shanti.

banks were yet to acknowledge: the power of pooled labor could represent capital itself. Once Krishnammal was able to convince the government of this truth, she was able to use this power to leverage the purchase of the land. Through her vision and an opportunistic practicality, Krishnammal saw a simple unvarnished truth: purchasing land at a fair price provided both landlords and landless what each desired. Once the landless *dalits* could be organized for struggle, something that had been wholly foreign to them, it was only a small step to organize them to own the land they had already been working for centuries. Through a combination of nonviolent struggle and shrewd financing, almost 11,000 formerly landless families now, it seemed, held the keys to their own futures for the first time. The shadowy outlines of Gandhi's self-reliant, self-sufficient village republics, the *Gram Swaraj* to which Krishnammal and Jagannathan had devoted their entire lives, would slowly begin to come into focus.

If our tale was allowed to have a fairytale ending, our story outline should have ended here, with the sprouting up of schools and nurseries, house-building projects[8], orphanages and children's hostels[9], women's self-help associations, farm implement cooperatives and agricultural experiments, small industrial workshops, new cultural flowerings, and campaigns against alcoholism and other social ills besetting the community. I have perfectly etched in my mind a 1990 picture of Krishnammal (I have a photograph, too!), lying stretched out on the masonry in front of an ancient stone bull at the great Thanjavur Temple—the same temple that would have prohibited even the approaching footfall of her mother—smiling, and looking totally relaxed, something between a cat sunning itself and a recumbent queen, having just signed papers that would result in 550 new families receiving title to their own land. And I have a second picture, taken two weeks earlier, of a similarly relaxed and

S. Jagannathan, with the editor's daughter, in Madras City Jail, December 1990.

smiling Jagannathan holding my older daughter (then age 3, and this being their first meeting) in the Madras City Jail, where he was imprisoned—as he often was—for leading protests against the state government's 'cheap liquor' policies.

History would deal them a different hand. In late 1992, Krishnammal and Jagannathan set out on a year-long *padayatra* to promote *Gram Swaraj* and to organize village assemblies. It should have resembled a valedictory tour, and likely did, until they reached an area where they found people in an absolutely desperate situation. "Our land has been taken, our water polluted, and the fish are dying," was their cry. As quickly as some of the wealthier landholders had gone to the West, so prawn farms, backed by multinational corporations, with World Bank loans, and government blessing, had moved into the breach. Large tracts of fertile land that had been traditionally cultivated for centuries were taken out of agriculture. Mangroves guarding the coastal areas from cyclones and tidal overflows were ruthlessly cut down. Land was salinated, and massive amounts of chemicals used, quickly reaching down into the water table, and destroying supplies of drinking water. Polluted water was discharged into the sea, decimating entire fisheries. All to provide luxury items for western tables.

It is the same story elsewhere, a new form of 'slash-and-burn' agriculture, though 'slash-and-flood' would be more accurate. It has destroyed entire coastlines in the Philippines and Ecuador, Thailand and Indonesia, and unleashed an epidemic of skin and eye diseases in its wake. It was a way, according to the United Nations Food and Agriculture Organization, to create job opportunities in depressed Third World areas, and to 'support people with a vitamin-enriched diet'. Except that where the land used to support 120 agricultural workers, it now supports two prawn farm managers, and only until the tanks give out, and the companies move on. It was supposed to improve the nutritional status of communities, but, as our author notes, not a single prawn has ever appeared on the table of the local people, although the price of prawns in American supermarkets has dropped from over $14/lb. in 1986 to under $5/lb. (adjusted for inflation) in 2003. (For a fuller account of global intensive prawn farming industry and its consequences, see

Appendix B: Prawns—An Unnatural History).

And so we have the continuing tale of our two aging heroes, who wanted only to supply a measure of rice, a house with a roof that doesn't leak, and a measure of self-esteem and self-worth to people who had known little but centuries of degradation, but now find themselves fighting the combined forces of multinational capitalism and the global marketplace. The odds are very long. Jagannathan is now about to turn 90 and has already, quite literally as you will read in this book, sacrificed his eyes in this titanic struggle.

* * * * *

Having done my best to place Amma and Appa in their social and historical context, I am acutely aware of how far away I am from having captured their essence. Social history is only the backdrop in front of which Krishnammal and Jagannathan have played out their lives.

It is closer to the truth to say that to know them is to experience the power of living myths. At first examination, Jagannathan evokes the pathos of a Don Quixote, jousting impossibly with windmills. Only he is much more hard-headed that Quixote, and he knows keenly that the windmills he battles against are all-too-real, even if others are not as quick to recognize them for what they are. He wins at least his share of the skirmishes and is now embarked upon a colossal struggle, which will likely consume the rest of his life. Krishnammal is, to cite a 1999 award given her by the Women's World Summit Foundation, India's Joan of Arc. They live in time, and yet out of it at the same moment. We are fortunate that the tool of oral history is perhaps the best way to get at the human qualities behind those who have taken on mythic proportions, and to allow us at least a hint at what turns ordinary human beings into such extraordinary ones.

If our heroes were painters on a canvas, the first and primary color for the entire work would be the color of freedom. Somewhere along the line, both Amma and Appa attached themselves to the rather unusual notion that, having cast off all semblances of slavishness, they could be the authors of their own lives, and in doing so, spend their lives enabling others to give authorship to their own as well. They think nothing of moving to a village hundreds of miles from their home, where they have never been and where they know no one, because they have read in the newspaper that people have been killed, and they truly believe they can make a difference. They will transplant themselves thousands of miles away to another state, where their own native language isn't even spoken, and spend seven months sleeping literally in pigsties, and living on boiled potato leaves, in order to impede keepers of temples from treating people unfairly. They walk freely out of police vans to which they have been confined, and lie down in front of trucks and bulldozers. They wear clothing made only of thread they have spun themselves, and if they haven't had enough time to spin, their clothing will be threadbare. They go to prison and there demand the right to wash their clothes, and make it possible for everyone else to do so as well. They make new bank rules for bankers, adopt and take it upon themselves to feed, clothe, house, and educate several hundred children at a time, and find laws and their application where no one thought there were any. It is disorienting, but ultimately liberating. No one who has ever met Amma and Appa goes away unchanged.

The source of this freedom is not easily knowable, although it is possible to catch glimpses of it. It is certainly not the usual response to life of a woman who grows up in the poorest possible household, with 12 children born into it, and headed by an alcoholic and wife-beating husband who dies, leaving a widow to work both day and night to fend for them all. But even here there are hints, as Krishnammal's mother finds and feeds handicapped people even poorer than herself, and begins each day facing the rising sun with a prayer. Krishnammal begins to experience small acts of kindness from those with backgrounds far richer materially than her own, and her experience of her own mother demonstrates that acts of charity and kindness do not have to be reserved to the wealthy. Anyone who ever meets Amma cannot fail to notice that even when she does not have a rupee in her pocket, she acts and speaks as if she is rich in abundance, knowing that she will be provided for. To the question "how many children do you have?" a common response from Krishnammal will be, "How many are there?" She is a queen without a palace, an empress without a treasury, a pauper whose beneficence animates virtually everything she touches. She herself identifies with the Tamil saint in a traditional folktale, one Manimegalai, a daughter of a prostitute who withholds her chastity from the king, is surrounded by a protective ring of fire, and is finally given a magic vessel—the *achayapatra*—which at her request provides food for the hungry.

Indeed, it was from this abundance of feeling that I myself met Krishnammal for the first time. Following a conference in northern India in 1977, she invited me to follow her more than a thousand miles to the south to her home in Gandhigram, which I did. I stayed for a week. Every meal, three times a day, consisted of rice and *rasam*, a fiery hot pepper broth of which South Indians are fond. While I thought that this diet was rather odd, I ate it happily. It was what they were eating, and it was tasty. Little did I know then that the reason for this rather sparse diet was that Krishnammal and Jagannathan had nothing else to eat at the time, he having just been released from being imprisoned by Indira Gandhi for more than a year, and both of them trying to put their lives back together again. To this day, when I return to Gandhigram, those who remember make jokes about the strange American who subsisted on rice and *rasam* and didn't know the difference!

With Jagannathan, too, we catch but hints. His early home life was far, far different from hers, especially in that he was always well provided for. But we begin with the story of a 13-year-old, home from school, organizing the village boys to carry a large photograph of Gandhi from village to village, and who throws his English-manufactured shirt and pen—gifts of his father—into a *swadeshi* fire, part of a movement to consume only those goods produced in India itself. At 15, he is beaten within an inch of his life by policemen wielding iron-tipped batons. He is to be imprisoned, locked in solitary, given rotten food, and degraded, along with, it should be noted, thousands of his compatriots, the very flower of India's youth. Choosing paths that might lead to personal sacrifice in furthering a higher cause soon becomes second nature to him. It is what any human being should be *expected* to do when faced with the suffering of others. It is as natural as breathing itself.

This quintessentially radical fearlessness can almost not fail to make us feel uncomfortable. We are safer viewing them as Quixote and Joan, or as Rama and Sita—the fortitude-imbued hero and heroine of the Indian mythological epic the *Ramayana*—rather than as an expression of the same modernity we inhabit. For just as they have steeled themselves in fearlessness, we have allowed ourselves to be programmed for safety and security. We experience with Amma and Appa the urge to respond when we come face-to-face with suffering; it is part of the nature we share. But unlike them, we have learned that we are safest and most secure in ourselves when we are placed in a position that when it comes to suffering, we don't have to see or experience it. Out of sight, out of mind. Krishnammal and Jagannathan, in contrast, find it difficult to hear of suffering without first exploring, then wrestling with it for themselves, and finally putting their entire spirits behind ameliorating it.

One of the gifts of oral history, however, is that it cuts down the distance between us, so we can better understand our heroes' choices. Fear, for example, is not always absent. Having been beaten, imprisoned repeatedly, and starved, having walked the length and breadth of India without a rupee and meditated with *rishis* in the Himalayas, having overcome all the usual fears and about to abandon his new bride for almost two years without a second thought, at the age of 36 and having celebrated an extremely unconventional marriage, Jagannathan is afraid to go home for a day to meet his parents. Krishnammal, having adopted a revolutionary's lifestyle, is forced to address the question, "How does a revolutionary raise her children?" (For one child, the answer was to bring him along; for another, the answer was to place her in boarding schools!)

Something else that makes us uncomfortable is Amma and Appa having come to their feeling of abundance by owning virtually nothing. Jagannathan's marriage vows,

> "Do not expect any wealth or comforts from me. We shall have no property. Even the vessels we use at home shall be made of mud, so that when we move on, it shall be easy to abandon them,"

read like they are taken straight out of some lost Indian epic—a forgotten *Ramayana*—not something from the year 1950. It is only up close that one can see the freedom this has provided them. Their daughter Dr. Sathya Jeganathan notes that she cannot remember a time in her entire life when her parents weren't simply "camping". In 1981, my wife and I, living at the Worker's Home in Gandhigram, discovered when we decided to do a little of our own cooking, that Krishnammal and Jagannathan indeed did not own a single pot. Having purchased some ourselves, we gave them to Amma and Appa when we left. Returning in 1990, we saw the same pots waiting for us, lying virtually unused for nine years. And while educators, activists, and political leaders from around the world had come to visit Krishnammal and Jagannathan since the 1950s, it wasn't until 1998 that Amma and Appa had any chairs for guests to sit on, a gift from their daughter. Now relocated most of the time in Kuthur for more than a decade, Krishnammal and Jagannathan still do not have even a bed, no less a room, they can call their own. Having virtually nothing in the way of material possessions personally, they also have nothing material to defend. Liberated from the tyranny of things, they are total free agents, free to seek leverage points upon which they can move the world.

This lack of possessions and possessiveness is also bound up with a high degree of fastidiousness regarding those items—food and clothing—that are the basic requirements of their existence. Besides Jagannathan's spinning for his own clothing needs, Krishnammal has for decades lived in hand-me-down *sarees* provided by her daughter. I have seen Krishnammal keep a collection of used paperclips and safety pins in her bodice, ready to be called on for use whenever needed. This fastidiousness, however, is not clung to solely as a matter of personal purity, but rather as a reminder that the goods we consume come with their own human and environmental price tags. What if, as they seem to imply, every piece of food, every stitch of clothing, every paper clip and safety pin we purchased in the market came with pictures of the human and environmental costs affixed to each? Would we, to use Jagannathan's clothing choices as an example, choose to have our own brothers and sisters, sons and daughters chained to the floors of Third World sweatshops if we knew there really existed other options?

In short, Krishnammal and Jagannathan have made their challenge to the global marketplace a personal affair, as much a spiritual as a political matter, and, in so doing, suggest that we do the same. The ideal of *gram swaraj*—the village republic, self-governing, self-sufficient in all its basic necessities, existing on the basis of mutuality, of democracy unfettered by so-called "free trade"—offers both a critique and a naked challenge to the ubiquity of the market. It represents the one form of competition that the market itself cannot tolerate: namely, the notion that somewhere, someone and something could actually exist quite comfortably outside its boundaries. Perhaps, just perhaps, free human beings might choose as a goal to encompass larger spheres of conviviality, and reduce those in which human beings and the natural world are bought and sold. Amma and Appa demand of us that we challenge the very idea of progress itself, and dare to seek an itemized accounting for this so-called progress' fatalities, not only in human and environmental casualties, but in the deadening of the human spirit, including our own. In place of free trade and free markets, in place of tiger prawns on the dinner table or in the buffet line, Jagannathan and Krishnammal offer us a real, living 21st Century alternative idea of progress—the possibility and potentiality of free men and free women. It only remains for us to decide whether to take them up on it.

—A Note on the Text—

The text of the first 12 chapters of this book are based on taped interviews conducted by Laura Coppo in Tamil Nadu, India in October-November 1999. The interviews were conducted in English, but English is neither the native language of Jagannathan and Krishnammal (which is Tamil) nor of Ms. Coppo, who is Italian. The interviews were then translated into Italian, and formed the basis of the book *Terra Gamberi Contadini ed Eroi: 70 Anni di Lotte Nonviolente di Una Straordinaria Coppia di Indiani*

(Bologna, Italy: EMI della Coop. SERMIS, 2002). In January 2003, I worked face-to-face with Ms. Coppo in the small village of Aramengo in the Piedmont region of Italy to turn the text back into English of a more idiomatic variety. We have, however, striven to retain some of the linguistic mannerisms special to our subjects, (you will, for example, notice the use of the term "big landlord") and which often makes them so approachable and endearing.

The differences in the way Appa and Amma have chosen to relate the stories of their respective lives should come through as obvious. Jagannathan frames his life story in a highly linear fashion, as if he has told it dozens of times before. He is also given to little outbursts of sarcasm, and sees irony at every turn, and lets the reader know it. Conversations, having taken place decades earlier, come through as morality tales, almost miniature theatrical dramas, which determine or dictate the next phase of struggle or of work.

Krishnammal, in contrast, is a character who finds herself in parables, or almost in fairytales. Although barely conscious of that fact, she is one of the world's great storytellers. Having studied the lives of the Tamil saints in her childhood, and who undoubtedly played so great a role in the early formation of her character, she speaks of her life almost as if it is similarly out of time. There are bursts of emotion and of color, and simple, uncomplicated, and direct links between thought and action. There is scarcely a 'strategic' or even 'tactical' consideration. In the West, we might think of her way of being as embodying a fundamental faith: she is illuminated by her own inward Light which is available to all, she is led to where she needs to be, and, she has learned through experience that when every available avenue seems blocked, "the way will open".

One of the more amusing aspects of having both oral biographies told in tandem are the contradictions unearthed. Krishnammal and Jagannathan do not agree about either the date or circumstances under which they met each other. Jagannathan is clear that he met Krishnammal for the first time in 1941, at a training camp organized by him, and was immediately smitten. Without telling anyone of his future intentions, he went to her village and saw her house and her family. And, according to his version, he declared his intentions of marrying her before his second imprisonment, in 1944. His account is very detailed on this score, but speaks of the visit of Gandhi to Madurai in 1941, at which time Krishnammal helped care for the Mahatma. The trouble with this account is that Gandhi did not come to Madurai in 1941, but in 1946! Krishnammal, in contrast, relates the date of Gandhi's Madurai visit correctly (and she should know, since she was very much involved in it, and there is a photograph), but is sure she did not meet Jagannathan until 1945. This date is impossible, as Jagannathan was in prison in 1944 and 1945, and the training camp in Madurai predates his imprisonment. Future scholars may ponder. For our purposes, this is the stuff of which legends—or at least good family arguments—are made!

Amma and Appa

It is 5 o'clock in the morning of what will be a hot mid-September day when I get off the train at Madurai Station. As I am too sleepy to engage in the required negotiations with a rickshaw driver, I decide to walk to the bus station. The city is waking up, and is already animated by intense activity. People in front of the little kiosks sell *chai*—the sweet spiced tea. Others are arriving by bus from nearby villages with crates full of fruit and vegetables to sell at the corner of some crowded road. Women buy garlands of white jasmine interlaced with red roses or delicate orange flowers to take to the temple or to affix to their long, black hair. The sounds of percussion instruments attract my attention to a small procession. About twenty women are walking to the Meenakshi Temple, whose high and colorful *gopuram* towers, built in the 13th to 18th Centuries, are visible even from here. On their heads the women are balancing clay pots filled with long, tender-green, freshly sprouted seeds. Someone explains to me that they are likely from a nearby village, and are carrying out a ritual designed to ensure a successful harvest.

My destination is Gandhigram, 'Gandhi's Village', where the "Constructive Workers' Home" is situated. This is the first of several *ashrams* founded by Jagannathan and his coworkers. I cross the dusty bus station, looking for a telephone to call Krishnammal and tell her about my arrival. I'm excited that I am going to hear her voice for the first time, and that soon I will reach my destination.

After receiving her greetings and instructions, I enjoy a cup of chai and a *samosa* (a fried stuffed pastry) before starting to look for the correct bus. This last operation is for once not too complicated, and I get on a nearly empty bus. But, predictably, within ten minutes the bus is absolutely packed,

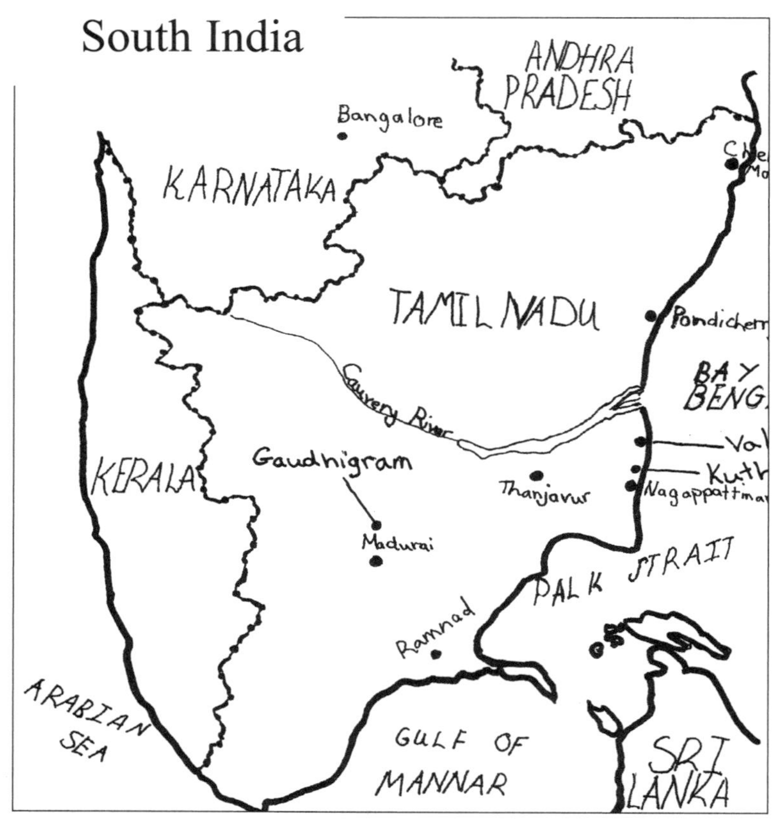

Map courtesy of Lauren McCann.

so much so that I have to acrobatically wedge myself into a corner, with my legs up in the air on top of my luggage. Being the only foreigner on board, I attract the curiosity and smiles of the other passengers, and I let everybody know where I am going, ensuring that someone will warn me when I reach my destination.

The driver takes his place on the rickety seat and performs a little private ceremony. He lights some incense, and places some flowers on the image of Lord Ganesh, the elephant-headed God of new beginnings and the remover of obstacles, whose blessings are needed at the beginning of a journey. Then he anoints himself on the forehead with red powder. He turns the cranky, old cassette recorder up to full volume, and starts what in my eyes is a mad, exciting suicidal race down a terrifying Indian motorway.

As is my habit, I decide not to look at the road—or at the obstacles that we meet along the way. Rather, I enjoy the view from the side window. I've never been to this part of Tamil Nadu (India's southernmost state), and I am enchanted by its beauty: paddy (rice) fields, coconut and banana trees; fields of flowers; tapioca and sugarcane plantations, vineyards; vegetable patches; and lush, green mountains in the background. At full speed, the bus passes villages consisting of a few houses, some made of brick with tiled roofs, most of them constructed with low mud walls, covered by traditional palm-leaf roofs. We drive past colorful temples, Catholic churches and graveyards, people working in the fields, bullock carts, children in uniforms on the way to school, squatting farmers waiting for the bus in unexpected corners, and more people, cows, sheep, and dogs sitting in the shade of huge banyan *(ficus religiosa)* trees. These are election days and the symbol of the Indian Communist Party, the most powerful party in this area, is painted on every wall, with an ear of wheat substituting for the traditional hammer.

After about an hour, the bus stops in front of several small buildings: two small village tailor shops, a barbershop, a tea shop. Suddenly, I am informed me that I have reached my destination, and I am convulsively disgorged from the overcrowded bus. In a jeep parked nearby, I see a hand waving and the smiling faces of some children. I meet Vallarmati, one of the youngest of Jagannathan and Krishnammal's workers, Karti, the driver who will take us up and down Tamil Nadu, and some of the children living in the hostel by the side of the Workers' Home.

We drive under an arch proclaiming "Gandhigram Rural Deemed University". Most of Gandhigram village is the university campus itself. The other buildings are a *khadi* shop—selling the traditional Gandhian handspun and hand-woven cloth, and other products of local village industries—a bank, a public phone, a chai shop, and some small brick homes. We drive along a dirt road flanked by primary and secondary schools. Then the jeep follows the road skirting the railway and turns in the direction of the mountains. After a few minutes, we reach the Workers' Home, Jagannathan and Krishnammal's headquarters, which I have seen so many times in videos and pictures. We stop next to a little house with a flat roof and a small verandah—the guest house, where a room is already prepared for me. Vallarmati opens the door and leaves me, saying: "*Amma* will be here in a minute". *Amma*, mother, is what everyone calls Krishnammal, just as Jagannathan is *Appa*, father. Soon I'll understand the reason for these terms of endearment.

The room is delightful in its simplicity. Everything I need is on the shelves. I find an ample supply of bottled water and a tray full of fruit. Before meeting Krishnammal, I want to wash away the dust and the tiredness of a long train journey, and with pleasure I pour a bucket of water over my head.

Krishnammal is sitting on the verandah steps. She is a little woman in her mid-seventies, with a wrinkled face and plaited gray hair. She is wearing a colorful khadi *saree* (the traditional Indian woman's dress made of a single wrapped piece of cloth), but, unusual for an Indian woman, no earrings or anklets, bangles or necklaces. The first thing that impresses me is the determination and the vitality I read in her eyes. I reach for her and she hugs me as if I were a daughter she has not seen for a long time. I feel immediately at home, and I am scolded for not calling immediately upon my arrival in India!

Krishnammal asks me about my trip and about some common friends, and speaks enthusiastically about my interview project. She explains to me how she had always wished to write about the people that played a fundamental role in her life; her mother; Vinoba Bhave, the saintly leader of the

Bhoodan (land-gift) movement; Jayaprakash Narayan (the shrewd former socialist leader turned Gandhian); and Jagannathan himself, but she could never find the time. "But now," she says "because you are here, I am on holiday, and I will find time to do all this." It is strange concept of holiday. In the following five weeks, I will see her running all the time, looking after her husband, after the hostel's children, the co-workers, the many visitors, the people coming from nearby villages asking for help. With a surprising energy she will work, plan, organize, take care, cook, scold, cuddle. She has the energy of a woman less than half her 70-plus years, or even less than that.

Krishnammal leaves, suggesting I rest for a while, and returns later, bringing my lunch. I am a bit embarrassed to eat on my own, whilst she waits for the opportunity to fit more food on my plate. But I will have to get used to it because that is her way: the guests eat first, served like kings and queens, and Krishnammal always eats last, when everybody else has been fed. "Cooking and feeding is my hobby," Amma declares, and there is no way to object to her extraordinary hospitality.

We plan to start the interviews today, and in the late afternoon I cross the field that divides the guesthouse from the Workers' Home. The Home is a large building with a wide, high red-tiled roof covering a pleasant open area with a cement floor. Two sides of it are partially closed by a low wall, and the other two contain three rooms each. Everything is painted in a pleasant sea-green that gives a feeling of freshness and cleanliness. I sit and wait: it is Sunday and some visitors have come to see Jagannathan, who is probably still resting. After a while Appa walks out of a room, and with surprise I realize he is almost blind. I knew about his eyes problems, but from the way he walks I get the impression that he can barely see at all.

Jagannathan is in his late eighties, with short, white hair, quite tall and thin. In the purest Gandhian tradition, he is wearing only a piece of *khadi* cloth around his hips and a pair of wooden sandals. He walks with difficulty, but his back is perfectly straight, making him appear taller than he actually is, and his skin has hardly any wrinkles. Like his wife, his expression is firm and determined, but when he smiles, his face reveals an infinite sweetness and a child-like playfulness.

Today he doesn't smile much. He looks very weak and tired, much more than I expected, and I wonder if I will ever manage to work with him, if he will feel up to telling me his story. I can't imagine that in a few days I will be trying to meet Krishnammal's eyes to let her know that I am exhausted after three hours of interviewing, while Jagannathan would seem ready to go on forever.

He has a reason to be tired. They have just concluded the latest act of the struggle that has kept them busy for the last ten years: a long campaign against intensive prawn farming that has been destroying the land, and with it the livelihood of the people, on the coast of Tamil Nadu. Jagannathan is slowly recovering from his "Prayerful Penance", 55 days spent on a regime of one meal a day, no breakfast or dinner. The objective of this penance was to obtain from the local politicians a commitment to apply a Supreme Court judgment that has ordered the immediate closure of all the aquaculture farms.

Krishnammal introduces the visitors to Jagannathan, a couple with two young daughters who touch Appa's feet, a sign of respect reserved in India to the elderly and to *gurus* (great teachers) The next guest is the Vice Chancellor of Gandhigram University, who spends some time in counsel with Appa. Last, I see a familiar face: K. M. Natarajan, one of the leaders of the *Sarvodaya Movement* whom I met the previous year in Italy, where he was one of the speakers at a conference on Gandhi. (Sarvodaya, meaning "welfare of all", is the name Gandhi gave to the constructive movement he created to work alongside the political struggle for independence. Among its many concerns are village-level development and the building of village-based industries, an end to the scourge of untouchability, the uplift of women, the protection of children, and prohibition.) After talking to everybody, Jagannathan is helped back to his room for further rest.

Finally, Krishnammal is free (or as free as she ever will be) and we walk back together to my room, where she thinks it will be easier to work without interruptions. It is getting dark. The black silhouettes of the trees contrast with the golden and orange colors of the sunset, and thousands of birds are singing their goodbye to this day. A pleasant breeze crosses the room, bringing along the smells of herbs and burning fires. Devotional music can be heard from a distant temple. Yes, I am not dreaming—this is definitely Mother India. A relaxed Krishnammal lies on the bed, her hand supporting her head, and starts. She wants to tell me about her childhood through the story of her mother, beginning what she considers to be a tribute to the people who left an indelible mark on her, directing her to a life of service to poor women.

Krishnammal: My mother

"I was born June, 26th, 1926 into a *harijan* family in the village of Ayyancottai, not far from here. My mother gave birth to 12 children. Only six of us survived. She was widowed at the age of 32. My father was a violent man given over to drink, and who beat her regularly. His behavior made me decide I would never marry.

At that time, the life of a widow was even harder than now. My mother would go to bed late at night and would routinely arise at three o'clock in the morning to join the group of women that went to collect green leaves in the forest. The leaves were the fertilizer for the fields of the biggest landlord in the area. The women had to walk seven miles to reach the hillside, and collect the leaves that they would then carry back in bundles on their heads another seven miles. They then would spread the leaves on the landlord's paddy fields. During the entire day they hardly had anything to eat, and in the evening they were dead tired. But at home the household duties were waiting for them. They collected water from the well, cleaned the house and utensils, and prepared the kitchen for the evening meal. Then they would gather at the house of the work leader to receive their pay. The leader was a very harsh and cruel woman. As I could read, I was put in charge of calling out the names of the women in turn to approach her next to receive their pay. It was a horrible and painful task for me. All the women waited anxiously for their turn to receive their meager wages, but the leader was very cunning and she would always find ways to criticize their work, and pay them less than their due. With great disappointment, they went straight to the local shop to buy something to cook. For those who were not widows, their drunkard husbands would be waiting for them at home, ready to complain and often to beat them. This was the way women spent their lives.

When the leader complained and insulted the women, I felt so upset. She offered me some coins for my job, but tears ran from my eyes. I felt helpless and my mind went in search of God's help.

The hardship for my mother wasn't over in the evening because she had to work through the night to clean the rice. I felt so sorry for her that I could not sleep, and I used to sit and observe her. She would beg me to sleep, but I couldn't. When it was time for her to leave the house to collect leaves, I used to sit and ponder over the hardships of life. Slowly, the desire to dedicate my life to the destitute women took shape in my heart. And God has miraculously answered my prayers, as I have spent my entire life with distressed women, working for their uplift.

I now look about it as surprising how a poor woman like my mother could realize her dream of bringing up her orphaned children better than the other women in the village, and gain the respect of the whole community. She was adventurous by nature, mentally and physically strong. She had many special qualities and she could play different roles on the same day: she was a loving mother, an excellent teacher for her children, a benevolent neighbor, a doctor that cured with traditional herbal medicines, and a very pious woman. Her favorite activity was to feed the hungry; she regularly fed a handicapped man who lived in our road. To avoid been seen, she used to hide the food in her *saree.*

I have inherited many virtues from her. I have learned to keep a positive attitude; to welcome everything that comes my way, whether good or bad, with open arms; to not reject anything but to endure patiently and surrender to God's will; to take things as they come, and go through them with faith in God.

Another thing I learned from my mother is that to remember God and our godly nature is to assure us a happy death, without suffering. At the time of her last breath, I was with her; she shook her head twice and then passed away, repeating God's name. What a happy end for my mother. I think that her hard life assured her a happy end. I am also grateful to her for taking care of my children when I was involved in our struggles.

My mother used to go out at dawn and stand before of the rising sun, singing the name of many gods and goddesses; she used to remain there for some time and then finish her prayer. I liked to stand behind her watching. The rising sun and the beautiful scenery were a pleasant sight for me: I felt that the whole of nature in its beauty was conversing and communicating with me. This ritual impressed me so much that it became my lifetime habit to sit outside in the early morning. While I am contemplating nature the whole plan of the day appears in my mind. Every day I plan my work with a prayer and feel there is a divine hand guiding all my activities. This is a moment for myself, to be on my own, merged in nature. I feel at one with the trees, the leaves, the birds and the mountains, the stars and the flowers, with the water in the tank.[1] This is the time when I am isolated from the rest of the world and I am perfectly at peace. Then, after planning my day, I am ready to go back inside."

Krishnammal is interrupted by Vallarmati, informing us that the children are ready for the evening prayer. The Workers' Home, like the several other ashrams created by Jagannathan and Krishnammal in the Kuthur area some 200 kilometers to the east, gives shelter to approximately 40 orphans and children coming from families that cannot care for their little ones—mothers who have lost their husbands or, more often, families with an alcoholic father.

Alcohol abuse is one of the most dramatic social

problems in the Indian countryside. Many men spend most of what they earn on alcohol, at the expense of women and children. Jagannathan and Krishnammal have been leading a long campaign against the government's policy of cheap alcohol, organizing rallies and protests to promote prohibition. In spite of this, the so-called "toddy shops" (purveyors of cheap fermented coconut liquor) are still very popular, and alcohol abuse continues to afflict many families.

The 40 children of the hostel of the Workers' Home, sponsored primarily by an Italian non-governmental organization, eat and sleep in the ashram, looked after by Krishnammal and the other workers, and during the day they attend the nearby school. Most of them are from harijan families.

Krishnammal invites me to join the prayer. It is dark now, and Vallarmati shows us the way with a flashlight. When we reach the house, I see Jagannathan sitting cross-legged on a mat on the floor, his eyes half-closed. He is sitting under a picture of Mahatma Gandhi and he is spinning, as he has been doing every day for almost 70 years. From four to six in the morning and every evening, Jagannathan spins. The simple loincloth he wears is made with the cotton he spun himself, and he has spun the cotton for every piece of clothing he has worn (when not traveling to cold climates) for more than five decades. Fifty years ago, during more than 40 days of meditation prior to his wedding, he spun the cotton used to make Krishnammal's wedding saree.

The children arrive carrying a lamp, and they sit in a circle, boys on one side, girls on the other. Together they sing some *bhajans* (devotional songs), and then a boy sings a captivatingly beautiful *bhajan* by himself. Finally they all join together in a *bhajan* written by Sri Ramalingam, a Tamil saint who lived at the beginning of the 20th Century, and to whom Krishnammal has been deeply devoted since her schooldays. She explains to me, "This song says that in each one of us there is a divine light. This can be temporarily obfuscated by many factors like suffering or pain, or hunger. But it is critical that people, and especially the poor and the oppressed, become aware of the divine light inside themselves. That's why the divine light ceremony is an important part of my work with women: I want to give them strength and faith in their own potential and in their own godly nature, because they are used to thinking of themselves as nothing, and deserving of nothing."

When the prayer is over, Krishnammal gives the children some advice on their studies, as they are soon to take exams. Then they will have a week of holidays and will go home to their parents or to some relative who will take care of them. I look at their smiling eyes, and I think that, despite their family situations, they are lucky to be here.

The following day, Jagannathan seems to feel better and we are formally introduced. He is friendly and merry. We talk for a while and he asks me when I want to start our interview. I say I am at his disposal, and we arrange to start the same day at four o'clock. That afternoon, I am sitting on the floor by his chair, pen in one hand and tape recorder in the other, anxious to hear his extraordinary story, and he starts:

Jagannathan: My family

"My village is in the far south, in Ramnad District, one of the most backward districts of Tamil Nadu. It is a very dry area, and drinking water is always a problem. There is no industry, and agriculture is very poor because there are no irrigation systems. We depend mostly on rain. Nowadays the rains fail, year after year. I remember that when I was a child, at least once a month there was rain and we could harvest at least some of crops. Not rice—which is very water intensive—but crops like *rahi* (millet) and so on. They grew abundantly, but now the area goes two or even three months without rain.

This District also had many *rajas* (princes). In colonial days there were 50. Under them, there were *zamindars* (landlords). After the British left, this *raja-zamindari* system was abolished. After

Independence, we had not only freedom from the British, but also freedom from the *rajas* and *zamindars*. That was an old and cruel system. Because our District had numbers of *zamindars*, poverty and slavery were much deeper there than elsewhere. This was the situation in the District where I was born.

The village of my birth is a small village. At the time, there were about 20 families. My father's father and his family were very poor. They possessed no land, nor any regular source of employment. So around 100 years ago, they migrated to another part of the District, where my great-grandfather had some relatives. One of these was the treasurer of the *raja*. Treasurers were powerful, like ministers, so he was a politically influential man, and the *raja* had given him a village as a gift. My grandfather and 20 other families migrated to this land, about a hundred kilometers away, to this village called Sirkali. It's a big village with a large water tank. They built their huts by the water tank, but when it rained the situation was difficult, and the banks of the tank were slippery and damp. So later on, my grandfather and 20 other families moved further from the tank, forming a new colony, where I was born.

My grandfather still had no land, but he had a bullock cart with which he earned a living. Every other day, he would travel about 20 kilometers to buy salt that he would then sell to the village shops. He was a good man, a hard worker. But in one of these villages, there were some criminals who used to steal goats and cows, and then they would sell them in villages far away. Because my grandfather was going to different towns to buy salt, these criminals suspected that he was giving information to the police about their thieving, and so became his enemies. One day, my grandfather was coming home with his cart full of bags of salt, and they killed him. They put his body into a bag of salt on the back of the cart. The bullocks knew the way and so they came home, but without the driver. My grandmother found the dead body on the cart. It was a real tragedy for my family, especially as there was no other source of income. My father, my uncle, and their two sisters were still at home with my grandmother, and they didn't know what to do.

My father was conversant in Tamil literature, knew all the religious songs, and had excellent handwriting. He was a very spiritual man and used to sit and meditate for hours in front of an image of Krishna. He had a chair in front of the house, and in the evening he used to sit there and sing. So when I went to sleep, I delighted in his singing.

About 50 kilometers from our village, there was a community of *chettiars*—members of a merchant caste—who used to go to Burma on business, often as moneylenders. My father became employed by them as an accountant, on account of his handwriting and calculating skill, and joined them on the 24-hour sea journey from Madras to Rangoon. He received a good salary, and after a while he returned and got married. In course of time, he gained his employers' confidence, and after five or six years they helped him start his own business. After getting married, he would come home every two or three years. After three years, my mother had her first child, and after five years I was born. Whenever my father came back, he used to bring some money and buy land, and then he started building some stone houses. We were wealthy enough to be able to go to school."

In the village school

"I began my education in the village school. The village teacher was my maternal uncle, who also worked as a mediator when there was a quarrel between villagers. We used to write on palm leaves. We would write with burnt wood or with yellow turmeric powder. The first lesson was in yellow, for prosperity and good luck, then in black. We also used to write in the sand. We had no books or notebooks, only palm leaves. The teacher used to write a line on a palm leaf. Then he would go away and we were to learn the line by heart that evening. From old Tamil scripts we learned sentences like "don't get angry with anybody". We also had to learn lines from songs. We also learnt arithmetic through songs; in fact, we learned everything through songs! The teacher was a good man, even if sometimes he hit us with the stems of the palm leaves. I was there until the third grade.

One of my father's sisters was married to a man who lived in

Ramnad, the town that gives the name to the District. He used to work for the Collector's Office.[2] So my father arranged for us to go to school in Ramnad, about 20 kilometers from home, and we stayed with my aunt. After leaving my first school in Ramnad, I attended a Christian high school. My father used to send money to my uncle so that he could take care of us. He also used to send nice clothes for us, and during festivals, we would wait for his presents anxiously.

I was not a bright student. I improved in the ninth and tenth grades when I became interested in English and in other subjects. I even acted in a Shakespeare play and I started writing articles for the school paper. Before that I used to spend all my time playing, playing, and playing!"

At the College

"Like my brother, I went to College, I think it was 1928. I was 16 and I went to the American Mission College in Madurai. My brother was at the National College in Trichi. At College, I mainly played a lot of tennis. I was a good tennis player. I had nice white shoes, tennis clothes... My father sent me money, and so I enjoyed the life of a pampered student in luxury and fashion. I used to wear a hat and shoes.[3] When I went home all dressed up for the holidays, my mother was so happy. "Oh, my son, so nice and fashionable!"

But during my second year something happened in my life. I started reading Gandhi, and the modern Indian philosophers including Swami Vivekananda and Ramakrishna. I gave up tennis, fashionable clothes, and the shoes, and I started down a more spiritual path.

A certain Dr. Foster came to the College to address a meeting. He was a Scotsman who became a Gandhian. He arrived wearing khadi and I was struck by this man, who was so simple and dressed like this, even if he was a foreigner. He spoke of service to the community. He was a very pious man and I was very much attracted by him. After his speech, I went to talk to him and he told me he had an ashram in Tirupatti, the *Krista Kula* (Family of Christ) *Ashram*.

Foster made a great impression on me and I decided to change my lifestyle completely. I shaved my head, and decided to renounce the world, and its pleasures. I had this unchanneled spiritual impulse. As an acquired discipline, I began to sleep outside by the river, rather than in the college hostel. So I went home for *Deepavali*[4] with shaved head and wearing only a piece of cloth down to my knees, and with palm leaves covering my head in the rain, as I had no umbrella. My mother was shocked, and there were tears in her eyes!

I read Gandhi's books, in which he suggested that college education was an education for slaves, preparing us for lives as servants to the British. He urged that young men leave their colleges and join the indigenous national schools.

At that time, the British government made a law establishing that there could not be any gatherings or meetings with more that four people. I suggested to some students that we disobey the law, and I wrote a leaflet suggesting that students leave school and disobey this order. I distributed it on the road by the College and in the students' rooms. But one of the wardens called me in and said: "All right, Jagannathan, we appreciate your spirit, but why do you tell other students to leave the College while you are still part of it?" That same day I had decided to protest against the British law and about 20 students joined me. We marched and chanted slogans. Next to the College there is a bridge over a river. When we reached the bridge, we met a group of policemen who started to beat us with *lathis* (iron-tipped wooden batons). I was the leader, so I was beaten badly. I fell on the ground and they continued to beat me. I fell unconscious, and then the police left me there. A group of people from the Congress Party brought me to their office. I was delirious for four or five days, and I stayed there with them, but soon I had to leave. I could not go back to the College, so I left my studies and went back home. My father was not there, and I didn't say anything to my brother."

After leaving college

"What next? I wrote a letter to Gandhi, saying that had I left my studies and asking whether I could join him in his ashram. This happened in 1930. He replied with a postcard, asking, "Why do you want to come so far away, where we don't speak your language? My own son Devadas is coming to stay in an ashram in Tamil Nadu, run by Rajaji (S. Rajalogolapanchram, a scholar, and later to be first Governor General of Free India, succeeding Lord Mountbatten.) So why don't you go to that ashram?" I wrote this ashram and waited and waited for a reply, but none ever came.

I stayed at home for almost a year. I dedicated myself to agriculture, because we had some land. There was already a man who worked the land with bullocks, and a girl taking care of the cattle. So I started plugging alongside this man, a harijan. We had so much paddy (rice) that year! My mother was so happy. But I was not satisfied. There were two water tanks on the east and on the west side of our small village In the early morning, I used to go to one of the tanks to sit and meditate. I wondered, "Oh God, what can I do? Shall I go to some other ashram?" Then in the evening I would go to the other tank.

Finally, I wrote Dr. Foster at Krista Kula Ashram, and he invited me to join him. I knew my mother wanted me to stay home, and that she would shed many tears. I knew she wasn't going to give her permission, and she would have told my brother who would have stopped me. So I left home without telling anybody and joined the ashram, 200 kilometers from my village.

My family searched, but they couldn't find me. I was at Krista Kula Ashram nearly two years. There were only unmarried men. There was also an Indian man, who studied with Dr. Foster in Edinburgh. The Scotsman was rich and he gave all his belongings to the ashram, so they had a nice church that from the outside looked like an Hindu temple, but inside there was a cross. At the ashram, I worked as a teacher. There was a school and a large hospital. I enjoyed ashram life. Foster and his friend were very pious people, and they were also nationalists. They loved Gandhi, were committed to nonviolence, wore khadi, and desired independence for India. They were nationalists and spiritualists at the same time, so my hunger was satisfied. I was the only Hindu there; the other 40 members being Christians. While I was there, some people tried to convert me, which I didn't appreciate. But I liked Dr. Foster and his friend, and I very much enjoyed ashram life."

While I was there, Ralph Keithan arrived. You see his picture there on the wall. He was here in Madurai as an American missionary. His wife Mildred was a physician. They both came from America to serve. Slowly they made contact with Gandhi, wrote him and met him. Even if Gandhi did not appreciate American missionaries very much, he liked Keithan, and he suggested that Keithan leave the American mission service, through which he was getting a good salary, a car, etc. But because of this correspondence with Gandhi, he had no time to resign, for he was thrown out by the mission board. So Keithan started to look for a place to work. He came to Krista Kula Ashram and asked to join it, but because he was married he was refused. I was really sorry about this, but in the ashram they had their rules. So Keithan went to Bangalore to work for an Hindu institution.

In the slums of Bangalore

"Because of this episode with Keithan and the pressure to convert me, in late 1933 I decided to go to this ashram in Bangalore myself, the *Dhina Sarva Seva Sangh. Dhina* means "poor", so it translates as the "association to serve poor people". In Bangalore, there is a large population of workers and poor people, from both Tamil Nadu and Karnataka. They were living in terrible slums, and the ashram was working with them. They also had a rural center for village service. Keithan and his wife were there, about 12 miles from Bangalore, in a village called Kangheri. I worked both with them and in the slums.

I held night classes for youth, and I was very happy, as in Krista Kula Ashram. There were other social workers working in the slums, about 40 of us. We had a very simple life. We shaved our heads, and carried a stick with a bucket hanging in the front and one hanging in the back, and we went from house to house to ask for food. People knew we worked for the poor, and they would put some rice in one bucket, and some *sambar* (spicy lentil soup) in the other. They knew us—"Oh, the Gandhi people have come!" they would say, and give us something. Sometimes they also gave us some oil, money, or even clothes. We lived like that. A very simple life. We received some money from the government for our schools and our medical programs. I loved working among the young workers.

Finally, in 1934 I wrote to my family to inform them where I was. Before I never had the courage. I was afraid they would have told me to go back home, but now after three years I wrote to my family, and also to my father who was still in Burma, to say that I was in Bangalore. They all wrote me, asking that I return home, but I said I couldn't because I had joined the ashram and I had to finish my service in the slum school. In that period I never went home, and my family left me alone, thinking I had gone mad in the ashram! That was 1933-36. Then in 1936, we began to agitate for prohibition in the slums, as people used to drink too much there. We organized intense propaganda. I used to organize meetings in the slums, but I also went to the villages to urge people not to drink, explaining how it adversely affects their health."

Wandering

"In 1936, in Maharastra in central India there was a national conference of the Congress Party planned to talk about prohibition, and I was sent there with another young man. The director of the ashram told us to go there and then, instead of coming back, to tour India for a year. He said he had no money to give us, but presentation letters for the ashrams where we could stay. So we were at the conference for three days, and then we left. Since we had no funds, we used to beg till we reached some Gandhian institution that could give us shelter, food, and maybe a little money.

We went to Ahmedabad (the site of Gandhi's own ashram), visited historic and religious places, and walked 45 kilometers a day. Sometimes we would sit in a temple and were given some money or something to eat. Then we went to the north of India, to the Himalayas, and to the religious centers of Hardwar and Rishikesh. We stayed in Hardwar for nearly two months to learn Hindi, and then from there we went to Rishikesh, in the foothills of the Himalayas, where there are many religious people and scholars. There was a Swami Shivananda Saraswati, a physician who had became a *sannyasin*, a sage who has renounced the world[5], living in a small building with three or four students. He was a great scholar who wrote many books and had traveled all over the world. Now there is a big ashram there, but when I joined it was only a very small place. In Rishikesh, there are three or four places where they used to feed *brahmacharyas* (young devotees) and samnyasins, so we had access to food. For three months we lived like that, and it was wonderful. Swami Shivananda used to wake us up chanting "Om, Om, Om...", then we would bathe in the Ganges, then pray, study, and meditate. It was such a great wonder to live with him!

In April, we set about on pilgrimage to the four traditional holy places in the Himalayas: Gangotri, where the Ganges has its beginning; then to Jamunotri, where the Yamuna River starts; then to the mountain temples of Kedarnath and Badrinath. It is about 100 kilometers roundtrip. Up and down so many mountains! In those days there was a thick forest that has now been destroyed, with huge, tall trees. In the cold, for nearly four months we walked in the Himalayas. After that, we wanted to go to Mount Kailash, the silver mountain and abode of Lord Shiva, one of the highest peaks in the world. The way was very difficult, and for 50 kilometers we would have had to walk on ice. But then we received a telegram from the ashram in Bangalore, requesting that we return.

Gandhi Students' Home

The reason they called me back was to organize student meetings for Dr. Kagawa[6]. Known then as "the Gandhi of Japan", Dr. Kagawa called upon students to simplify their lives and work with the poor in the slums, with whom he identified. He invited them to create student settlements in the slums. In those days, he was very popular all over the world. Kagawa came to India for two months to spread his message. Then he left India, and we decided to continue this student work in the slums. Keithan and I started what we called the "Gandhi Students' Home". We collected money, and we built a big building. Keithan, his wife, and his three children lived on the second floor, while I stayed downstairs with the students, where I lived from 1937-1939. I would bring students to see the conditions of the slums, and then we would study economic conditions. We also held one- and two-day camps with students from Bangalore city, as well as conferences and meetings, and the work was quite intense. About 120 students came as volunteers. They had to pay to stay in our hostel, which was much cheaper than those at the colleges, but it was more disciplined and the work was hard.

In 1940, I summoned up enough courage to start this kind of work in Tamil Nadu. I wrote to my family, and went back to my village and organized the Gandhi Students' Home, near the American College where I had studied. By the river there were some old buildings which I restored, made some rooms and asked the students to join me. I appealed to them: "Let's dedicate ourselves to service!" Keithan often came to help. The 25 students who joined me were young people from middle-class families inspired by Gandhi. I also organized one-month camps during summer holidays, in the slums but also in the countryside. Students used to collect money and food for the villages, where they then would engage in health propaganda and other kinds of service work.

In 1942 the Quit India Movement began, launched by Mahatma Gandhi to convince the British to leave India once for all. But I think you've had enough, and we can stop for today..."

I had started with the idea of taking notes and recording Jagannathan's words at the same time, but soon I had to drop the pen, sit on the floor and allow myself to be carried away by the narration. In front of my eyes, the dancing images of a man slowly leading home his cart full of salt, of children learning by writing on palm leaves and singing, of a young man dressed like an English dandy who goes home for his school holidays. I saw Jagannathan's face light up as he told of his spiritual awakening, and about his simple life of service in the slums of Bangalore. I saw him inspired as he remembered his pilgrimage to the Himalayan peaks, surrounded by centuries-old trees, glaciers, and ashrams. The vitality, the strength, and the passion of this man makes one forget that he is almost 90, so much so that even now I can't conceive of Jagannathan as an old man. When I think of him, the first characteristics that come into my mind are his wonderful, childlike laugh, the determination in his eyes when he tells about his struggles, and the sweetness in his voice when he calls for Krishnammal.

Meeting Gandhi

As days go by, Jagannathan is feeling better. I start taking my meals with him, and he always asks how many *dosas* (thin lentil-flour pancakes) or *idlis* (steamed lentil and rice cakes) I have managed to eat, and is very pleased that I enjoy the Gandhigram cuisine. After lunch, he asks for one of the chocolates I brought from Italy, following a suggestion made by his son Bhoomi, "If you want to make him speak, bring him chocolate. Even Gandhians have their weak points." It is intriguing to think of chocolate as a bridge across the cultural divide.

Time passes slowly in Gandhigram, in what seems like a leisurely country rhythm. Life starts very early. At five in the morning, the hostel children are ready for their prayers. The farmers who live in the ashram and take care of the land and the cattle have already milked the cows and water buffaloes, and are leading them to the pastures to graze. In the kitchen, the women, with the help of Krishnammal, are preparing an abundant breakfast for the children. After lunch, served around one o'clock, a long siesta fills the hottest hours of the day, the heat now made more severe by the drought. This year the monsoon is very late, and the peasants are worried. The soil is so dry it is impossible to till, and the animals are clearly suffering, especially the newly born calf and water buffalo, who seek some relief under the shade of a cotton-silk tree. Life in Gandhigram starts up again in the late afternoon when the children come back from school and receive their tea of roasted chickpeas. This is the time of the day when Jagannathan continues his story.

Jagannathan meets Gandhi

"Before telling you how I joined the 'Quit India Movement'

and about all that transpired as a consequence, I want to tell you about my meetings with Gandhi, and how I was inspired by him even as a young boy.

While in high school in Ramnad, I would go back to my village for the holidays. There, I would collect the village boys of my age and carry a big photograph of Gandhi. I was only 13. About 15 or 20 boys joined my processions, and we used to go to nearby villages, singing songs about Gandhi and his national movement. So even as a boy I used to organize marches! My father, a nationalist, was so proud of me!

When I was studying in Ramnad, my house was on the main road, where in the evenings we used to play some kind of village cricket. Once, a procession of people from the Congress Party came our way, marching and chanting slogans about Gandhi. So the boys and I followed them until they came to a crossroads. Speeches were made urging that all clothes or objects produced abroad should be burned. In those days everything was imported from England, so Gandhi started a Swadeshi Movement to encourage the use of local products. During this demonstration, it was explained that the Indian village cotton industry had been destroyed by the British, forcing importation of cloth from British mills.[1] Then several people started to make a fire with their clothes. At that time, my father was sending me clothes from Burma, so I was wearing a colorful, foreign-made, poplin shirt, and I had a pen maunfactured in England. That day I threw these two things into the fire. I still remember watching my shirt burn. Then I wrote to my father that we should not wear foreign clothes, and to send me only native-made cloth, and he started sending me clothes that were produced in Burma. In this way, I joined Gandhi's Swadeshi Movement.

While I was in Krista Kula Ashram in 1932, Gandhi came to Tamil Nadu during his tour for the removal of untouchability and the abolition of caste, a struggle that is still far from successful. On his way he came to our ashram for a public meeting. After the meeting he went to rest. I gave him a note. I wrote that of all the *avataras*—the messengers or incarnations of God that have come in this world, such as Rama, Krishna, Buddha, etc.—it seemed to me that Christ was supreme. Christ suffering on the cross for the sake of humanity was a superior notion, and I wanted to know his opinion. Gandhi was very tired after the meeting, but his assistants told him there was a young man who wished to meet him. He was already lying down, just about to sleep, but he invited me to come close and sit down, and he spent about ten minutes with me. He told me that God was incarnated at different times for different purposes. During the time of Rama, thousands of years ago, what was required was to inculcate the ideal of a just kingship, so God manifested himself as the ideal king. In those days, kings used to marry two or three women, while Rama was faithful to his one and only wife. Then he renounced his kingdom and went to the forest. Than came Krishna, the second *avatara*. He was a king but he became a spiritual master, manifesting another side of rulership. Then came Buddha, who was born a prince, but who renounced the kingship for a higher calling. So Gandhi explained the *avataras* to me one by one, and how they came into the world for different purposes. In different times the incarnations are different, as God says in the *Bhagavad Gita,* "I take different incarnations in different times all over the world according to the circumstances. I take birth for the sake of the world." Gandhi explained all this to me, and I was extremely pleased with his response.

After Bangalore, I came back to Madurai to create a students' ashram and organize summer courses and camps. In 1941, Gandhi came to Madurai. Around 2,000 young volunteers were to receive Gandhi and control the crowd, and I was in charge of organizing them. There was a huge, unmanageable crowd, perhaps around a million people. That evening Gandhi was pushed hard. Even the police could not do anything, and we could not control the situation. We were all crushed! Gandhi walked onto the stage, raised his hand, and the crowd calmed down. It was extraordinary how he could take control by only raising his hand: his spiritual power was enormous. Then he spoke, and there were devotional songs—*bhajans*, and I was stunned by his power. On this visit to Madurai, he was lodged in a big palace, and Krishnammal will tell you how she was there, welcoming Gandhi, and taking care of him for three days. At that time she was a student in Madurai College. But I was crushed in the crowd!

Even before meeting Gandhi in Krista Kula Ashram, I remembered a college friend who ran a national school in a village, and once I went and stayed with him for a few days. While I was visiting, it became known that Gandhi was planning to drive through that village. My friend and I became determined to cause Gandhi to stop in the village, so that the children could see him. But a stop there was not planned as part of the program. Because Gandhi was collecting money for the untouchables, we collected some money, thinking he might pause to receive the donation. About 120 children waited for him along the road. He was in the last car. The car halted, and I had the money to give him. I was so pleased to touch his hand that I had the impulse to give him something else. I had a gold watch my father had sent me, so I gave it to Gandhi, who was also collecting jewelry for his campaign. My father was very pleased as well. I told you how he went to work in Burma, but in course of time the Burmese realized they were exploited too, and so they drove the Tamils out from Burma with a people's movement. My father understood in advance that something was going to happen, so he sold the land he had there, and came back home. On his way back he met Gandhi, and gave him some money. He looked upon my involvement in the freedom movement with satisfaction.

So these are the contacts I had with Gandhi. And in this period I had another important contact!"

Meeting Krishnammal

"Krishnammal joined one of the many student camps I organized in 1941. I always thought that I would live my life as a bachelor, but I changed my mind because when I was in Krista Kula Ashram, and also in the ashram in Bangalore, I learned of immoral relations existing among the social workers. So after this experience, I came to think that to be a good social worker one needs to have a good companion; otherwise one is tempted. But I wondered who could be my companion? So Krishnammal arrived in this camp where there were 25 other students. Now Indian women always wear jewels. Even the poorest girl has something. But Krishnammal stood out from all the others because of her plain dress. She wore only white sarees with a small border and no jewelry, and I was very much attracted by this simplicity. I immediately thought of marrying her. I thought that if one had to have a companion, she should be like Krishnammal.[2] She was very good at singing devotional songs, and was a devotee of Ramalingam, the latest Tamil saint, who lived about 80 years ago. Even now she goes every year to the place where this saint and teacher lived. Ramalingam brought back the traditions of old Tamil literature, explaining it in a very simple fashion, and introducing the cult of light. Thus I was also very much attracted by Krishnammal's spirituality. During the month I observed her, she was very kind and gentle, with a high spirit of service. I didn't tell anybody that I wanted to marry her, but I went to her village and saw her house and her family. But still everything was only in my mind."

The 'Quit India Movement' and prison

"On August 9th, 1942, Gandhi started the 'Quit India Movement'. He launched it because the British government had involved India in World War II without even consulting us. How could Britain claim to be fighting for freedom, yet hold India in bondage? The 'Quit India Resolution' stated that we had had enough of British rule, that we wanted nonviolence, and that we did not desire to be involved in the world conflict. Before this, Gandhi had launched a civil disobedience campaign consisting of individual satyagraha, choosing Vinoba Bhave to be the first *satyagrahi*. Jawarhalal Nehru was a much more powerful Independence leader than Vinoba, but Gandhi chose Vinoba because he was such a spiritual man. Gandhi's followers walked from village to village to campaign against India's involvement in the war. I was involved in this movement too, and first of all I walked to my village where my father joined the satyagraha. I was so proud he was in this movement, too, and he was proud of me!

The British government responded by arresting all leaders of the movement. Thousands of people were imprisoned. At the time, I was in Madurai in the Students' Home with about 30 students. I told them I was going to join this movement, and that they would be quite capable of running the Students' Home themselves.

When all the leaders were arrested, people became angry and violence broke out. Telephone lines were cut, train rails uprooted, post offices set afire, and there were no leaders to control the situation because they were all in prison. The government responded with repression. In Madurai, they imposed a curfew order, so that after 6 p.m. nobody could go out. If anybody went out after six in the evening and before six in the morning, the order was to shoot on sight. I was unsure what to do. As Gandhians, we did not approve of violence, even against property, but at the same time we didn't want to respect an inhumane order such as the curfew. I organized a secret meeting with some other students, and we decided to rebel against that order. One evening after six, some of us started marching and chanting slogans. We were ready to be shot, because we wanted to broadcast our message at any cost. We marched along a road that is usually very crowded, but was deserted because of the curfew. The police saw us and approached. We were shouting, "Get out of India, Quit India!" All the policemen were English. I thought they would shoot us. Many policemen arrived and we went on shouting. But they didn't shoot. The policeman in charge ordered that we be brought to the police station, where we would be flogged. At the police station, we were prepared to be flogged, but the investigating police discovered that my brother was a magistrate. When they came to know that, and that my family at the time was quite wealthy, the police didn't flog us. The next day we were taken to the magistrate. I was convicted and sentenced to 15 months in prison.

I was sent to a prison in Andhra Pradesh, a state in east central India. It was a trying experience, my first prison experience among many to follow. The prison was overcrowded, with 1,500 prisoners, 300 in each block. The gates opened only when we had to wash. We were given rotten food, rice so full of worms that we couldn't eat it, despite the orders and threats of the prison authorities.

We had limited water to wash. Inside the building there were no latrines. There were pots that got filled at night, so it was wretched. They wanted us to suffer. For two hours in the evenings and mornings we could go out a bit, but then we were locked in like animals again. This was special treatment for political prisoners. But we kept up our spirits anyway. We sang songs and told stories. Because I was a good prisoner, I was released from prison three months early, at the end of 1943."

Organizing meetings

"But how to continue the movement? There was violence all over the country. After a year, many people were out of prison and there was a national meeting, secret because the British had banned all meetings. Both Keithan and I participated in this *All India Satyagraha Conference,* where we discussed how to stop violence toward people and toward property. Because many leaders were still in prison, it was decided that I was to be in charge of the satyagraha movement in Tamil Nadu. They asked me to organize political conferences at the district level, secretly of course because meetings were forbidden.

At the time, my brother the magistrate was also working as a recruiting officer, recruiting soldiers for the army, while I was recruiting volunteers to fight the government! So when I went home, my brother was there in his khaki dress recruiting soldiers, and I was wearing only a piece of homespun cloth like this. My mother used to comment upon the fact that she had two sons who took very different roads!

I started with my home district. I went from village to village organizing meetings and then I moved on. People were afraid and wouldn't come to the meetings, but Keithan and I kept at it. Everything happened secretly, because we might be arrested at any time, but accepting the principle of nonviolence means to be ready for that, too.

Then I organized the first political conference. There were about 300 people. We gathered in the morning at five o'clock and we raised our flag. The police arrived and arrested all 300. Because our principle was nonresistance, the participants were instructed not to run away and not to oppose the police. But I escaped, because I couldn't be arrested as I had to go on organizing these political conferences. I organized meetings in four districts, and nearly 3,000 people went to prison. So the political leaders who were in prison came to know that a certain Jagannathan and the people of the Sarvodaya Movement had started a movement of nonviolent resistance.

After four district conferences, I summoned up the courage to organize a state-level conference in Madras. Everything was organized secretly. By that time the police had come to know I was the one who was organizing the meetings, so they were looking for me, but I eluded capture. I never got off trains in the main stations where the police were planning to arrest me. In Madras, we expected all the leaders to attend, and with all these people the police would have understood there was going to be a meeting, but somehow we managed to get people to arrive from different locations, and welcomed them in different areas of Madras. We told everyone to keep the place of the meeting secret, and to come to the beach from different directions. The previous night we had buried the national flag under the sand, because before starting any conference we would raise the flag and sing the national song. I asked a leader from Madras to preside over the conference. In Madras, people often go for a walk on the beach in the evening, so coming from different directions we could arrive unnoticed. Then at nine o'clock, we suddenly gathered in one place, raised the flag and started singing. The police were caught by surprise. They called more policemen, and the 500 participants were all arrested. I stood aside because I did not want to be arrested.

For about eight months, I had managed to escape arrest, but that day the Tamil Nadu Governor was traveling by train to Madurai. There was a big ceremony at the station, with red carpets on the ground and everybody waiting for him, so I thought it would be clever to come back home on that same train, because the police would be busy with the Governor. Generally, I never got off at the large Madurai Station. But that day I thought they were not going to notice me, so foolishly I got off there. I was immediately caught by two policemen! In my pocket I had a circular letter for the *All India Satyagraha Conference*, as I was not expecting to be arrested. They took me to the police station, and I was worried about the letters that had the names of so many people, so I said I had to go to the urinal, and threw the letters away. I was not convicted, because they could not find any evidence against me, but I was placed in "administrative detention", which simply means one is put in prison without due process."

In prison again

"This time, beginning in 1944, I was in prison for two years. I was transferred two or three times: first in Madurai, then to Kerala, then to Thanjavur, in the area where we are working now. There were leaders from Andhra, Kerala, Tamil Nadu, and I was among them. Being in detention was a bit better than being a convicted prisoner. We have some facilities including a room, and better food that we could choose and cook ourselves. Detention is for more respectable people! I had a bed, a chair, a table, and slowly my conditions improved.

I forgot to tell you one thing. Before I was in prison, Krishnammal was living in a hostel. She was a student. I went to see her in the hostel and I told her plainly, "You know I am a public worker and that all this time I've been a bachelor. But now I want a married life, because to be a good public worker, it's better to have a wife. So I would like to marry you." She simply smiled. She didn't say yes or no, but this meant at least she didn't dislike me! So in this period before my second imprisonment, I was happy.

During those two years in prison, I also managed to take leave. I wrote the government that my father was ill and I wanted to go and see him, and I was authorized to go to my village for a month, but a policeman had to come with me. So I had a bodyguard! The condition was that I could not engage in any political activities. Then I had to go back to prison. But I will tell you the rest tomorrow: now it's time for me to go for my evening walk".

Jagannathan calls Vallarmati. He tells her something and she runs to call Krishnammal's nephew, a kind boy with a sweet smile who always accompanies Jagannathan on his evening walks. When he arrives, Jagannathan puts a hand on his shoulder, and there they go, in the warm, golden colors of the Indian sunset. I look at them as they walk away, and I can't help thinking about the pictures of Gandhi walking with his hand on his nieces' shoulder, the same white, simple clothes, the same strong, sinewy legs that walked for miles, the same untameable spirit.

The following day I finally manage to catch Krishnammal again. Even if she keeps insisting that she is happy to be on holiday, Amma has thousands of things to do and sometimes I spend the whole day waiting for her, while she proclaims, "Now I am free", and then disappears again into the kitchen or wherever her help is required. One of her secretaries has just arrived from Kuthur and has started working on an article Jagannathan is preparing for a local magazine. But each of the typewriter keys needs to be lifted up manually after every use!

Today, Krishnammal received notice that she is being awarded an international prize for her life of service to women, and she is happy because it will bring some money for the ashram that is urgently needed just now for the children's hostel. She proudly shows me the letter she had just received, and tells me, "Every time something seems to go wrong and we are having great difficulties, a divine hand comes to our aid. This has happened throughout my life, and that's the reason why I never worry too much."

We walk back to the guest house to get on with our work, followed by Karti the driver. He is in charge of my daily coconut water. He breaks two coconuts for us, and we drink the refreshing liquid.

We sit, finally! I get ready to take notes and record, but Krishnammal takes some papers out of her pocket and tells me that with the help of her secretary she has already written down what she wanted to tell me today. As I am wondering how they found time to do that, Krishnammal starts reading.

In the meantime Krishnammal...

"Thanks to my mother's efforts, I was the first member of my family to go to school. I really loved it. Up till the seventh grade, I studied in the village school, but then my family, especially my elder brother, decided it would be good for me to receive further education, and they sent me to study in Madurai.

The city atmosphere was completely different from the village. As I had not learned any English in the village school, I was fearful. But the headmistress, Mrs. Alice Maharaja, was very kind and encouraged me with her love. She accommodated me in her own house for a few rupees, so that my family could support me. Mrs. Maharaja told me that if I had had the best marks in knowledge of the Bible, then I would have had the highest marks in all the other subjects and I would have become the leader of the class. The headmistress was pleased with me and rewarded me with boxes of pencils and colorful ribbons.

At the end of the eighth grade, I should have gone to high school, but that of course would have meant more expense for my family. Luckily, I was very dear to Mrs. Maharaja, who introduced me to a person that would play a fundamental role in my life: Dr. Soundaram Ramachandran. Dr. Soundaram came from a very rich, high caste family, but under the influence of her mother and Gandhi, she championed the cause of destitute women. She was very adventurous by nature, and she committed herself to fight for the rights of young widows. She educated and enlightened them, and made the necessary arrangements for them to live a dignified life. Without any benefit to herself, she identified completely with the lonely, lowly, and distressed women in society. Inspired by the Tamil nationalist poet Subramaniya Bharati, she sought to bring out their noble qualities. She was convinced that women are not a bundle a flesh and bones, but have extraordinary moral and spiritual strength. And what about their virtues of compassion, kindness, love and affection for the whole family, for their often-alcoholic husbands, and their selfless sacrifices to maintain the family?

These thoughts always dominated the mind and heart of Dr. Soundaram, who bravely attacked the caste system and was completely against the old customs and habits that enslaved women. Mrs. Maharaja introduced me to this woman, telling her, "This girl will bring prestige to your name," and showed her all my prizes and certificates. With a broad smile, Dr. Soundaram accepted me and took me with her. Thanks to her, I was able to continue my studies and live with 20 other women in the Meenakshi Hostel that had been created by Dr. Soundaram herself. Thanks to her loving words and encouragement, I felt at home.

Soon, Dr. Soundaram started involving me in all her social service activities. She was busy working as a doctor, but in addition, during the night she used to go out to collect prostitutes from the streets. She invited them to leave that life and go with her, offering to take care of them and give them a future. The pimps who were involved in this crime shouted insulting and humiliating words to her. I was scared and I suffered for her, but Dr. Soundaram faced them boldly and released those women from their pimps' clutches.

Spiritual development

"I also loved the hostel warden, who showed great interest in my spiritual tendencies, and encouraged them. With her help, I studied many books about Tamil saints and I was impressed especially by the story of the 18 *siddhas* of the south. The *siddhas* are saints who attained levels of divinity and freed their souls from the chain of rebirths. They followed the path of simple living and high thinking, walking from village to village, and living by begging. They brought long-lasting good to society: they established the method of *siddha*[3] medicine, on the line of the ancient seers, the *rishis*, and healed people both physically and spiritually, without gathering any wealth for themselves. The story of two of these saints touched my heart in a special way. One is the story of

Manimegalai, daughter of the prostitute Mahadevi. During her young days, she developed a deep aversion to the profession of prostitution. When the king became aware of her intention not to follow her mother's path, he arrested her and put her into jail. In jail, he tried to spoil her chastity, but the divine power of the girl protected her: a circle of fire appeared around her and stopped the king from reaching her. Then she followed the path of Buddha, and from a lotus tank she received as a gift a wonderful vessel called the *achayapatra*, which at her request provided food for the hungry. Whether truth or legend, I believed this story and I admired Manimagalai.

The other saint who inspired me was Pampatti Siddha, a snake-charmer with a high-minded philosophy of life expressed through his rustic songs. He used to compare the life of man to a gardener who prays to God intensely for a water pot to water his garden daily. But when his prayer is answered, instead of using the pot for its intended purpose, he handles it carelessly and dances roughly, so much so that the pot falls and breaks: the gift is lost forever. In the same way, people who pray and do penance without realizing the real purpose of life, waste this precious gift in trivial enjoyment and petty things.

The example and sweet songs of Pampatty Siddha helped me understand the real meaning of life and the purpose of my living. My high school days passed in this state of mind. Then I began my college studies, living in the women's hostel. The area surrounding the hostel offered me an enlightening atmosphere. I used to spend the early hours of the day in that magnificent natural setting. I never felt lonely because nature in its beauty joined with me in praying to God. What a wonderful manifestation of the Divine Spirit! The tall palmyra trees, the various hues of the flowers and of the green leaves, the varied scenery of the sky with its different colors at sunrise were a delight for my mind. Then, with a peaceful and calm spirit, I could begin my daily studies.

In the meantime, I looked for a way to dedicate myself to social work. The College started a study center whose members used to meet every Wednesday morning to spin and discuss Gandhian ideas. During one of those meetings we decided to offer a literacy class for the youths of the nearby slum, and I started teaching."

Krishnammal and Gandhi

"In my second year of college, I was blessed with the unique opportunity of meeting Gandhi during his visit to Madurai in 1946. His visit was an exciting and thrilling experience. The whole of Tamil Nadu, it seemed, started gathering in the area of the meeting three days before his arrival. Reaching that area was beyond our imagination because of the huge crowd, but I had a nice surprise! Dr. Soundaram came to the hostel and took me with her to receive Gandhi in a secret place, outside Madurai city. She put me in charge of serving Dr. Susila Nayar, a physician who was attending Gandhi's personal needs. I was given a car and a VIP pass. I was often in the presence of Gandhi, and I was able listen to his conversations with eminent leaders from all over India. One day, Rajaji, one of the leaders of the Congress Party, asked me who I was and told me to leave, but Dr. Soundaram immediately said I was her daughter, and I then felt she was even more than a mother to me.

The next day we moved by train with Gandhi to visit Palani Temple. In the temple, I sat right in front of Gandhi, and I was asked to sing a devotional song. Sitting with Gandhiji was a privilege, and I also had the opportunity to meet Gandhian leaders. The spirit of Gandhian work had began to grow in my mind and, at the end of my college days, I was ready for social work."

First Satyahgraha

Today Jagannathan wants to tell me the story of the Workers' Home: how the idea took shape, when and how the ashram was created, what its role was, who was involved in the project. For what now looks like little more than a quiet country farm has for more than 50 years been an active center for the diffusion of Gandhi's model of society and economy; a place where the idea of the first land satyagraha took shape; a place visited by Nehru, Vinoba, and Gandhian leaders and scholars and activists from all over the world.

On the walls of the Workers' Home, there hangs a picture of a young Jagannathan together with Ralph Keithan, the American missionary follower of Gandhi, who took part in the freedom struggle, was banished from India, and returned after 1947. At that time he joined Jagannathan in the project of creating a center to educate young workers in Gandhian ideals, and train them in the techniques of nonviolent struggle. Keithan spent the rest of his life with Jagannathan and Krishnammal, providing them with help and inspiration.

Jagannathan: The Workers' Home

"In 1947, we were about to become an independent nation. Gandhi was negotiating with the British government. There was so much joy in the prison. Everyone was thinking about this coming freedom, their own and that of the country. The political leaders were all excited at the idea of participating in the elections and becoming members of the new government.

But I was not happy. I kept on thinking: "What is this freedom? It is not freedom for the common man. This freedom is not for the untouchables or the village poor. This freedom is only for the upper classes, the rich, the educated. This is not real freedom for the people." For two or three months I went on thinking in this vein. I knew that if political freedom was about to come, there would still be no economic freedom for the majority of people. I had always been working for poor people, in Krista Kula Ashram and in the ashram in Bangalore, among the untouchables and the wretched, and I was wondering when economic freedom for these poor people was going to arrive. In the end, I decided that once out of prison, I was going to start working for the economic freedom of the common man. I began to question, "Why are these people so poor?" And the answer was obvious: they don't have land. It is the landless that end up in the city slums. India is an agricultural country: 70% of the people live in the villages, even as the few in the cities become rich. There are the landless, the untouchables, the poor. But without socio-economic freedom, where is freedom for them? They are slaves of the landlords, so the only real revolution can come through access to the land. Even before Vinoba's movement, I had this conviction.

I should also tell you what happened to Keithan while I was in prison. As already mentioned, he was working in Bangalore. During the Quit India Movement, there was a large meeting to decide what to do to stop the violence that exploded after all the leaders were put in prison. Keithan was also there. In the period during which I was organizing secret meetings, he received a deportation order. His wife boldly decided to stay in India, but later she and their three children also received deportation orders. Keithan consulted Gandhi, who advised him to respect the order and go back to America to let people know what was happening here. Keithan left. After freedom, when the first Indian Government was formed, we thought: "Now Keithan should come back to India." So the Governor General Rajagopalachari invited him to return to India.

In January or February 1947, we were all released, and in August, India became an independent nation. The first thing I did after I was released was to go to the districts where the land problem was worst, and there we started organizing the *Gandhi Kissan Sanghs*, Gandhi Agricultural Workers Associations. Then I thought of offering training for village youth on the land problem, and we organized some week-long camps. We selected some of the participants for longer training of six months, one year, and even two years. Keithan, who by that time had managed to return to India, joined me and ran the training on Gandhi's constructive program, on nonviolence, and on satyagraha, the techniques of nonviolent protest and noncooperation. But we were also offered practical training in weaving, spinning, gardening, digging wells, etc.

After I started this work, Dr. Soundaram, a doctor from Madras who in Gandhi's central India ashram in Wardha married Dr. Ramachandran, a great Gandhian fighter and philosopher from Kerala, decided she wanted to settle here. She wrote me saying she wanted to start an ashram in Tamil Nadu to work with village women. She asked me to find a place for her, so I started surveying the whole district to find a proper location. Then she came to see for herself. She was a wealthy woman so she arrived in a car, and Krishnammal was with her!

I had selected several locations. One evening, we met in a nearby weavers' village. I told her I had found a place on a hill, but she replied, "Oh, you are a recluse, you are a sannyasin, I want to start an ashram for women, so I need a safe place by the road, near the train station, not on a hill!" A group of nationalists living in a nearby village donated 13 acres of land. Then we made contact with the people that owned land in that area, and purchased some more. In the beginning, we worked together, but slowly her program changed. With other people, she founded Gandhigram Rural University, an institution that did not have the collective, cooperative spirit we desired. Later, Dr. Soundaram got involved in politics, and became a member of Parliament. Both Keithan and I did not approve of this direction, so at that point I officially resigned from Gandhigram, even if I went on cooperating with them.

In the meantime, I was looking for a place to settle and offer training in a more systematic fashion. Keithan and I dreamed of a community on the model of Gandhi's Tolstoy Farm in South Africa, based on the ideals of simplicity and self-sufficiency. We appealed to the village people and we received some of the land here as a gift, and partly we purchased it. It was all forest, full of trees, and there was lots of work to be done. First of all, we needed money.

So I started going from place to place looking for some funding for our training center, and in Madurai we found a very good man who helped us. He was from a rich family but very devoted and simple, a real nationalist. When we started this Workers' Home, it consisted of Keithan, Dr. Soundaram's husband, myself, and this man from Madurai who became the chairman, while I was the secretary. It was a good period because we had just attained freedom, and people had high hopes for the future and were willing to help.

It took a year to collect the funds we needed. First, we built a mud hut with a detached palm-leaf roof for me, while Keithan and his family lived in a house nearby, and then we started the training. We appealed to young men to come and work for the freedom of the common man. The first project was a two-year training program on work in the villages. About 30 people from the nearby villages joined us.

We worked hard. We built the well you see near the ashram. We held seminars to consider how to strengthen the rural sector of society. We offered regular classes, did constructive work in some villages, and built this place. Each morning at 4 a.m., Keithan and I would go with his jeep to a hill nearby to collect the stones we used to build these walls. It was very difficult, as we had to load and unload the stones, and our hands were full of bruises! We would bring the stones and cut them. We also dug the foundations ourselves. In 1948, the building was completed.

We also went to the villages, seeking to understand the problems of the people, how they were living, and so on. We studied the problem of the landless people: at the time, it was a new kind of study. Industrial labor was already well organized, especially by the Communists and Socialists, but it wasn't like that in the agrarian sector, mainly because farm laborers were spread throughout all the villages, while industrial workers are all concentrated in the same place and hence easier to organize. We wanted to find our own nonviolent approach to the land problem, a non-party-based approach. But at the same time, we were interested in creating a nonviolent movement of factory workers. So we paid a regular salary to a trained worker that gave birth to a nonviolent Gandhian organization called the *Indian National Trade Union Congress*. With him, we also started an ashram for young workers by the riverside. Youths would come, have some training, read, play games, and then go to work."

Kumarappa

"Dr. J.C. (Cornelius) Kumarappa was a Gandhian economist promoting a model of small-scale decentralized economy similar to that made famous in the West by E.F. Schumacher.[1] We invited him to the Workers' Home to give classes on nonviolent Gandhian economics and the contrast between it and with both Chinese- and Soviet-style communism and capitalist economies.

Kumarappa came from a Christian family in Kerala, but was educated in America and was employed there at a rather high salary. He lived in the United States for 30 years, but when Gandhi initiated his Swadeshi movement focusing on village industries and on khadi as instruments against British exploitation, Kumarappa came back to India and joined him. Gandhi had started a Village Industry Association and asked Kumarappa to become its secretary. Gandhi gave him the entire responsibility for organizing village industries, and Kumarappa, who was a scientist, started experimenting not only with spinning and weaving, but also with oil and rice production, flower cultivation, the building of mini-mills, papermaking, pottery, and many other small-scale industries.Then he started a training center in Wardha, in central India, later to become a large institution, and began publishing a monthly newspaper on small-scale industries.

Kumarappa was deeply convinced of the philosophy of decentralized industries. He suggested a real economic revolution to parallel the political one, and became very popular all over India. Whenever Gandhi was arrested, he was also arrested, because the government perceived the threat to its power posed by this decentralized, anti-capitalistic economic approach.

Kumarappa trained and inspired a large number of Gandhian workers, and even here in Gandhigram there is a center for the production of paper and other items established by him. He was a very strong and gentle man. He became my close friend, and we were both interested in the land problem. He returned many times to Gandhigram, and trained many students with an aim to integrate nonviolent Gandhian politics with nonviolent economics, based on small-scale industries.

Kumarappa was later to join the *Bhoodan* Movement, but was to leave it because of his disagreement with Vinoba (Bhave)'s methods. He loved Vinoba, but he disagreed with him because of what he perceived to be Vinoba's lack of practicality. But more on that later. Right now I want to tell you how we had our first success using satyagraha, people's power, in a nonviolent struggle."

The first satyagraha

"About 20 kilometers from here, there is an area irrigated by a river, and in that area sugarcane is grown. There was and still is a century-old small-scale industry. The sugarcane gets crushed with small machines: the canes are introduced in a simple mechanism, and bullocks walk in a circle turning a wheel. The wheel in turn crushes the canes, squeezing out the juice. The juice then gets boiled in large pans, the result being lumps of sugar called *jaggeri*. It is very sweet and fruity, and more healthful than the more refined product.

So in 1949, when we were walking from village to village, we came to know about a problem. About eight kilometers from Gandhigram, in a place called Kodai Road, some wealthy people invested in a sugar mill for the industrial production of sugar. Many of them were Workers' Home donors. But because there were already many people processing sugarcane traditionally, these industrialists looked for a way to force the people to bring their cane to the mill. So they appealed to the government, requesting a law requiring a license to produce *jaggeri*. The government, supposedly inspired by Gandhi, enacted such a law. Before, farmers were free to produce: it was a small-scale industry employing many people. The law was clearly an indirect way to force the cultivators to submit their sugarcane to the industrial mills. People didn't know what to do and they wanted to protest against this law, so we offered to organize them. Keithan, Kumarappa, and I agitated in the villages, saying this was a slavish order, similar to the British tax on salt!

Gandhi demonstrated to the world that it is possible to achieve freedom by nonviolent means. According to his technique, one should not make the opponent suffer, but one has to be able to suffer oneself to convert the opponent. Think about his historical salt satyagraha. Sea salt is produced by drying marine water in the sun, but the British government had imposed a tax on salt, and required a license to make it. So Gandhi started a movement against this iniquitous tax, a mass satyagraha during which people were beaten badly (as is portrayed in the movie *Gandhi*.) The British were not made to suffer; instead we took suffering upon ourselves. And in doing so, we ourselves were strengthened and changed, for we experienced an inner independence even before the British granted the outward one. This is our great inheritance from Gandhi.

Why should the government interfere with a 100-year-old industry? We told the people they should disobey this order, held many meetings, and found 300 volunteers who were ready to protest and disobey that law. But what did the police do? In each small mill producing jagger, there are two or three iron balls that crush the cane, and the police started confiscating them from the people who refused to buy the required license, together with the big pots used to boil the sugarcane juice. The people started getting nervous and did not know what to do, because the sugarcane needs to be crushed within a short period of time, before it dries out.

At that time, we didn't have a jeep but we were always walking. One late afternoon at four o'clock, I was walking to a village when a police lorry arrived to take the machines away. I had no clue what to do to prevent this, and certainly no plan, but all at once an idea came. As soon as the police van was about to leave, I ran and lay down in front of it, so the lorry could not go past. It was a sudden idea, but people were so encouraged by this gesture that many arrived and laid down in the road in front and back of the van so that it could not move at all. The police called for help, and by seven o'clock an police officer came and started shouting, "If you don't move we will beat you, we will shoot you." And he also said, "This is an order from our national government—you are Gandhians, how can you disobey the order?" And we answered, "Yes, this is our government, but how could they give such an order, interfering with the people's economy and their livelihood? It is a slavish order, worse than a British order!" So we went on arguing and till midnight nothing happened. Nobody moved. By this time there were 2-3,000 people who had arrived from other villages, and there were also nearly a hundred policemen.

Finally, the police phoned the Madras Government, explaining that some Gandhians were offering satyagraha. The Agriculture Minister ordered the police to return the equipment to the people and said he would arrive the next day. The police obeyed and departed.

The next day the Minister came, and held talks with Kumarappa and Dr. Soundaram. I didn't go, but stayed with the village people. Kumarappa explained that that order was unfair, that we were Gandhians and wanted to promote village industries. Furthermore, what did it matter whether it was our national government or a foreign government that was destroying village industries? The British destroyed India's spinning and cotton industry, and in the same way the national government was bent on destroying the indigenous sugar industry for the sake of the capitalists. The Minister agreed with us, and canceled the order for the law's enforcement. We agreed that those who wanted could bring their sugarcane to the industrial mill, but those who did not want to were free to do as they pleased. The Minister asked us not to agitate among the people to boycott the mill, and we came to this compromise.

This 1950 satyagraha was our first large-scale one, and for the first time we disobeyed the national government. We succeeded in that both the traditional industry and the new mill went on, and they are working even today. Unfortunately, it was a satyagraha that that cost the Workers' Home many of its large donors

When I think back upon the incident, I try to imagine what might have happened had I not lain down in front of the van. It is unlikely that the people by themselves would have had the courage to do so. But I had that inspiration and many people followed me. Women put their babies in front of the wheels to stop the van. Everybody was ready to die. I had no reason to have ever expected this spirit at all. I thought that the police would simply drag me away and the lorry would leave, but people responded in a spontaneous and authentic fashion. In the evening, women went to cook for us and brought us food on the road. At eight o'clock dinner was served! It was a tremendous experience. By God's grace I had the courage to do what I did, and people responded with enthusiasm. This lesson has been repeated for me again and again."

While Jagannathan tells his story, the phone rings. Vallarmati runs to answer: it is Bhoomikumar ("Bhoomi"), Jagannathan and Krishnammal's first child.

Bhoomi was born in 1953, at the time of the *Bhoodan* Movement in Tamil Nadu and took part in it when he was one. At the age of three, he was the youngest participant in Vinoba's *padayatra*. Now Bhoomi is a doctor specializing in child psychiatry, and he works in Cambodia for Caritas. He has set up a clinic for children with psychiatric problems (often victims of war), after working for many years as a physician for ASSEFA (Association of Sarva Seva Farms), an Indian nongovernmental organization Jagannathan will tell me about later.

It was Bhoomi who suggested the idea of a book detailing the story of his parents' lives to Elena Camino, his friend and one who is responsible for an Italian branch of ASSEFA. He has always supported and encouraged me since I started working on this project.

As Jagannathan speaks and jokes on the phone with Bhoomi, Krishnammal tells me, "Bhoomi is worried about his father's health, and he would like us to go to see him to have a little holiday. But how can we leave when our workers are all involved in the campaign against intensive prawn farming? We can't move, the people need us here." More on that later. And then she starts scurrying hither and thither, as usual.

CHAPTER 4

Wedding Stories

Today we are going to Madurai. After innumerable changes of plans, it seems that we are leaving in the morning to attend a wedding. In the afternoon, Krishnammal has arranged for me to meet K. M. Natarajan, one of the leaders of the Sarvodaya Movement who has worked very closely with Jagannathan.

The bride is one of Jagannathan's nieces, but he is not coming with us, partly because he does not feel very well yet and it is an unusually hot day, but also because, as he says (echoing Gandhi's late-in-life convictions), "I don't like this kind of wedding. I only approve of intercaste marriages."

This instead is a wedding between cousins, a tradition that has always been strong in Tamil Nadu, but that now is getting stronger because of the dowry problem. The tradition according to which the bride's family has to offer gifts to the bridegroom's family has recently exploded to such a degree that now families often find themselves in major debt to ensure their girls a good marriage. It is a phenomena that involves all social classes, and that has rendered the birth of a baby daughter a sad event for those who cannot afford a rich dowry. A woman who marries with a dowry that does not satisfy the husband's family runs the risk of becoming a scapegoat in her new family, or of being sent back home with some excuse or, in some dramatic but not entirely rare instances, of being killed. Marrying a member of the family is a partial solution to this problem for, at least, as Krishnammal explains, "money stays in the family."

We leave early in the morning, with the jeep stuffed with people coming to the wedding and people from the ashram and its neighborhood who have to reach different destinations on the way to Madurai. For each passenger who gets off, at least two seem to get on the vehicle, but, in the standard magic of Indian transport, there always seems to be room for everybody. The last stop is at the house of one of Jagannathan's sisters. She is old and sick, but she lives surrounded by the love of her children and grandchildren in a house where four generations live under the same roof. Several of these generations seem to have climbed onto the jeep to come to the wedding. Shaking my head in disbelief, I count 14 people squeezed onto the seats.

As the jeep races at full speed trhough the city, Krishnammal tells me the story of her marriage with Jagannathan.

Krishnammal tells the story of her wedding

"I remember that Dr. Soundaram didn't want me to marry Jagannathan, because she thought of him as some kind of sannyasin who ate only raw vegetables. But Jagannathan had worked for her husband Dr. Ramachandran during the Quit India Movement, and he thought I should marry him, especially as he didn't want Jagannathan to become a sannyasin for real, disappearing into some religious ashram and abandoning social work.

Because I was the first woman to graduate from college in my community (actually the first harijan woman to graduate in the entire state), many young men wanted to marry me. I was a bit afraid of Jagannathan because he had too much of the sannyasin in him, but I accepted him, because otherwise my family would have forced me to marry some rich man, with no involvement in any social concerns, and that was not for me! My relatives and, especially, my brother opposed our marriage. Dr. Soundaram did not trust Jagannathan, but I knew our marriage was going to work because we had the same aims in life.

The day of the wedding, just before the ceremony here in Gandhigram, I sat in a room in front of Ramalingam's image to pray and I wondered, "Why should I marry?" As a child, I had decided I would never marry because I had witnessed the terrible life my mother had led with my father. Dr. Soundaram came to look for me, and waited behind me until I stood up, ready to go. The ceremony was very simple: Keithan put a hank of cotton he had spun himself around our necks, and we were married.

Just two days after the marriage, Jagannathan left. I knew he was going to wander around, but I couldn't imagine he was going to do it so soon! For three months, I didn't hear anything from him. At that time, I was living in Gandhigram, teaching destitute women. My mother got worried! One day she came to bring some clay vessels. Traditionally, when two people get married there is a ceremony in which we boil some milk in a new pot, and this is a symbol of a new home starting. But Jagannathan was not there. My mother got angry and said: "Everybody is talking about you—you married a sannyasin and he left you!" But I never cared about what people said.

Jagannathan came back after three months, and suggested I apply to a teacher training program because he could not stay with me and was going to leave again. He had decided to join Vinoba's movement (see the next chapter). He had this call to go and join him while he had been alone in Gandhigram. So I went to study in Madras, but soon I was in trouble. Our families were not supporting us. Jagannathan was away, and I had no place to go during holidays when the hostel was closed. Jagannathan wrote me nice letters, but he made no arrangements for my food or housing! Finally, he wrote, instructing me to go to his sister's place for the holidays. Later, I received a letter from him saying: "Until you join Vinoba's padayatra, there can be no family life for us." So I finished my exams, and without even getting my certificate, I left to join Vinoba."

Jagannathan and Krishnammal's wedding broke virtually all the rules it was possible to break. First of all, it was an intercaste marriage. Even today, a high caste man marrying an untouchable woman would be an extraordinary event; 50 years ago it was virtually unthinkable. Jagannathan chose his bride, when today a large number of weddings in India are still arranged by the families. And the people who supported their wedding, Dr. Ramachandran and his wife, were not even their relatives.

They were not married by a brahmin priest, as tradition would require, but by their friend Ralph Keithan, the American missionary who was working with them in Gandhigram. There was no dowry and no big celebration, no gold, silk or expensive presents, but only a simple thread hand-spun by Keithan to symbolize their union. Not long ago, when Amma and Appa celebrated their 50th wedding anniversary, they refused the traditional flower garlands and asked instead for a garland made of oranges that they later distributed among the Sarvodaya workers who were there to celebrate.

Jagannathan and Krishnammal never bothered to register their wedding legally, and the only family member who was at their wedding was Jagannathan's brother. Truly a revolutionary wedding for two revolutionary souls!

The wedding I am attending, in contrast, is a proper, traditional, though thoroughly modern wedding, with hundreds of guests, a stage decorated with pink and blue paper flowers and two enormous golden thrones where the shy couple is sitting. In front of them, the *pujari* (holy men hired to make sacrifices in the name of the couple) recite *mantras* and carry out the proper ceremonies. The most important moments of the ceremony are highlighted by a group of musicians playing long trumpets. Their powerful sound drowns out, if just momentarily, the loud 'Bollywood' music that huge amplifiers blast inside and outside the building especially rented for the occasion. Below the stage, in the place of honor, sits Jagannathan's brother, more than 90 years old. He is the same brother that so many years ago recruited soldiers for the British army, and now, following tradition, has become a sannyasin and lives in the country near Trichi, in an ashram run by women who also maintain a hostel for orphaned girls, many of whom are blind. Relatives and friends are queuing in front of the holy man dressed in orange to touch his feet and receive his blessing. This transformation from magistrate and government servant to holy man is still well within contemporary Indian norms.

It is unbearably hot, inside as much as outside, in spite of the fans. I try to go unobserved and hide in a corner, but a young girl spies me, grabs my hand and starts introducing me to many other girls, all smiling, each of whom wants to know my name, where I am from, if I have any brothers or sisters, and, particularly, whether I am married and have children. Then it is lunchtime and I feel I'm about to faint, especially because I've just been told that the wedding festivities will last for two more days! But Krishnammal decides it is time for us to go, and with relief we head towards Natarajan's home. There we experience a power outage and sit in the dark, until finally, the power restored, I regain my strength under a fan.

That night when we return exhausted after the intense day in Madurai, I tell Jagannathan the version of the their wedding story Krishnammal told me, and he can't resist adding his version.

Jagannathan tells the story of his wedding

"At the time of the sugarcane satyagraha, I was working here, and Krishnammal was working with Dr. Soundaram, taking care of poor women who had been left by their husbands or became widows, and she was also teaching in a hostel for poor children.

In July 1950, we got married. My relatives didn't like this marriage, because she was from an untouchable family, and her family didn't like me, because Krishnammal was a college graduate while I had left my studies. So her elder brother told her, "This fellow is a Gandhian—he doesn't have anything—so why would you marry him?" They wanted her to marry some official or something like that, but her mother supported her. My family was staunchly opposed.

It was the 6th of July. Keithan was there. Kumarappa and all the workers were there. From my family, only my brother came for the wedding. Our marriage was very simple. We briefly prayed in front of a lamp, and it was done. My brother called me over and spoke to me. "You don't even have a ring! I will give you mine", he urged, but I didn't want it because Krishnammal would not wear any jewelry at all. Generally, in our marriages we have a thread with some gold to give to the bride, but we had no gold! So we took some turmeric—a symbol of welfare—and I tied some pieces of turmeric on the thread. Then we had a prayer, and Keithan put our heads close together and placed a cotton garland made of thread he had spun himself around our necks. After this ceremony, we only had some puffed rice as snacks, and it was over.

After the marriage, Dr. Soundaram ordered us to go to our villages and meet our people. I didn't want to, but she insisted, so we went in Keithan's jeep. I was terrified! How was I to face my mother and my father? I thought they would just scold me! My father was a nationalist—he would only wear khadi, he met Gandhi, took part in individual acts of satyagraha—but he was not ready to accept intercaste marriages. At that time, he was working in a town six miles from my village, so we went to see him first. When we walked into his office and told him we had gotten married, he was furious! He told Dr. Soundaram, "You are a millionaire, you can afford an intercaste marriage, but how can I face other people now?" Dr. Soundaram just smiled back and said, "But you are a Gandhian, a nationalist, and you should welcome this marriage. She is an educated girl, a nice and gentle girl who devotes herself to public service. If you are a nationalist, a Gandhian, you should be pleased about this match." My father answered, "All your philosophy is nice but it cannot be put into practice in the villages. You are a city woman. There things are different." But when we asked for his blessing, he consented. "All right," he said, "you go to the village and I will join you tomorrow".

So we arrived at my village where my mother and sisters were. You see, a mother's love is so wonderful. My father was angry, but my mother knew I was there with my bride. She was happy and smiled. She knew I was a very disobedient fellow. I had left home for so many years without telling them where I was. I was a wanderer, and she had wept so much for me, I was the only child who gave her trouble, but now she was happy that I had married. She went to the prayer room, and welcomed us with burning camphor. I would have never expected this. I thought she would have been angry, too. But a mother's love is so superb, so supreme.

That night my mother organized a feast for us, a nice meal. Than she took me aside to the prayer room, and asked me what I gave Krishnammal for the wedding. I answered that I had tied some turmeric to the wedding thread. She started crying. "I spent thousands of rupees for your brother's wedding. We bought so much gold for the bride, bangles, rings, and so on, but you didn't get her anything! So I will give you a thousand rupees—go to the temple in Madurai and get something for her." (I didn't.) The next day, my father arrived and he was accepting. We ate together, and that evening Krishnammal and I left for Coimbatur where we stayed for two days. So this is the story of my marriage. But now it's time to go to bed. It's late and you must be tired from your journey."

Vallarmati and Karti arrive to prepare Jagannathan's bed. He sleeps in the open space under the roof of the Workers' Home. Karti places the bed between four columns. It is a simple wooden table covered by an old saree. Then he ties the four sides of an old mosquito net to the columns. Jagannathan slips under the net full of holes; he will be awakened by the first daylight.

Exhausted, I go to bed, too. When I reach my room I realize that tonight I am not going to be alone: a group of children sleeps on the flat roof. After throwing a few buckets of water over my head, I too disappear under my mosquito net. For a while I stare at the geckos chasing insects up and down the roof and the walls and then I turn the light off, musing that to my own wedding, I won't invite more than ten people.

The Nonviolent Revolution of the Walking Saint

Today I am going to hear the story of Jagannathan and Krishnammal's involvement in Vinoba Bhave's Bhoodan Movement, and of the indelible mark that this experience has left on their lives.

Vinoba[1] was born in 1885 into a brahmin family, and earned a doctorate in engineering. In 1916, he joined Gandhi and lived in his ashrams for his entire life, actively taking part in the nonviolent freedom struggle to free India from British rule. Gandhi considered him his spiritual leader, and as such Vinoba became famous all over India. After Gandhi's death, Vinoba refused to take part in the political life of India. Despite offers he received from the national government, he went on living in the Wardha Ashram until, in 1951, he started his extraordinary land reform movement. Followed by a group of cooperators that became more and more numerous, Vinoba walked the length and breadth of India appealing to whomever owned land to give a part of it to the landless poor, victims of centuries of oppression, and at the mercy of the large landholders who held them in virtual servitude. In a period of 13 years, Vinoba obtained four million acres in gifts, establishing a precedent—though by no means a final victory—for a nonviolent approach to the land problem, and, in so doing, headed off a revolutionary attempt by several Maoist groups who had initiated a campaign for the violent expropriation of land in central India. Vinoba wrote, "My mission is not to prevent a revolution. I simply want to avoid a violent revolution and promote a nonviolent one. My aim is to produce a threefold revolution: a change in people's hearts, a change in their lives, and a change in the social structure."

During the period he spent in prison before Independence, Jagannathan had already decided the issue of landed property was critical. In Vinoba, he found a master who declared, "The future peace and prosperity of the country depends upon a solution to the land problem."

Jagannathan: Vinoba's movement

"At the time of our wedding, Vinobaji had inaugerated his movement for the redistribution of land. After Independence, the Communists had started organizing tillers for a violent revolution as in China: kill the landlords and expropriate their land. In 1950 near Ahmedabad in Gujarat, violence had exploded. Landlords were killed and their properties set on fire. Jawaharlal Nehru, Prime Minister at the time, sent the army to suppress the revolt that the Communists had been organizing secretly for two years, but the army failed. Gandhi was already dead, and Vinoba was in his ashram, wondering about the reasons for this violence after India had attained freedom through nonviolence. He decided to walk in that troubled area to bring peace.

One morning—it was April 18, 1951—Vinoba went to a village and entered the area where the untouchables lived. There were no men, only women and children. He asked where the men were, and they explained to him that the men were out working as day-laborers. Vinoba sat with these poor people and asked them about their needs. They said, "We are 80 families. If we could just have one acre of land each, we would be satisfied." Vinoba replied, "I can't bring land from Wardha and give it to you. Nehru can't bring land from Delhi. It is only the local people who can help you. I can give you money or bullocks, but how can I give you land?"

After leaving the slum area of the village, Vinoba went to the area where high caste people lived, and that evening organized a public meeting, inviting the harijans as well. There was a big crowd. Vinoba appealed to the rich people of the village. "You have big houses. You gave me good food and hospitality, and I am thankful to you, but this morning I was in the slum area, and it was so dirty, so poverty-stricken, everybody was so thin. Those poor families asked me for 80 acres of land, but how can I give them land? Only you can do that." This was his first appeal for Bhoodan, for land gifts. At that point, a man stood up, and said, "I offer you a hundred acres." Vinoba couldn't believe his ears. He asked him if his family was in agreement. The man said he would have to convince his four brothers. Vinoba told him to consult with his whole family, and if they all agreed, to return the next evening to tell him. The man went, consulted his family and all the family members agreed with his donation. This was the first land gift.

In one of his books, Vinoba wrote that generally he used to go to bed at eight o'clock and wake up at two in the morning, and that when he was asleep he was like a dead body that gains new life in the morning! But that night he could not sleep, thinking about those poor people who gave him inspiration for his appeal, and about the man who spontaneously gave even more than that which had been asked of him, and in all this he saw the hand of God. He understood that from that moment on, his mission would be to ask for land as a gift, and so the Bhoodan Movement was born. In a month, Vinoba collected about 30,000 acres, and the newspapers started talking about his march.

In the meantime, the Communists who had started the violence had been arrested and imprisoned. Vinoba went to meet them and explained how it was possible to get land without resorting to violence. After a while, the killing and the arson against the homes of landlords ceased, and peace was reestablished. In the Parliament, Nehru announced, "The Communists started a violent upheaval. I sent the army, but the army could not solve the situation. Then Vinoba, a single man, reestablished peace by walking in that area. A miracle as happened. What our army could not suppress, this disciple of Gandhi managed to stop by himself."

With Vinoba

"I read the news in the papers. As I told you, I had already realized myself that the land problem was fundamental. I remembered that in May 1948, after Independence, there was a national conference of the Sarvodaya Movement in Coimbatore in Tamil Nadu. All the major leaders were there. I sent a note to conference, indicating my belief that the main problem in India was land, because this is an agricultural country, full of landless laborers and poor people. I was very disappointed because nobody took notice of it.

In the meantime, after the satyagraha against the sugarcane mill, the wealthy donors who had given money to start the Workers' Home and who provided monthly donations for our maintenance, began to question our approach. "What is this Jagannathan doing, fighting against our national government like a Communist?" One by one, their donations stopped.

I did not know what to do. It was a very difficult time. Many workers left. To eat, I had to walk from village to village asking for food. It was a terrible situation, and we suffered this way for almost one year. Luckily, we had a vegetable garden, so we could collect some vegetables and greens and we managed to survive.

In that period I was sleeping in the Worker's Home. One morning at four o'clock I came out here, facing this side where the moon was shining. Suddenly I heard God's call, "Jagannathan, you should go to Vinoba". It was a sudden thought. I had never considered it previously. So I discussed it with Keithan and I told him, "There is a miracle happening, a new nonviolent way to the land, and I want to go and join this movement. I want to share and understand this experience." So Keithan wrote a letter to Vinoba, and Vinoba welcomed me.

But what about Krishnammal? She was a college graduate, and I suggested she enroll in a one-year teacher training program in Madras. She agreed. Dr. Soundaram also agreed, and because Krishnammal is from a disadvantaged class, she received a scholarship. I said goodbye to her, and went to join Vinoba. See, it is all God's will. It was a sudden thought that morning, a sudden impulse, as when I lay down in front of the police lorry. In all this I see the hand of God.

When Vinoba was walking near Hyderabad in central India,

Nehru called him because the first Planning Commission was to take place in Delhi, and he wanted Vinoba to fly there and share his ideas. Vinobaji meditated for some time, and then replied he could not leave the movement, that, he said "had started by the will of God, so I can't break with God's call in favor of Nehru's call." He added that he would come to Delhi, but not by plane, only by walking, and that if they wanted him they had to wait for him to arrive. Nehru accepted, and Vinoba walked all the way to Delhi, where he arrived four months later. On the way to Delhi, he collected nearly 100,000 acres of land! In Delhi, they organized a big bungalow for him and the people who were walking with him. But Vinoba wanted to stay in Gandhi's *Samadhi*, the place where Gandhi's funeral pyre was, and now a large open space. So tents were arranged, and even the Planning Commission meetings took place there. Then Vinoba left and continued his padayatra.

I joined Vinoba in February 1951, after he left Delhi. It was a wonderful experience for me, a new pilgrimage. What a gift to be with such a spiritual giant! Gandhi was also a spiritual being, but Vinoba was a giant, even more spiritual than Gandhi, and more learned than he. He learned Arabic to read the Koran, and studied Hebrew to read the Old Testament. He was a Sanskrit scholar, and he knew all the Vedas, but he wanted to know about other religions as well, and to read the texts in the original languages.

He wrote several books on the *Bhagavad Gita*[2] and on other Hindu scriptures, but also on the Koran and the Bible. Vinoba used to sell his books at public meetings. After meetings, there would be queues of people waiting to buy his books and have them autographed. He would sign "*Ram Hari*" (Praise God). Hundreds of books were sold every day.

Early morning at four o'clock, we would start walking. There were about 20 people, though sometimes the group was bigger. From four to five no one could talk; we had to meditate and walk. It was a silent, prayerful march. Everything was quiet, in tune with nature that was still asleep. We were like disciplined soldiers marching.

In the morning, Vinoba ate only curd and honey. At 6 o'clock, he would sit somewhere along the road and eat. The people of the

Vinoba Bhave, the "Walking Saint", December 1978.

villages knew we were arriving, and they would prepare breakfast. We would have our food in the fields, and then start walking again. After breakfast, we could speak. Many people came to talk with Vinoba: politicians, economists, Gandhians, village people, even major national leaders. When we reached the villages, there were always so many people, and Vinoba was always at risk of being crushed. So I always tried to be at his side. When we walked in the dark in the early morning, usually there were three lanterns to carry, one in front and two at the sides of Vinoba. I always tried to carry the lantern to be close to him, and hear what he said. In the evening, I would hide one lantern somewhere, to take it back in the morning and walk by his side again.

The march would go on like that, and then we would reach a village, and people would organize a reception for him, and stand at the side of the road singing. Vinoba would talk to the crowd, and then move on to another village. Slowly even the less wealthy people started answering the appeal to donate land. Vinoba started asking, "Why should only rich people donate land? Why can't poor people give a little piece, too?" In the period when I was walking with him, he would appeal to people like this, "This is a sacrifice to God, a sacrifice for the community, so everybody should sacrifice, not only the rich."

Each time we entered a new state, we would meet the local people involved in the Bhoodan Movement. When we entered Uttar Pradesh, Vinoba gave as his objective the collection of 500,000 acres of land. We walked in Uttar Pradesh for one or two months, a rich area because it is criss-crossed by the river Ganges, and when we would reach a village there would be queues of people ready to donate. Vinoba requested people write on a piece of paper what they desired to donate, with the agreement of their entire family.

During the public meetings, Vinoba prayed. He spoke like a saint and melted people's hearts: he could melt iron, like fire. He melted people's heart with his spiritual power.

Sometimes, when during his meetings somebody offered him bananas, biscuits, and so forth, he would start an auction. He said, "One acre of land for this banana!" And so many hands would be raised. Westerners who had joined the march were amazed that people would line up to get a biscuit for one acre of land. It was madness, a spiritual madness: people were mad, mad after God. It was a wonder. You can give money, food, even your house, but in this country (and elsewhere) people are usually madly attached to their land, but Vinoba knew how to melt their hearts. Not through the power of law, nor the power of the government, but through spiritual power.

This was the nature of the movement, and how I loved being a part of it! I was the fellow that, when in prison, wanted to give land to the landless, but without knowing how. What was the way? Oh, this is the way!

After walking, Vinoba would take a bath and rest, and the most important people of the village would come to talk to him. I could see how in a few minutes he could move them. A man would come, wearing a silk shirt and gold rings, and perhaps offer five acres. Vinoba would look at him, with all this gold and silk and offering only five acres, and would say, "You are giving this much, thank you, but how many acres do you have?"

"Five hundred acres."

Vinoba would reply, smiling: "Don't you think that if you have five hundred acres, five acres is a bit too little to give, and a bit too little to receive?" Then he would ask: "How many brothers are you?"

"Four brothers."

"So imagine a fifth brother is born: won't you give him land even though he is the last one?"

"Of course, I would certainly give him land."

"Then, you see, I am your last brother born in your house. I am the youngest of your brothers."

The man would be so happy that Vinoba pronounced him a member of his own family that he would donate a hundred acres. So within a few minutes the man who wanted to give five acres was signing on for a hundred.

One day, as we were walking, a cyclist who was coming downhill from the opposite direction crashed against Vinoba, who was walking in front. Vinoba was hurt and could not walk, so we thought, "Now Vinoba will have to rest." But he would not stop. He only put on some bandages, and the next day he wanted us to continue the march, and we had to carry him. We built a palanquin, and he sat on a chair on top of the palanquin, and four of us, two in the front and two in the back, and carried him along. In those days, only kings and very important people were carried like this. Vinoba did not like it very much, but there was no other way. I was also one of the fellows who carried him. I remember that one day, because of some incorrect calculations, we had to walk 22 miles to reach the camp. It was nearly midday when we reached the place, carrying him the entire way. Some village people came and helped us, but it was so hard! So Vinoba said: "No, that is too much for you.

Tomorrow I will travel by bullock cart." So for the next several days we used a cart pulled by a bullock. The padayatra never stopped. If it was raining when Vinoba woke up, he would not wait for the rain to cease. He would start singing bhajans and dance in the rain, and then we would start walking again. We were all amazed by him.

I wrote articles about how people responded to Vinoba's appeal, some of which appeared in English-language newspapers. Vinoba was happy that someone was writing in English. I also wrote down, in English and in Tamil, his extraordinary speeches on spiritual issues, for example, how people's attachment to the land was man's original sin, because the land belongs to no one. Just like the sun, air, water, the five elements, so the land is God's property. One cannot purchase the sun, nor the air, nor the sky, so why should land be treated any differently? It is a sin against God. This was his philosophy. He believed that land had to be common property, and that private ownership of the land should be abolished.

I was ten months in the *yatra*, this extraordinary spiritual pilgrimage. At that time I became very proficient in English. I translated his speeches and sent them to England, one or two a month. I was so happy. But one day Vinoba called me and asked:

"How long have you been on this padayatra?"

"Ten months," I replied.

"It is time for you to go back to Tamil Nadu and start the movement there," he instructed.

I replied, "How can I start a movement, a humble man like me? There are so many great people that could do this; please, write to them, they can do better than I can"

Vinoba smiled and asked me, "Don't you know the *Ramayana*? Who helped Rama to fight against Ravana? Monkeys and squirrels. When Rama built the bridge to reach Lanka, the monkey God Hanuman brought big stones, while squirrels rolled in the sand, so that it got caught in their fur, and then they would run into the sea to wash so the sand would be deposited on the sea bottom. Thus was Rama helped by monkeys and squirrels. You are my squirrel. I am creating a story like the *Ramayana*, a story of a nonviolent revolution: there may be more important people involved, but you are my squirrel."

I would have never expected this, and replied, "No, please, Vinobaji, I don't want to go. I am so happy here in your *yatra*," but he remained firm.

Finally, I said, "All right, I will go, but I must ask you for one thing. My wife Krishnammal is undertaking a teacher training course and she has almost finished. I'll ask her to come and walk with you, and only then will I go".

He agreed. As soon as Krishnammal arrived she became ill, but I had to leave anyway because Vinoba told me to go; they would take care of her. She was saddened, but I had to leave five days after she arrived. I told her that I had been collecting Vinoba's speeches to send them to the newspapers, so I suggested she continue with this activity. At the beginning she could not speak Hindi, but she slowly learned. We met again in March 1953 in Bihar, where Vinoba went for a conference. From there we came back together to Tamil Nadu to start the Bhoodan Movement there."

In Krishnammal's story, the disappointment at having to remain far from her husband is evident.

Krishnammal: With Vinoba

"Just after finishing my studies, I left for Varanasi, and on September 11, 1952, I met Jagannathan. We went immediately to bathe in the Ganges, and as soon as I immersed myself in the water, I felt the cold penetrating my bones, and I got sick. Vinoba had decided that Jagannathan had to go back to Tamil Nadu and start the Bhoodan Movement there, so he had to leave. Vinoba's march had to continue—the next day at four o'clock in the morning he started walking again and I found myself there, all alone in a room. I was sick for almost three months, and when I rejoined the group I was so weak that they sent me back to an ashram in Varanasi to recover. I was so sick that could eat only *idlis* (bland, steamed lentil and rice cakes, a popular breakfast food in South India.)

I spent my time praying to be strong enough to walk again. I was in Varanasi for a month and then I joined Vinoba in Patna. There, a woman doctor from the south checked me and put me a special diet: raisins with some lime early in the morning, and then only rice and curd, for a month. I got better, but I was very angry with Jagannathan, who left me there when I was sick. I never replied to his letters, which were only full of information about the villages' problems.

I walked with Vinoba in Uttar Pradesh and in Bihar. Bihar is a state that could have been rich because of its great natural resources, but people there were exploited by outsiders from Gujarat. Rich forests had been cut down, and fertile land purchased by people that did not reside there. In Bihar, there were still tribal communities living on the hills in close contact with nature, and many untouchables, the weakest part of the population. The absentee landlords used them as bonded labor. Moneylenders came from outside, and politicians were corrupt. Even today, compared to other states, the caste system is still very strong, and social injustice more extreme in Bihar.

Vinoba's padayatra started at four o'clock in the morning. He was followed by about 50 people coming from various parts of the country. I was in charge of carrying one of the lamps that lighted his way, and I was lucky because it was something that everybody wanted to do. From four to six we walked in silence, absorbed in ourselves. Then at six o'clock, there was a break when Vinoba would ask questions of all the people who were walking with him. Knowing 14 languages, he could do this using people's own tongue. He knew the songs of the Tamil poet Bharati and the poems of Ramalingam. Sometimes he asked me questions about these poems, and I was ashamed because he knew more than I did! I had a very pleasant time with him. His only food was a small cup of milk or *dahi* (a diluted yoghurt drink) taken 18 times a day, and every time he drank he sang a chapter of the *Bhagavad Gita*, so that by the end of the day he had chanted the entire book. His graceful look and divine nature attracted people all along his way. Village people lined up to receive him with devotional songs. After the morning break, we walked again from nine to 12.

Vinoba belonged to the old tradition of the Rishis, the ancient seers. He renounced private life to work with Gandhi, together with his two brothers. The spiritual heir of Gandhi, Vinoba wanted the country to achieve *Gram Swaraj* (village self-rule) through Gandhi's constructive program, to bring about change in the social life of the people. He thought that India should achieve economic freedom in a nonviolent manner. In all his meetings he explained to the people that Gram Swaraj means self-sufficiency and freedom for the villages, decentralized political power, justice run by the village courts, and land to the village community.

His march was a way to find and harness the charitable energies of people in society. Rich and poor responded to Vinoba in the same way, and an army of volunteers left their homes to dedicate their lives to the achievement of Gram Swaraj. Many were inspired by Vinoba's speeches to accept the landless poor as members of their families, and people were inspired to rid themselves of a good part of their property."

Krishnammal is interrupted by the arrival of an exhausted-looking woman who is carrying a basket with some fruit and vegetables on her head. She walks with effort under the burning sun, a worn saree with no blouse underneath, bare feet on the burning ground. Krishnammal assists her in climbing the steps to the Workers' Home verandah, and helps her to lie on the floor, putting a rolled saree under her head. Vallarmati runs to get her a glass of water. I am struck by the contrast between the loving way Krishnammal takes care of the woman and the firm way she talks to her, almost as if she was scolding her. Krishnammal must notice my perplexity because she takes the opportunity to explain, "I told her she is mad to walk under a sun like this, she will get heatstroke! She walks from her village to sell these few vegetables, but if she gets sick who is going to take care of her—she doesn't have anybody in the world!" After a while the woman tries to get up, but Krishnammal insists that she get some more rest, then buys the entire contents of the basket and lets her go. Amma follows her with her eyes, and then continues, "The woman is a widow; her children are dead. She doesn't have anything and barely survives by selling the few things she manages to grow. Her look is haggard, and she can only think about survival. But in her there is a divine light, as in each one of us. I have dedicated my life to these women. The aim of my life is to make sure they have that minimum necessary to have a dignified life, so that they can raise their heads and think about God, too".

CHAPTER SIX

The Land Movement in Tamil Nadu

The next day, I reach the Worker's Home very early, anxious to listen to the rest of Jagannathan's recounting of the land movement in Tamil Nadu. The verandah is deserted. The children are probably having their breakfast at the hostel, and Krishnammal is with them. I hear Jagannathan's voice reciting what seems like a prayer, and I go to look for him. I find him standing in front of the area dedicated to *puja* (worship), a small niche in the wall that shelters some images of gods and goddesses and one of Sri Ramalingam, so dear to Krishnammal. There, an oil lamp burns day and night to symbolize the divine light in each of us. Jagannathan recites a verse in Sanskrit, than claps his hands, joins them, brings them over his head. Then he bends down to touch the floor, lifts himself up again and bends backwards, and then down again... This is the *Surya Namaskaran*—the "greeting to the sun"—one of the most classical and complex yoga exercises that Jagannathan practices every morning for 40 minutes with a flexibility that my 30-year-old old body has long forgotten. I sit quietly watching him, mesmerized by his perfect concentration and by the precision of his movements. When he finishes, he calls for Krishnammal. I tell him she is not there, and I help him reach his chair on the verandah. Soon Krishnammal arrives, bringing our breakfast; we eat with appetite, and then Jagannathan restarts his story.

Jagannathan: From Bhoodan to the common ownership of land

"I was sorry to leave Krishnammal again, but I couldn't do otherwise. I was obligated to obey Vinoba. So I left her and came back here. It was 1952. I immediately had to face the problem of how to begin collecting land. Before I left the padayatra, Vinoba had transformed his Bhoodan Movement into the *Gramdan* Movement. *Gramdan* means 'village gift', and Vinoba had started inviting people to renounce all private ownership of land in favor of the village community. He spoke to the village people, saying, "Lord Krishna was born in a village—Gokulam Village—where everybody was happy because they lived as one family. Why don't you live like that, sharing everything as in a spiritual commune?" So Bhoodan is the gift of some land, while Gramdan is the gift of one's entire property to the village community, to live as one family.

One day, Vinoba was in a large village where there was a man who alone owned 500 acres. There were other owners with medium holdings, and many having small ones. During a meeting in the village, Vinoba related how, as a boy, Lord Krishna used to steal butter from his mother to share with the other children of the village. Vinoba thaen retired for the night, and the next day he continued his march. But the large landholder gathered the people of his village and told them, "Vinobaji is a saint who reminds us that we should live as one family. I am prepared to give all my 500 acres to the village community." Vinoba had already left, but his message had reached the heart of a man who now was prepared to give up his land. Can you imagine a similar revolution happening anywhere else in the world? After this man's declaration, many others said they wanted to follow his example.

The next day all the important men of the village went to Vinoba and told him, "We are ready to surrender our 1,300 acres of land to the village community and live as one family. We want your blessing." Vinobaji was astonished. He had only given the message and gone away, never expecting that one village was immediately going to announce Gramdan. He was as surprised as he was the day he was offered 100 acres of land for the first time. He stated simply, "God is leading a great nonviolent revolution, and the country is ripe for the next step."

So before I left him to come back to Tamil Nadu, Vinoba told me, "It will take me many years before I reach Tamil Nadu, but when I come I want hundreds of Gramdan villages. Tamil Nadu is such a spiritual place, with hundreds of temples like those found nowhere else in the world, and people who are so devoted to God are going to be devoted to this movement, too." I did not know what to say, as I expected I would not be able to get even a few acres, but I left anyway."

The Bhoodan-Gramdan Movement in Tamil Nadu

"Initiating the Bhoodan-Gramdan Movement in Tamil Nadu was very difficult, because land is not easily given. People like Vinoba have this great spiritual power, but I was only one of Gandhi's disciples. But Vinoba put me in charge of this, so I had to take it on. First, I organized a meeting of workers of the Sarvodaya Movement from the whole state. Then I planned a walking tour starting from Rameshwaram, the place where, in the *Ramayana*, Rama built the bridge to reach Sita in Sri Lanka. We thought it would be useful to have a national leader to guide the tour, so we called upon Shankar Rao Dev, fomrer Secretary of Congress Party prior to Independence, but who had left politics to join the Sarvodaya Movement. Dev was a good speaker, but being from Maharastra, he couldn't speak Tamil, so he spoke in English and had a translator. We had to organize everything. We marched 15-20 kilometers a day, and then we would reach a camp where we had food and some meetings, and at the end we collected the land that was offered.

This *yatra* (pilgrimage) started in 1952 on October 2, the day of the anniversary of Gandhi's birth. At the time, Krishnammal was with Vinoba and no one could help me. We wanted to start well, and it was important that on the first day we could collect a good amount of land, so I ran here and there, asking for Bhoodan. Rameshwaram is in Ramnad, my home district. In Ramnad, there was a *raja* (prince), and I approached him to ask him for land. It was very hard but I managed, and I explained that the Bhoodan tour was starting from his district, and so we were expecting a good gift from him. After long discussions, he promised to give a thousand acres, but it was only a promise. Another man from a different district promised 120 acres, so we started with the expectation of these two donations. On the first day at about seven o'clock in the morning we had prayers, and then had a meeting attended by nearly 200 people. But the land-gift from the raja and the other man was yet to be officially announced, as the two men had just promised. And there I felt God's guidance again. While we were praying, we received a telegram from the raja, saying he was offering a thousand acres, so his promise was maintained.

It was a good start. We commenced our pilgrimage at six o'clock, later than Vinoba. My own village was on our route, and I wanted my father to give some land, but it was very difficult to get land from him! Anyway, he said, "I will come to meet this leader, this Shankar Rao Dev.". He came on the third or fourth day, but he did not promise anything. But, at the end, he donated, too. After about a month, we reached Madurai and Coimbatore districts, walking every day. In the first month, we collected about 3,500 acres, not a big thing, but it was an achievement anyway. I did not expect I would be able to get even that much.

Shankar Rao Dev left us, and I started walking by myself from village to village. At this time, K. M. Natarajan, who had just finished his studies, joined me. He was my first assistant, and even today we are still working together. He came to me when he was so young, and he took on many responsibilities: office work, translating speeches and sending them to the newspapers, and sending a tally of Bhoodan to the papers every day so they would announce how much land had been given. We started walking in the villages where in the past I had organized my summer camps with students. These were areas I knew, but I had an unexpected response from the people, who offered much more land than I thought they would. For a month, there were Natarajan, two or three other people, and myself—nothing like Vinoba's tour. Sometimes, there was someone to receive us, and sometimes nobody gave us food. I asked Vinoba to send me a woman who was walking with him, who spoke English and Marathi but could not speak Tamil, so Natarajan would translate. I woud arrange for the meetings and collect bhoodan. When we got land, I announced it in the evening meetings.

In February or March 1953, there was a national conference

of all the people who participated in Vinoba's movement. Every year, Vinoba called for an assembly of workers to discuss the Bhoodan Movement, to ascertain how things were going in the different states, and discuss how to proceed. We called it *Sarvodaya Sammela* (Sarvodaya Roundtable). People would come from all over India, generally 3,000-5,000 people to meet and talk for two or three days. I attended that conference in Bihar myself, and there was Krishnammal! Oh, I was so happy! We met again after her year on the padayatra. That was such a rich experience for her. I think that Vinoba liked her even better than he liked me, because of her simple lifestyle, and because she could sing beautiful songs. She became a favorite of Vinoba's and learnt Hindi so well! At that conference I told her, "Now it's time for you to come with me, with Vinoba's permission, and help in the movement in Tamil Nadu". We had been married now for several years, but only then did we make love for the first time, because before we were always separated! And on November 24th, 1953, Bhoomikumar was born, in the middle of the Bhoodan Movement

Krishnammal continued walking even when she was eight months pregnant. At the eighth month, at a Tamil Nadu state conference held in Thanjavur, even our Chief Minister came. When he saw that Krishnammal was with me and she was pregnant, he said, "What is wrong with you, fellow? She is already eight months pregnant and you are allowing her to walk? She should be resting! You shouldn't allow her this kind of physical exercise." She was so dedicated to the movement that she didn't want to stop, but after this advice she came here to Gandhigram to rest, and I went for another yatra. So Bhoomi was born here in Gandhigram, in the hospital. I received a telegram when I was about 100 kilometers away. I finished my work and then I returned to Gandhigram. It was Vinoba himself who choose the name Bhoomikumar, meaning son of mother earth.

In 1954 and 1955, we organized many more padayatras. Krishnammal used to carry the child and walk, so Bhoomi also traveled with us even when he was only one year old. It was very difficult for Krishnammal, I thought, but she managed it with the assistance of some women from the north, Vinoba's disciples, who joined our yatra. As soon as she was up and walking, she began addressing meetings.

After three years from the commencement of the movement in Tamil Nadu, we had collected about 100,000 acres. We had covered many districts, even if not all of them, walking and walking. This is the required technique: one cannot drive in a car to ask for land. Some suffering and a spiritual approach is necessary. This was a godly movement, and to melt the heart of the people we had to walk the same way one walks to go on pilgrimage to a holy place. Each village *is* a holy place. It was a spiritual approach to the land problem, starting from the point that land is a gift of God like the sun, air, and water. Our aim was to change people's hearts.

During these three years, we also distributed the land. We had been waiting for Vinoba to come, and we knew we were not going to have time to distribute while he was here, with everything to arrange and organize. During his marches, Vinoba did not have time to distribute the land—he only collected—but we decided to distribute each time we received land to avoid having people make promises and then change their minds, or having their sons refuse to relinquish title, as often happened.

In 1955, a year before Vinoba came, I arranged a meeting with Kamaraj—the Chief Minister of Tamil Nadu—and all the Congress leaders. Jayaprakash Narayan (JP) came as well. JP was a very popular leader because he had left the Socialist party and renounced all political power to embrace the Bhoodan Movement. Like Rama, who renounced the throne and went to the forest, or like Buddha, who was a prince and renounced the throne for higher purposes, JP, in line with this tradition, gave up power and gained great respect as a result. I organized a joint 15-day tour for JP and Kamaraj. It was a tour by car and thousands of people joined the meetings, and everywhere there were huge crowds.

Kamaraj appreciated the Bhoodan Movement, and he loved me very much, as I loved him. He came from a very poor harijan family; his father died when he was little and they had nothing. His mother sold food in the street, but the son became a powerful and respected politician. He was not educated, but he was a very simple and inspiring speaker. This tour created a good atmosphere for Vinoba's movement.

In March 1956, Vinoba entered Tamil Nadu. Every time he entered a state it was a big affair: ministers and politicians would come to meet him, and all the authorities would be there. When he arrived in Tamil Nadu, he was received by Kamaraj and other state officials and representatives from all parties except the Communist Party. The Communists did not believe in nonviolence and in our movement, and they thought we were only getting bad land, useless for cultivation. Vinoba used to respond by saying that while it might be true we were being given dry land, even that bad land had been kept as private property. So it was a beginning; next time the landholders would give us good land. And with people's labor, we could make it good land. We would clear it of brush, move stones, cut down trees, and then start cultivating. When the Communists attacked the Bhoodan Movement, we never did any propaganda against them. Vinoba only responded quietly to their criticism. But the fact was that of all the land we got, at least 40% was good land, excellent for the cultivation of rice and corn. Most of the land was not irrigated, because nobody would give irrigated land, so the first thing to do was to dig wells. But Vinoba believed that step by step it was possible to move and heal people's hearts and make them give better land.

When he entered Tamil Nadu through Chengalpattu in the northern part of the state, Vinoba wanted people to give up private ownership of their land in favor of the village community. Before Vinoba came, I tried hard to achieve Gramdan. In 1955, we had a workers' meeting in Chengalpattu, where I told that Vinoba was now asking for Gramdan, and that at least on the day he came we had to be able announce that one village had declared Gramdan. The meeting went on for three days, and then a man named Ramakrishna Reddy arrived and said, "Jagannathan, I am prepared to give all my land in the village of Kaliyampoondi, but the other landlords may not agree to give up theirs, so please come to my village." So we went and camped there for three days, meeting the other landlords. Some were ready to participate, but others did not want to, and the three days were a failure. So Ramakrishna Reddy asked us to come to another village, Vaiallur, where he also owned land, and where all the families were small owners and untouchables.

So we moved to Vaiallur and organized many meetings. Reddy explained that he wanted to donate his 94 acres of fertile land, and many people of his same caste, small holders, agreed to donate as well. But among the 32 untouchables of the village there was one, named Subhan, who owned only one acre but did not want to join the Gramdan because he did not trust us. So to convince him, Reddy touched his feet. This was an extraordinary act, because a man from the higher castes man never touches a harijan, and especially does not touch his feet, because this gesture is a sign reserved for great respect. But he did so, and this gesture convinced Subban, so the first Gramdan was announced.

We had convinced everyone, but then they still had to sign a paper stating that they were giving their land to the community, and renouncing private ownership. Everyone signed, but the problem was that Ramakrishna Reddy's land was under his wife Sitalakshmi's name, so she was the one who had to sign. He went to his village to get her signature, but she refused. She asked, "How can I do this? I have five children. What will happen to them? I can't sign". This news discouraged us completely because we had expended such great effort, and Vinoba was about to arrive. But Reddy said he was going to fast to convert his wife. He fasted for some days, and his wife was in tears, and on the third day, she said, "You know that when Rama went to the forest, Sita didn't let him go alone. She left a comfortable life in the palace to be in the forest with him, wearing rough clothes. As Sita followed Rama, I am going to follow you, so I will sign. Rama renounced his kingdom, and my husband renounced his property, so I will follow."

That evening we held a prayer meeting in the small village temple there. After the prayer, something wholly out of the ordinary occurred that demonstrated how economic revolution can bring about social revolution. Reddy and his wife came before the image of the temple Goddess and said, "Oh Mother, this land is yours," and offered their land to the village Goddess. And all the other people that were giving land did the same, placing the land documents in front of the temple altar. Then people prostrated themselves in front of image of the Goddess, and an extraordinary thing happened: Reddy prostrated himself at the untouchables' feet, and after him other caste people did the same, and everybody embraced in fellowship. It was a sign of an extraordinary change, and we were amazed.

Such a glorious thing it was when people started giving up their private property, with no violence, while in other parts of the world so many people were being killed, and still are getting killed, because of the land. Reddy's gesture had a tremendous impact. Even now, when I remember this episode tears come to my eyes.

The movement continues

A young man named Manickam joined us. He was a young graduate who now worked for the telephone department. He was devoted to Vinoba and knew everything about the movement. He came to see me because he wanted to leave his job and join us. He came to Vaiallur, and was so moved by the amazing atmosphere created that, during a meeting, he stood up and said, "I had in my mind to leave my job and join this movement, but now that I see with my eyes what is happening here, I want to donate my life to this village. I will live here and serve this village, and all the money I have I will use to serve you. My family will move here to work for you." What a man he was! He was with us for very many years (he died in 1999) and lived in Vaiallur, helping the people for more than four decades.

After the declaration of Gramdan, there were 127 acres belonging to the village community, but now it had to be decided what to do with them. There were about 30 harijan families that had no land at all and so we thought, as a first experiment, to attempt a collective farm, with everyone working the land as one family. Another solution might have been to divide the land and distribute it on the condition that it could not be sold, but our enthusiasm was so great that we decided on a collective approach. It was very, very difficult. The first three or four months things went well, because of the enthusiasm. But then problems began because we did not know where to get money to buy the seeds, tools, manure and the items that the village people could not produce themselves. People were working the land collectively but nobody was earning anything, whereas before the untouchables families were working other people's land and receiving a daily wage. So we approached merchants in Madras, which was close by, and they donated food and other items to the revolution that was taking place. It went on like that for some months, but then quarrels started because, if before people had to work to make a living, during this experiment they were getting food anyway, so many became lazy and stopped working. Jealousy and conflicts grew, and after one year we abandoned this experiment.

I believe this kind of experiment can work only if the human mind is perfectly developed. People must abandon their selfish instincts and learn to think in collective terms. Otherwise it will end in failure. In Vaiallur, collective approaches were tried prematurely, and we failed. This is the sad story of the first Gramdan. Now Vaiallur has changed; the land has been distributed and everybody is cultivating individually, but people still recognize the work we have done and what we, and they, have achieved.

In April 1956, the Sarvodaya Movement Workers Conference was held in Kanchipuram, home to one of the great temples of Tamil Nadu. More than 100,000 people were there, and we had to face the problem of how to feed and host all these people every day. Fortunately, the Chief Minister took charge of the whole thing, and he put me in charge of the reception committee. At the end of the conference, Vinoba said, "Before we move, I want to fast for three days, to prepare myself spiritually for my tour in Tamil Nadu. This is such a spiritual part of India, with huge, old temples, so I am expecting a great response for Gramdan, and I want to pray." I was sad that he wanted to fast here, thinking I had done something wrong, but Vinoba said it was just his way to make himself fit for the padayatra.

After his arrival, the Gramdan Movement accelerated. The first day of his padayatra, forty villages were declared as Gramdan. Then all the Gandhigram students started going to the villages to convince people to join the movement. In that way, more and more villages announced Gramdan. I think that at the end of the tour they were 4-5,000. Vinoba was here for 11 months, before heading for Kerala. In 1957 he left, and I was now free from the responsibility of organizing Vinobaji's camps. It had been a difficult task—so many people to feed every day!

At the time, Bhoomi was three years old. He followed the tour with us, so he was on tour with Vinoba for an entire year! We taught him some songs and slogans, and he would sing them before meetings. Vinoba liked this very much. I believe Bhoomi's continued commitment to service for the people (he is now a child psychiatrist who works in Pnomh Penh, Cambodia) stems from these early experiences, and the impact Vinoba and the others had upon him, even when he was very young. It is such a blessing to me that my son could have an experience such as this."

I am anxious to hear how Krishnammal remembers this period of her life, when she had a small child to look after. It is so interesting to hear the story from both of them, often because the way they remember things is so different, and their style of delivery so contrasting. Jagannathan narrates as if he had written the story of his life already a thousand times in his mind. Sitting on his chair, at an agreed-upon time, he gives himself over to the past in a logical manner, always making sure that what he says is clear to me and I know exactly where we are. He remembers names and dates with precision, and every day, he start his narration exactly when it was interrupted the day before. Once in a while he asks me if everything is clear, if the tape recorder is working, if I have to turn the tape over, or if I am too tired to continue.

Krishnammal narrates in an enthusiastic and often chaotic manner, without following any precise temporal order, but moving here and there in time and space. Her story is the stuff of emotion and extremely lively images that have latched onto her memory, and her mind and heart. Often, in order to understand her, I have to stop and ask at least "where" and "when", and sometimes I think that I should ask her to be more precise in her narration, but then I realize it would be of no use in any case. She has to be chased and caught. Sometimes a fact or a visitor reminds her of an episode in her past and she starts narrating, whether we are in the car, in a temple, on a train, or conformably sitting on the verandah of the guesthouse. In the middle of a story, she holds my arm with her hand, as if to ensure that I am hanging on for the ride, and I can hardly write anymore! Often, very often, she is interrupted by someone who calls her, some guest who has just arrived, or a phone call. I take notes the best I can and then, asking her lots of questions, I manage to recreate the picture and put her narration into some more linear arrangement.

Krishnammal: The land movement and Vinoba's march in Tamil Nadu

"During the Bhoodan Movement in Tamil Nadu, I was in charge of creating and guiding women's groups in the villages, and in forming committees to ask for Bhoodan land. Jagannathan and I worked in different districts, and I used to see him very rarely. Jagannathan was carrying on many padayatras at the same time, with the help of different workers; we were preparing the whole of Tamil Nadu for Vinoba's arrival. We had no home, no money, no family life, but our work was very exciting. People always responded well to our message, because we were Gandhians and we were Vinoba's people, so the villagers were anxious to welcome us. I always carried little Bhoomi with me, and when I didn't get any land in a village, I refused to take food.

During the movement, we received so many kingly gestures, but we also had some bad experiences. I remember one evening in a village near Trichy where we had gone to conduct a public meeting, a big landlord welcomed us and gave us food. But that day I saw that when the untouchables of the village came to get their daily wages, he refused to pay them with the excuse that it was already dark, and according to the tradition one should not give money after sunset. I got upset, and that evening during the public meeting I spoke against his behavior. One of his men started shouting at me, saying we were welcomed and I had no right to speak like that. But how could I keep quiet after what I had seen? So that landlord threw our things out of his house, and that night we had no food and we had to sleep in the street, little Bhoomi with us!

In another village of the same district, there was a rich Hindu monastery that owned good land. When that evening we had our public meeting, we said that the temple land should be given to the people, before they got too angry and started a violent revolution, as in China. The temple people got angry and threw us out!

When Vinoba came to Tamil Nadu, I was in charge of organizing the camps in the villages. Vinoba choose to visit as many places as possible here, and so he used to walk in the evenings, too. There were always at least 50 people with him. I used to go by jeep to select the villages, find a place, and then organize the reception and the public meeting. The next day, while Vinoba was walking, I used to go ahead to arrange reception and food in the next location. Vinoba only wanted to stay in public places, such as schools or temples. In Coimbatore District, he walked twice to get more bhoodan and gramdan. How could he not be tired? We were all exhausted, but Vinoba never rested. If he had some time, he used it to read, making an extensive study of Tamil literature, the stories of the saints, and the devotional songs.

There were always so many people standing in queues to offer land gifts. People were totally attracted by Vinoba's spirituality. In the villages it was like a festival, people chanting and giving flowers. It was a new awakening of the people to Gandhi's message. There were also people from England, the U.S., and other countries marching with Vinoba. Bhoomi was always with me—he was three years old. He didn't go to school before the sixth grade. I used to be his teacher.

The last segment of Vinoba's tour was Kanyakumari, the extreme southern point of India, where the three oceans meet: the Pacific and Indian Oceans, and the Bay of Bengal. Vinoba was there for three days and, inspired by the pacific atmosphere of the place, he spent most of his time in deep meditation. The morning of the third day he woke up very early and started running around in an ecstatic state. I was worried because he was running very fast and I was scared he could fall in the water. I started shouting and I called Jagannathan. Vinoba walked into the water, climbed on a rock and sat on it, but it was dangerous because he could have been hit by waves. So Jagannathan and I held each others' hands and stood in front of him to protect him from the waves. After sitting in meditation for a while, Vinoba stood up, collected some sea water with his hands and facing the sun he made a vow that he was going to walk till he had attained Gram Swaraj, village self-rule, for the entire country.

It is an enormous privilege to have met and cooperated with a saint like Vinoba, and I always think that it is such a blessing that Jagannathan and I are still working towards Gram Swaraj."

The experience with Vinoba and the land-gift movement are among the subjects dearest to Jagannathan. He did, however, understand deeply and took great pains to explain to me what he saw as its limits and defects. It is a very interesting subject, especially because of the difference of perspectives between Jagannathan and Vinoba regarding the use of satyagraha to obtain land and fight injustice. Even today, this often distinguishes Jagannathan's methods with those of other Gandhians. Jagannathan tells me more about Vinoba's movement and Kumarappa's painful departure from the Bhoodan Movement.

Jagannathan: Kumarappa and the limits of the Bhoodan Movement

"When Vinoba arrived in Tamil Nadu in 1956, Kumarappa joined his padayatra, following the tour with the spirit of a scientist who wanted to understand the nature of this movement. He said to Vinoba, "This is a great movement. It is mightier than the movement Gandhi had against the British, because you are also fighting against capitalism, and you have almost succeeded in moving from the simple land gift to the abolition of private property in favor of the village community. It is an extraordinary thing, something that has not happened in any other part of the world." But then he added, "Vinobaji, I am a scientist, a practical man, while you are a spiritual man and a philosopher, so I want to invite you to come down to ground level. You should continue to collect these gift papers, but you should also distribute the land. Otherwise it will be of no use. You should receive the land first, then distribute it to the landless, and then immediately start projects to make it fertile and cultivable."

One night, there was a fire in the nearby forest, set by farmers to clear out the forest undergrowth to let the new plants grow better. Vinoba said to Kumarappa: "See the fire in the forest? I will set fire to the old, to this old system of land ownership. My duty is only to set fire. Another generation will come to plant a new forest. I can't take on that work now. I can only set fire and destroy the old system." Kumarappa answered, "No, this is not practical. It is a waste of time, and the movement will waste itself if the land is not distributed soon. When the men who gave land die, how many of their children will maintain their fathers' promises?" But Vinoba didn't listen. So Kumarappa, who had known me for a long time, told me he was going to leave Vinoba's movement because he wanted to look for some land to start some experiments in cultivation. He asked me to join him, but I could not go because Vinoba was here in Tamil Nadu and I was organizing his tour.

With Vinoba, we collected so much land, but when it was time to distribute, many people had already changed their mind and refused to keep their promises. Unfortunately, Vinoba did not accept Kumarappa's suggestion to collect, distribute, and then help to start cultivation. And the people did indeed need to be trained in techniques to make the bad lands fruitful, as well as requiring tools, bullocks, manure, and seed.

This was an extraordinary movement, but on the practical side, it had its limits. Kumarappa thought that this was going to bring it to ruin, and left the movement. He died here, with his heart broken because the national government had abandoned Gandhi's ideas and was becoming more and more capitalist-oriented. Kumarappa was sad and angry to see this imitation of the American economy, which he knew from firsthand experience, and on many occasions he attacked the government, as during the sugar-mill satyagraha.

I loved Vinoba and the spiritual basis of the movement, but at the same time I am a practical man and I wanted to see the condition of the landless improve immediately. I think that if Kumarappa and Vinoba had worked together the movement would have had a bigger and certainly longer-lasting impact. Differently from Vinoba, Gandhi had given Kumarappa lots of space, and in his place would have asked Kumarappa to take charge of the distribution and the scientific application of agriculture that he could not undertake himself. Gandhi would have given this kind of freedom to Kumarappa, and Vinoba should have done the same".

I would like to know something more about Vinoba's movement. First of all, I ask Jagannathan about the people who donated land and their motivations.

"Generally, in a village there are different groups of people owning land. The upper classes own 50 or 100 acres or more. Then there are the middle class, the small holders, and the landless. Four groups all together. The landless comprise about one-fourth of the population, the small holders another third, and the rest would be owners with medium- or large-size holdings. The landless and the small holders were eager to join the movement because they hoped to benefit from this cooperative spirit. They thought it could bring an increase in production, and an immediate benefit to their lives. The upper classes did not accept Gramdan easily, even if there are exceptions like Ramakrishnan Reddy who offered all his land. Vinoba decided that if 75% of the people of a village accepted Gramdan, and at least 50% of the land come under Gramdan, then the whole village could be called a Gramdan village. The government accepted this definition, so this meant that a village could be a Gramdan village even if 25% of the people had not joined, and 50% of the land had not been donated. But the fact that a village was recognized as Gramdan by the government was important because this way the distribution of the land was legally recognized, and it was possible to ask for funding to buy agricultural inputs, including animals, tools, and manure."

I asked him what happened to all the villages that had declared Gramdan?

"It was possible to get funding and ask for loans only if the government recognized the village as Gramdan, but generally the government is very slow in its actions and the bureaucracy so complicated that before the procedures were completed, people were starving. This was the main reason that made the experiment of common property fail in many villages. Suppose it is the rainy season and people want to put manure on the field. They have to write an application to get manure from the government, and then it may take three or four months to get it, so it arrives when it is not useful any longer. There was and there still is a lot of corruption in government—the local officials don't move if you don't bribe them. Corruption and long waits created many difficulties. In addition, while recognizing Gramdan in principle, in practice the government-run banks would not recognize collectively owned land to be used as security for loans. There was therefore no way for the community to access needed capital to make significant improvements.

There was a revolution in the villages, but not in the bureaucracy, and this created many obstacles. Only a parallel revolution in the government could have helped Gramdan.

Another problem is that to have an effective impact on people, Gramdan has to spread in a large area and not in isolated pockets, as happened in reality. Further, because in a village 50% of the land and 25% of the people may have not been part of the experiment, there were always selfish interests in the mix. Generally the best land was not given, so it was very difficult to improve Gramdan. It was clear that to have things working, the other 50% of the land should have been donated. But how to get it was the question. Vinoba said to leave it. But unless there is some nonviolent action to change the old system where the rich always own the best land, there can be no real revolution, and there will always be conflict. That selfish section of the society will always be a disturbing factor. Vinobaji avoided confrontation with them, while I think that this conflict should have been conducted through nonviolent means. Gandhi always tried to solve conflicts with satyagraha. Vinoba instead was too soft, and did not want to give trouble to the newly born national government. I did not agree with him.

So Vinoba's movement did not put down deep roots. Only in Tamil Nadu did we face up to these problems with many satyagrahas. This strengthened the movement, and that is the reason why now when we organize our actions against the prawn industries, there is massive participation, because people have been trained in satyagraha."

Towards Village Republics

It is my last day in Gandhigram. Tomorrow we are leaving for Vinoba Ashram in Kuthur, where Jagannathan and Krishnammal spend most of their time since they became involved in the campaign against intensive prawn farming.

Vinoba Ashram is the headquarters of LAFTI—Land For The Tillers' Freedom. LAFTI is an organization born in 1981. With it, the Jagannathans have formalized their activity of a lifetime. Krishnammal, LAFTI's secretary, explains to me that creating a proper organization had never been a particular desire for her, but it became necessary when she started receiving donations, funding, and loans both from private sources and from the Indian Government itself to buy land and sustain their rural development projects.

From a recent report, I read the long list of LAFTI's activities:

- LAFTI assists in the organization of the *Gram Sabhas*, or village assemblies. These are constituted by all the adult members of the communities—women and men—and meet monthly to discuss community problems and evolve an 'action plan' for the month. The Gram Sabha collects a contribution from each family, and deposits it in a common fund for community use.
- LAFTI facilitates the creation of *Mathar Sanghas*—women's organizations—whose purposes range from discussion of family issues and children, small savings, health, and nutrition to programs like 'Backyard Horticulture' and other small income-generating activities. One of their salient features is the 'Lamp Worship',

the simple form of community prayer with a lamp that plays a fundamental role in uniting the village woman and in giving them courage and self-confidence.

- LAFTI is engaged in the construction of brick houses using local materials and shared labor. The houses that are built are always owned in the name of women to guarantee them security and decisionmaking power.
- LAFTI promotes village crafts and the birth of training centers and small productive units for carpentry, brick-making, mat-weaving, soap production, etc.
- LAFTI facilitates programs of reforestation, and the composting of domestic waste.
- LAFTI promotes literacy through the creation of schools and adult education programs.
- LAFTI directs campaigns against the distribution of cheap liquor to help reduce the plague of alcoholism in the villages, and to push the government in the direction of prohibition.
- LAFT continues its land distribution campaign, which has always been at its core. The organization continues to buy and distribute land at low cost to the poorest families through a system of loans and credits.
- Finally, LAFTI spearheads a campaign against intensive prawn farming that has polluted the water and land resources in the areas occupied by the coastal villages. In the last ten years, this has engaged the Jagannathans and LAFTI workers more than any other activity.

But I've jumped too far ahead in our story. It was to be more than decades, and hundreds of marches, protests, fasts, and imprisonments before LAFTI was to arrive on the scene.

Thinking about our journey, I realized I have been so absorbed by the intense work with Jagannathan and Krishnammal that I still haven't explored the area around the Workers' Home. I borrow a bicycle to get as close as possible to the Sirumalai Mountains, the hills in the background of Gandhigram. The story of these mountains is linked to the

Indian epic, the *Ramayana*, in which, during the terrible battle between Rama and the demon-king Ravana, the monkey-god Hanuman was sent to the Himalayas to search for a special medicinal plant. But once on the Himalayan peaks, Hanuman did not recognize the herb he was asked to find. So he grabbed a whole mountain and flew with it all the way to Rama. During flight, a piece of the mountain fell and became the Sirumalai range, famous for the medicinal herbs that grow on its slopes. I bicycle through palm trees, sugarcane plantations, vegetable gardens, flowers fields, fields ploughed and ready for sowing. I stop in front of a vineyard and I think how much this fertile, quiet, clean, and serene India differs from the hell of her big cities. There, eyes and throat burn from the pollution, the stomach churns from the smell of rubbish and open sewage, and the heart shrinks at seeing the thousands who live at the margins of the new well-being, from which they will always be excluded, pushed always lower down by the rise of a middle class that drives cars, wears jeans, and eats at a still-beefless McDonald's.

I would like to go further, but the road is getting too bumpy, the heat too intense, and the time to continue Jagannathan's story is approaching, so I decide to go back on this bicycle that is too big for me.

Jagannathan: Constructive program and satyagraha

"After Vinoba left, we moved back here to Gandhigram, and Keithan had an idea. Twenty kilometers from here there is an area called Batlagundu, where about 300 villages had declared Gramdan. So Keithan suggested we move there, and intensify our activity. We would facilitate the birth of village assemblies, so that people would consult with each other and decide how to run the Gramdan, distributing the land, or cultivating it collectively. We would work with the tillers to find seeds, manure, tools, and everything they needed to start cultivation. And we would facilitate the birth of small-scale village industries. So we moved to a village called Kannavapatti and established an ashram there. K.M. Natarajan was chosen as secretary of a new organization created to help implement Gramdan.

In the years that followed, I organized many satyagrahas for the land. Some had the objective of making people respect their donation papers, because many people had promised land but never got around to actually giving it. Other satyagrahas were directed against social and economic injustice, such as when we discovered that the land of a temple was cultivated by a single large landholder instead of it being distributed to the landless as it should be by law, or the times we came to know that a certain landlord had much more land than the government allowed under recent land ceiling acts.

Vinoba was opposed to these satyagrahas. He maintained that if people didn't give the land they promised, it was better to let it go. But I thought that it was critical that the promises made were kept so that people wouldn't lose faith in nonviolence as a means to obtain land to cultivate. Many times I went against Vinoba's will and organized satyagrahas, so in Tamil Nadu the Bhoodan-Gramdan Movement became a true people's movement, not Vinoba's movement only.

One of the first satyagrahas took place about 15 miles form here, where there was a very rich man who owned coffee and cardamom plantations. During Vinoba's padayatra, he promised one fifth of his land, and the announcement of his donation appeared in headlines in the newspapers, and because of it he became very popular. We also became friends. When Vinoba arrived in his village, he visited the man's house. But when the padayatra moved to the south, this man never actually gave the land, only putting us off with promises. I was very worried, and I said so to Vinoba, who told me to leave it. But how could I leave it? He had promised! I told Vinoba, "This land has not been promised to you personally. It has been promised to the people, and they are waiting to have it. It is the poor people who are being cheated!" He answered that even if that man had promised, we couldn't know if in that period his family was having some difficulties. I decided that I was going to organize a satyagraha anyway. Vinoba opposed me, insisting, "No, don't do it. If the landlord is hard, he will become harder. As a reaction, his heart will harden again". I replied, "Vinobaji, I agree with you for what concerns that man, but what about the hundreds of poor people who live in that area and are waiting for the land? Have you considered their hearts? Don't you think they will be disappointed? They will be desperate, and maybe they will resort to violence. If the land is not distributed, they may start thinking that nonviolence is not the way." I discussed the situation with the other workers and said, "This rich landlord became popular with his donation, but now he is cheating the people, and he is cheating Vinoba. I think we should take nonviolent action. Let us gather a thousand people from the villages nearby and march around the village where this man lives, and organize meetings to discuss the whole thing. But be aware that, unfortunately, Vinoba doesn't approve of my position."

The first initiative was a thousand-person march, followed by a public meeting attended by 5,000 people. The village people insisted that they desired the promised distribution of land. I explained that I had had several meetings with the man, but he was still not surrendering the land. Vinoba himself wrote the man a letter, asking him to respect his promise, but he did not even answer. I also said, "This land gift is not for me, neither is it for Vinoba, nor for his family. He did not ask for this land for his sake, or for my sake, but he asked it for your sake. Vinoba's movement is not his movement or my movement, but it is yours. I am your nonviolent agent. With nonviolence, we obtained the promise of the land. Now it is your duty to go and ask him what happened to the land he promised you. I suggest you set up a committee of five people, and invite this man to a public meeting tomorrow".

The next day, there was a meeting where these five representatives asked him clearly to show them them the land he intended to donate. He was so surprised, as for five years he had managed to delay, but under the pressure of the people he finally decided to give up the land. Everything ended like this, with no violence and no need for further action.

When I told Vinoba that the land had finally come and had been distributed, he was so pleased! Vinoba was a philosopher, a giant in spirituality, but his feet were not planted firmly on the ground. And this became the weak point of the movement. His movement was the movement of a great saint, but it never really became engraved in people's hearts. This I regret even today.

It was 1957. After this successful satyagraha, we came to know about a conflict between some rich landlords from Madras who owned land in the Batlagundu area, and the tillers who were cultivating it. Members of the Madurai Landlords Association let everybody know that they were not going to rent their land to anyone who joined Vinoba's movement. The tillers had taken part in the Bhoodan Movement and in the large demonstration we had organized in Madurai, when 20,000 people marched to ask the landlords to join the movement and requested Gramdan. So the landlords became angry and decided to serve legal notice to evict 122 people who cultivated their land as tenants.

The people were desperate. They didn't know what to do and asked us for help. They told us it was time to put manure on the fields, and that those rich people from Madras said they were going to do it themselves. So we decided to organize a satyagraha. When the landlords arrived with their trucks full of manure, all elegant in their silk shirts and golden rings, we sat all around the fields to stop them from entering the land. They became angry and started to take the manure with their hands and throw it on us—horrible city manure. But we did not move. We stayed in our place without reacting. At the end they left, but they called for the police, who started to arrest us.

At the time, Kamaraj was still Chief Minister in Tamil Nadu. When he got to know that many of us were in prison, he was very angry, and sent the Home Minister Shri Kakkan, who was a harijan himself. Shri Kakkan organized a meeting with the landlords to learn why they wanted to evict people. They answered it was because they were asking for land for Gramdan. He asked if the tenants were taking land from them, and they said no. He asked if they were not paying their rent, and they answered they were paying. He asked why they were evicting them if the tenants were just expressing a wish, without forcing anything on anybody, and paying their share. In the end, the minister asked the landlords to

S. Jagannathan with children, Tamil Nadu, circa 1960.

cancel the eviction notice and they did.

We had another important satyagraha in a village called Vellampatty. Near Vellampatty there were 32 acres of land that had been donated by the rich people of the area to the big temple dedicated to the goddess Meenakshi. It was paddy land, very fertile, on the river delta. There is a law that says that if temples receive gifts of land, they can directly cultivate only 25 acres, and the rest has to be given in tenancy to the landless poor, who have to give the temple a share of the harvest. So those 32 acres should have been cultivated by landless people, while in Vellampatty they were in the hands of a very influential man, a relative of the Agriculture Minister, who already owned much of the land in the village, as well as a biscuit factory, a press, and a cinema.

When we came to know about this issue, I went to meet this man and asked him to respect the law and give land for tenancy, but he refused. I also met the Agriculture Minister, but he showed no interest. So I decided we were going to have another satyagraha. We informed the people that by law they had the right to cultivate that land, and so they had to take it back. We entered the land, but were immediately arrested—Keithan, myself, and all the people with us. But this was not the end of the satyagraha because Natarajan started going around the villages looking for other people who were willing to join the protest, and every day, for a whole week, the land was occupied by people who were regularly arrested. I think that at the end more than 700 people went to prison. When Kamaraj came to know what was happening, he sent Shri Kakkan again. Kakkan came to the village and ordered that the 32 acres be distributed the following day to 32 landless families. Than he came to the prison and ordered us released. He was moved to tears, because he was so ashamed that we people of the Sarvodaya Movement were in prison when Kamaraj was Chief Minister.

I had known Kamaraj since he was a student in Keithan's Harijan Hostel. Whenever I decided to organize a satyagraha I would tell him beforehand, as Gandhi used to do with the British, and Kamaraj used to tell me all the time, "No, this is not a good time, even if it was my own father organizing a satyagraha now, I would send him to prison!" He tried to involve me in politics, but I always refused.

These are only some instances of our satyagrahas in the Batlagundu area, where we worked for ten years, until 1967."

At lunchtime, Krishnammal introduces me to Lila, one of the LAFTI workers, who has come back to work after being unwell, and asks me if I want to talk with her. Lila is an affable woman in her fifties. I instantly notice her look, a mixture of the sweetness so typical of many Indian women, and the courage and determination of Krishnammal's eyes. She comes of a wealthy family from Kerala, where she studied to become a teacher and then, through a trust created by Dr. Soundaram, took up a teaching position in a village in Tamil Nadu, the same village where Jagannathan and Krishnammal organized one of their most important satyagrahas. She remembers, "It was December 1972 when I met Amma and Appa. I was 19. They were organizing a satyagraha in Vallivalam for the distribution of the temple land being illegally cultivated by a big landlord, the most powerful person in the village. People there were extremely poor. There were not enough houses, food, or employment, and everyone lived in mortal fear of this man. I decided to join the protest and I was so inspired by Amma's efforts that since then I have continued working with her for the poorest, against injustice. I have been through much in these years. Together with Krishnammal, I have fought, putting my life in danger, and being sent to prison so many times!".

Krishnammal interrupts to say she is brave, even too brave, so much that often she gets into trouble. Lila smiles and continues:

"I am married but I have no children. It took my husband some time to accept my choices, but he has come to understand and now he is proud of me. I remember that once the police came to arrest me, and he told them that there was no way I should go to prison with an empty stomach, and so he went to the neighbors to ask for two *dosas* (thin, lentil-flour pancakes) to send with me. If it were not for Amma, by now I would be a quiet schoolteacher, with an easy life. My sister is a teacher, and she makes eight thousand rupees (roughly $200) a month. My salary is thousand rupees, but I made this choice because I've seen too much injustice, too much suffering".

She relates the tale of the Valivalam satyagraha, where she was wounded by one of the men the local landlord had sent to cultivate the land, replacing the protesting village people. She tells me about the campaign against prawn farming, when the *gundas* (hired thugs) threw her in a ditch and threatened to bury her alive, or when, together with Krishnammal, she was surrounded by the same gundas who doused them with kerosene and threatened to burn them alive. She tells me about her terrible experiences in Indian prisons, where they were treated like common criminals. She relates all of this in a light-hearted manner, often breaking into laughter.[1] She becomes very serious only when she talks about her moral debt towards Amma and Appa. After her story, Lila goes to Jagannathan, and together they start talking, again bursting into laughter during their animated discussion. Krishnammal brings us back to Batlagundu.

Krishnammal: Batlagundu

Batlagundu was then the most backward district in Tamil Nadu. The situation of the untouchables was awful because they were totally at the mercy of caste Hindus, and had no recourse. They were often starving. They lived in tiny huts, without doors, only a pole across the entrance to which their children were tied so they couldn't go out while the parents were at work in the fields. The huts would fill up with water and mud every time it rained. The entire harvest would go to the owners of the fields, and there was nothing left for the people.

At the beginning, my work was mostly focused on helping the untouchables, I organized many padayatras against the caste system, and to affirm that land had to belong to the tillers: our slogan was that those who did not cultivate their land had to renounce it and give it to the village community. It was very difficult work, because it challenged a system of cultivation that was centuries old. People were afraid the landlords would take revenge and leave them with no help, because it was to the landlords that people would go when they needed loans to marry their daughters or for proper ceremonies for the dead. This was and often still is the system in Indian villages.

The first satyagraha I organized was in Koniapatti village between 1957 and 1958. In this village, all the small holders had lost their land because they got into debts with the richest group of caste Hindus of the village, and they could not pay the money back. The debt was for a total of 4,000 rupees. After losing their land, the men of the community had to move out of the village to find new employment, so the women and children were at the mercy of their creditors, who treated them like slaves. Often, the women were molested.

When I heard about this situation, I decided that the best course of action would be to find the 4,000 rupees to pay off the debt. I went to Madurai and got a loan from a Gandhian friend, promising to return it in four months. But when I offered to pay the debt back, those high-caste people refused to take money from me. They said, "Who are you to come and interfere?" they insisted. "We are neighbors, and we are just helping each other." This was their mentality, and they also managed to make the poor of the village believe the creditors were their benefactors!

I was determined not to give up, and for three months every morning I went to that village and sat there in full view, with the money well-hidden in my saree, waiting for them to accept my offer. Instead, they began to threaten me, and with a few rupees they bought off the untouchables, who started to treat me badly, spitting on me and telling me to go away. The climax occurred when I was approached by a young man who had lost his land because a water buffalo he had in custody was killed by a train and he didn't have the money to pay for it. He summoned up the courage and asked me for help in paying back his debt. But because here land is worth more than money, the owner of the water buffalo didn't even want to hear about it, and his wife became so terribly angry that she started beating the boy. He did not react because she was a woman—and of a higher caste— but she beat him so badly in the liver area that he died of internal bleeding. The family of the boy started to say that I was responsible for his death.

However, this episode made people change their minds about the landowner, and slowly they started to understand how they were exploited by him. They began to trust me and to accept money to rescue their land. But having their land back did not solve all their problems, since they were so poor they could not afford to buy tools, seeds, and draft animals.

I decided to approach the government. I went to the Collector's office and said I was not going to leave until they gave me the money to buy a bullock for each family in the village. It was an audacious demand, because usually the government was willing to assist only two families in each village, but I wanted help for all of them. For a week, I went there every day, until they agreed to help. But what a problem! When I went to the market with the village people to buy bulls, I discovered that the sellers had banded together to inflate the prices. So I went to the market on my own, bought the bulls and brought them back to the village. The people started cultivating cotton, and when it was ready I explained that they should to wait to sell it, because immediately after the harvest, prices are low. So they stored some of it, but then I discovered they were secretly selling it off bit by bit. In this first satyagraha, there were many problems, but at the end I had managed to free these people from slavery, and this gave me the strength to continue down this road.

In 1964, something terrible happened in my own village. Untouchables had lost their land by accumulating debts, and some of them began to steal to survive. One day, the high caste people of the village decided to teach them a lesson and called the Madurai police. The police came at night and acted so violently that eight people were injured, and one man was killed. Then they took the old people of the village and they made them march to the police station with a garland of slippers around their necks, in order to humiliate them. They buried the body of the man who was killed 15 kilometers away from the village, and then brought the injured people to a place where they were fed and their injuries cared for, fearing that the people would testify against the police. When I heard this, I filed a case against the 13 guilty policemen and I managed to have the body of the dead man exhumed to prove he had died because of the beatings. At the end of the trial, the policemen were found guilty, but the district judge called me and begged me, as a Gandhian, to forgive the policemen. Otherwise there would be 13 more families without any income. So I forgave them, and they were not fired.

After this episode, we organized many meetings with the untouchables of the village, and create a situation where they trusted us and approached us when they were victims of injustice. In that area we also started a school, and slowly people started recognizing our role in the area and we started working together. Today, the economic situation in the entire Batlagundu area, which had been the most backward area in Tamil Nadu, is very sound."

Peace mission in Ramnad District

"In India, there are some communities that the government recognizes as 'backward' and, like untouchables, have particular advantages in obtaining employment in the public sector, or admission to schools and universities, and so forth. In the Batlagundu area, there were many conflicts between untouchables and these backward communities. In Ramnad District, the untouchables and one of these communities had serious violent clashes resulting from the fact that untouchables were not allowed to enter the temples during religious festivals. Previously, the two communities had always had good relationships. But there was one backward community group—the *Nadars*—who had became rich in trade and felt threatened by one of the other communities, which was was guided by a strong and good leader who was working hard for the uplift of his people. The Nadars were afraid of him, and so they instigated the untouchables against his community, providing them with food and weapons. The riots were terrible: for a full month even the police could not enter the area. The wells were poisoned and the roads destroyed. The government tried to negotiate peace by organizing many meetings, but after one of those meetings the leader of the untouchables was killed. The Chief Minister Kamaraj thought he knew who was responsible for that, or at least he knew where they were from, and ordered the police to kill them. There was no due process, it wasn't even clear who was guilty, but the police shot five people from the village suspected by Kamaraj. The people of the backward community thought the government was against them and reacted with fury, killing all the untouchables they found.

When we read about this in the newspaper, Jagannathan stopped eating and sat all night without speaking, as he does when he has to make an important decision. Then he told me he had decided to go in the area of the clashes. But I didn't want him to go there on his own! So we both went to Gandhigram and spoke to Dr. Ramachandran who had a *Shanti Sena*[2], a peace brigade of young students. But he said it was too dangerous to send them there; he first wanted Jagannathan to bring back a report of the situation. So we went to meet Gandhian groups in Madurai, but we could get no help. Even the leader of the backward community told us it was just crazy to go there, but Jagannathan didn't want to listen. We went back to Batlagundu to meet Keithan, and we found him ready to jump on the jeep and go: he felt we had to leave that night, so he had already planned everything and was ready. They went together, but they couldn't reach any village. Jagannathan was furious. In that period, it was impossible to talk with him!

In the meantime, Dr. Soundaram came from Delhi, and decided to go to the area of the clashes with me and 20 young women from Gandhigram, who had already helped us during the Bhoodan padayatra. It seemed impossible to enter that area, as there was police everywhere, but in the end the police let us in, thinking that the presence of women might help.

We found a terrible situation. People had run away terrified and the villages were almost empty. Wells had been poisoned and there was no water to drink. But the clashes were over, so we started working to convince people to come back. It took us three months, but finally peace was reestablished.

These episodes made us reconsider very deeply what we were doing. In Batlagundu, we had started working for the untouchables, but now Jagannathan pointed out that struggling only for the untouchables was going to created conflicts between different communities, and as a nonviolent movement we should work for the whole community. So we focused on the idea of Gram Swaraj, or village republic, to bring together the concerns of all the different groups in a community. We worked to form many committees, first of all the *Gram Sabhas* (village assemblies)—composed of five members, representatives of all communities and chosen by all the members of the village, then women groups, youth groups, and so on. We tried to act in a way that people would learn to think about the welfare of all, and get used to making decisions together. In those years, we were helped by a British Quaker, Donald Groom, who took charge of the construction of irrigation wells, so that many Bhoodan lands that were dry could be cultivated."

Krishnammal: Working for the government

"From 1958 to 1962, I had the opportunity to play a new role. The government created a new program for social welfare, and in every district set up a development office charged with coordinating programs for helping the poorest in the villages. Dr. Soundaram had created a separate wing of this office for the welfare of women and children, and I was asked to head the effort. At first I refused, because I have always been opposed to many of the government's policies, but they convinced me with the promise that I would be able to make decisions and act as I saw fit.

I became responsible for ten *Gram Sevika* (village service) *Centres*. We worked in the villages with the main objective of creating women's associations, and helping women start small businesses. The women of that area really needed to be educated: they didn't even know how to cook a good *sambar* (a thin, South Indian curry made of lentils and vegetables)! They had always been oppressed—as a result of poverty, caste, and gender—and our aim was also to awaken them spiritually.

At that time my secretary was a young man named Logannathan. We moved continuously from village to village camping somewhere, with no fixed place to live. Bhoomi was still with me, and in this way received his education! We created strong contacts with the people as we were involved in every aspect of village women's life: weddings, funerals, caring for the sick and preventing disease—everything. Logannathan was a very good writer, and also he used to collect sayings from Gandhi, Vivekananda, and other spiritual masters to make large posters that we would display at our meetings. We also ran eight centers for women's and children's health. As chairman of the project, I earned five hundred rupees (approximately $20) a month—much more than I could ever imagine spending on myself—and with these funds I used to buy clothing for the children of the entire area.

We also organized nurseries for children whose families were working in the fields. Logannathan enjoyed working with children as well. He used to write little poems about the children who were making trouble, and then he would read them in the class without identifying the name of the child, who would nevertheless understand that he was the subject of the story.

In 1962, my daughter Sathya was born. After her birth, I stayed in the hospital for only a single day, and then I went back to the ashram. I kept her with me for only eight months, and then I had to leave her with my mother because I had too much work. Poor Sathya, I never had enough time for her. Even now, she suffers because we are far from her. She always tells us to take a holiday and spend some time with her, at least now that we are supposed to be old! But we can't, and holidays never existed for us.

So our work in Batlagundu went on till 1968, when we moved to another district. Satyagraha after satyagraha, Jagannathan and Keithan were always ready to protest! And how many marches, with hundreds and thousands of people! One day with the *Sarvodaya Mandal* (organization of Sarvodaya workers, of which Jagannathan was president), we organized a padayatra all the way to Madurai. Other groups joined in, so at the end there were 20,000 people shouting: "He who does not cultivate should not own land! Land to the tillers!" We arrived in Madurai without having given warning to the police, and they had to open the schools to give us a shelter."

In those years an important meeting took place, that even now is responsible for creating a link between Krishnammal and Jagannathan's work and groups in Italy. In 1967, Jagannathan and Krishnammal were contacted by an Italian professor, Giovanni Ermiglia, who had arrived in India inspired and attracted by Vinoba and his land-gift movement. Ermiglia had decided to collect funds to help projects working to cultivate Bhoodan lands. At first, he worked to create a Bhoodan cooperative in Karnataka with Ramachandran Rao, who had worked with Jagannathan in the slums in Bangalore, but the project failed. Rao told him about Jagannathan's work in Tamil Nadu, and Ermiglia went to meet him.

Their meeting signaled the birth of the idea of a development project for Bhoodan land named ASSEFA—Association of Sarva Seva Farms—and Krishnammal's young secretary Logannathan was put in charge of the project. Jagannathan was its president until 1993.

ASSEFA was born as a project specifically directed towards land and agriculture, but now it has become the largest non-governmental organization in India, active in six different Indian states. Its projects were transformed slowly from helping single families to those involving entire village communities. Education, health, and development are its main objectives. ASSEFA works with communities to encourage the birth of village assemblies and women's associations to promote and support its projects: agricultural development, the creation of small cooperatives for milk and vegetable production, crafts. One of the main objectives of this association is to spread an alternative educational model among the village children, a model that explicitly promotes their intellectual, physical, and spiritual development, is more connected to the reality from which the children come, and that can educate them in nonviolence and respect for diversity.

In the course of time, ASSEFA became such a large development organization, with such wide experience, that often the Indian Government began to use its managers' expertise for its own projects. Not everybody is enthusiastic about these changes, though. Jagannathan tells me that ASSEFA has become almost like a large corporation, losing its revolutionary spirit in the process. Now it is only interested in development, and does not question the roots of poverty in the Indian villages anymore. He was ASSEFA's president for a long time, and he tells me about his decision to resign in 1993, when his campaign against the government's policy of selling alcohol at a low price embarrassed ASSEFA's leadership, since they receive considerable funding from the government itself. There is some bitterness in his and Krishnammal's voice when they talk about the 'new generation' of ASSEFA managers, because they feel they have been forgotten and a bit betrayed, but then they remind themselves and others that there is no point in creating polemics when their ultimate objectives are the same: helping the poorest members of the society. He explains to me, "We have our own methods, and they have theirs, we are not in competition or in confict. My objective is revolution, Logannathan's is development. I think that in a country like India, that is still mostly based on agriculture, there cannot be justice and equity if the land belongs to the few, and the many are still exploited, and the government goes on promoting policies in favor of large capitalists and multinationals. Such policies result in the country becoming more and more deprived, even if the rich city dwellers are doing well. I struggle for a nonviolent revolution like Vinoba, and so I have decided to walk a different path from ASSEFA."

I follow all of this with a bit of discomfort. I would have liked to imagine the post-Independence Gandhian movements in India as united. Instead, there are different views and painful separations. At the end, though, I realize this is quite normal. Indian philosophy itself teaches us that the paths to liberation are many, and each individual has to choose his own.

K. M. Natarajan one day told me, "There are many Gandhian institutions that are not particularly interested in nonviolent struggles, but are more into constructive work, like khadi production, village industries and so on. There are activists like Jagannathan and Krishnammal, Sunderlal Bahuguna[3], or Medha Patkar[4], who are always in and out of prison, ready to put their own lives at risk for the cause they are fighting for. Then there are scientists like Vandana Shiva[5], who work in the same direction but with their energies devoted to research and education. There are intellectuals like Arundhati Roy[6], who has embraced the cause of the people who are fighting with Gandhian methods against the construction of a system of ecologically and socially destructive dams on the Narmada River. She wrote an essay about the struggle that became famous, but Jagannathan would likely tell her, "What are you doing there, writing books? Join the movement, jump in the river!" He is a revolutionary, but not everybody is like him, and, in the end, we need Vandana Shiva's research and Arundhati Roy's essays, and Sunderlal Bahuguna, Medha Patkar, and Jagannathan's sacrifice."

Traveling to Another Ashram

Today we are leaving for the Thanjavur area, where Jagannathan and Krishnammal have concentrated their activity for the last 30 years. In Gandhigram, everyone is packing. Krishnammal runs back and forth as usual, organizing, cooking, giving instructions, scolding, or cuddling the hostel's children. It is not clear to me how long we are going to be away from the Workers' Home, and I get ready for any eventuality.

At three, we finally leave, and after a six-hour journey by jeep we reach the Kuthur Workers' Home. It is already dark and we are exhausted. We unload the jeep and go straight to sleep, hoping that heat and mosquitoes are going to be merciful.

In the following days, we will all stay in the ashram's guesthouse. While Jagannathan and Krishnammal have been living in Kuthur for a long time, they do not have their own place, and not even their own room. They deposit their few things in this small house, sharing it with visitors.

When I wake up in the morning I walk out on the verandah. It is dawn and the birds are celebrating the arrival of the new day. Flocks of green parrots fly around the palm trees, a kingfisher lands on a bamboo pole, and the air is full of the shrill whistles of the myna birds. The hostel children (yes, there is *another* children's hostel here—this one for girls) are watering the vegetable patch with the water collected in the ashram's tank, now almost empty. The monsoon is very late and, as in Gandhigram, water is becoming scarce. The part of the ashram where the guest house is located consists of a large, square, fenced area, on the sides of which are showers, the vegetable patch, a lean-to which shelters some antique (though still working) and very picturesque tractors, the kitchen, and a small house with the traditional palm-leaf roof where the children take their meals. I continue my exploration, crossing the small dirt road from where we arrived the night before, and in front of me there is a gate, with a sign reading, "Land for the Tillers Freedom (LAFTI)—Vinoba Ashram". I walk in, and under a beautiful, round gazebo, I see Jagannathan sitting cross-legged under a large portrait of Gandhi. His eyes are closed, and he is spinning. I sit down quietly, observing his perfect, meditative concentration, as he repeats a gesture that for him must be automatic and as natural as breathing. The sound of the *charka* (spinning wheel) captures me too, and my spirit is filled with peace and calm.

In a few minutes, a meeting of the LAFTI workers is going to take place. I see the workers entering the gate on bicycles, motorbikes, or on foot, or coming out of the rooms that surround the courtyard. These, I discover, are LAFTI's offices. Unfortunately, only a few of the workers speak English, and often I will have to ask Krishnammal to translate for me. I am invited to the meeting. The workers, each in turn, gives a report on their activities, and then Jagannathan speaks, without ceasing his spinning. Someone brings me a pile of articles on aquaculture that have been published in the last years by Indian newspapers in English and Tamil, and I sit in a corner to have a look at them.

Krishnammal has told me that the following morning we will begin out tour of the villages where LAFTI has been working for decades. The first will be the village whose terrible tragedy brought Krishnammal and Jagannathan to this area. So after the meeting, we sit on the guesthouse verandah and Krishnammal tells me the story of Kilvenmani.

Krishnammal: Kilvenmani and Thanjavur District[1]

"On Christmas night in 1968, I was sitting by myself in Gandhigram. The moon was shining high in the sky. I could not sleep, and I kept on thinking about how humanity seems not to have understood the importance of Christ and his teachings.

When I woke up the next day, I read a terrible story in the newspaper. In a village in Thanjavur District, 44 harijan women and children had been burnt alive in a hut whether they had sought shelter to escape the attacks of local landlords and their henchmen. I immediately called Jagannathan, who was somewhere else on a padayatra, and as soon as he reached me, we left for that area. In Tiruvallur, we stopped in the police station to find out what happened, and then we went to the village. We were the first to go there. No one had been allowed in previously. The bodies were lined up in front of a tree. On the trunk of a tree there was some blood. It was the blood of a baby, thrown out of the window of the flaming house by his mother in an attempt to save him. A landlord had grabbed him, put him against the tree, and killed him with a knife. We both cried at this terrible sight.

I had never been in this area before, known as "Tamil Nadu's granary". It is an area rich with temples, where the land was in the hands of the brahmins and of two other rich communities, but the untouchables did the cultivating. They were day laborers, received miserable pay, and they lived in the *ceri*—a squalid area reserved to the untouchables—located outside the village. They were forced to sign agreements with the landlords, declaring they were ready to work for them and to provide all their manure for the landlords' fields. It was a feudal system: the landlords chose the brides for the untouchables, who were so poor they had to eat animals that had simply died rather than being butchered and other horrible food, and of course nobody went to school.

In 1947, the Communists started to organize the harijan community, and thanks to their commitment there were some improvements, but the result was also great tension, and repression from the police. In the ceri, there were daily police raids. Police were called without reason by the landlords, and they used to humiliate the untouchables by forcing them to walk on their knees all the way to the police station, and to endure other similar humiliations. In that village, so many years after Independence, there were no signs of the government's presence. People lived only at the pleasure of the landlords.

When we found ourselves in front of the scene of the massacre, Jagannathan became angry. He said it was the Communists' fault because they created so much tension, but I suggested that at least they had tried to do something. The untouchables had to meet with the Communists secretly, because if the landlords had discovered such meetings, they would not be given employment anymore.

For me, it was like a call from God, and I decided I had to stay there to help these people. Jagannathan was against it because he said we could not abandon all our projects in the Batlagundu area. At that time, though, he had been nominated as director of Sarva Seva Sangh, the national organization created by Vinoba, and he had to tour all over India, so I was free to do as I was led. I came to work in the Thanjavur area.

For a month I could not sleep, I was so horrified by what happened and by the intolerable situation of the untouchables. I had to move between different groups: the landlords, who had a green flag as their symbol, and the Communists with their red flag. First of all, I made contact with the Communists to better comprehend and study the situation. We used to meet in secret places, putting our lives at risk. One day I was going to visit the family of a man who had been killed by a landlord. On the way the police stopped me, took me to the police station, asked me lots of questions and searched my pockets. They let me go only in the evening. The Communists started thinking I was a member of the Congress Party, and they didn't want me to enter the village anymore. But I found a way to approach the people: I started to teach English to the children, and slowly I won their trust. I choose to stay in a place near Kottongodi temple, near Valivalam. I asked the people there only for a bed to sleep, and a pot of water, and from there I could observe the situation.

In the meantime, with the help of Sarva Seva Sangh, we created five Gandhi Peace Centers in that area, but we met strong opposition from the Communists. I wanted to organize a padayatra, but the workers of the Sarvodaya Movement who were helping me, suggested not to do so because it might create further conflict. I tried anyway with the help of an important leader of the Sarvodaya Movement, Shankar Rao Dev, but the Communists didn't allow the people to participate. So I tried to make friendship with the women, and when I could count on their trust, I organized a year-long padayatra to talk about Vinoba and spread Gandhian philosophy. During the padayatra we reached the house of a man named Chandran's house. Chandran has worked with us ever since, but at the time was a Naxalite.[2] He thought that the only way to change things was to fight the landlords with violence. He asked me, frankly, "What are you Gandhians doing for these people?" I asked him to join us to see with his own eyes, and he accepted."

Krishnammal has to go back to her work, and she invites me to ask Jagannathan to tell me how he remembers those years.

Jagannathan: Kilvenmani

"As Krishnammal told you, many poor women with their children were killed in that terrible episode. The fire was started by the landlords, high caste Hindus. The farmers were organized by the Communists, both 'right wing' Communists—supporters of the Soviet political line—and 'left wing' Communists—followers of Chinese Communism. Those groups formed the two main political parties in this area, CPM and CPI-M.[3]

The conflict was as follows: the farm laborers wanted an increase in the daily wage they were receiving to work in the paddy fields, but the landlords had refused. The Communists organized a strike. When the strike began, the landlords called in people from other districts to collect the rice. There were some high-caste Hindus among them, while traditionally farm laborers are only members of the depressed classes or harijans. One of these caste Hindus worked as the landlords' agent, and was in charge of calling people from outside to collect the rice. On December 24th, this man was killed, and the landlords decided to take revenge. The following night, the landlords and their henchmen attacked the ceri in the dark with guns, and carrying petrol to burn down the houses.

They started to shoot and burn down some houses. Everyone escaped, and the women, the children, and the elderly took refuge in a small hut. The landlords locked the door, poured petrol all around, and set it aflame. All were burnt alive. We ran to the place, arriving the morning of December 26th. The bodies were lined against palm trees. Krishnammal started crying, I could not control myself and I cried, too.

There were 74 harijan families living there, and they were terrified. The Communists said they would take revenge, and the caste Hindus also wanted revenge. We were in between; we were new to the area and did not know anybody. We explained we were Gandhians and we didn't have anything to do with politics, but they didn't believe us, and so for months our efforts were futile.

We went on patiently. Slowly, the people began to understand, and became less hostile. We started talking about Gramdan, and told them about our experience in Batlagundu, explaining how we had managed to redistribute land through nonviolent action. In spite of the difficulties and with much sacrifice, we continued to work in that village for two years.

In this period a German industrialist, by the name of Meyer, contacted us. He had heard about our movement and wanted to help us. We told him we needed land to distribute among the poor, and bullocks and tools, and he offered us money to purchase land in Kilvenmani. There were some landlords who owned land in that area, but who lived 15 kilometers away. We went to talk to them, explained what had happened and we managed to get the land for a low price, and distributed it among the people. It was 1971 when we distributed one acre each to the 74 families. For them it was paradise. They had been fighting for a few mere handful of rice and they got land, good land, paddy land. It was a revolution. But struggles in that area had just begun: tomorrow I will tell you about the great satyagraha in Valivalam."

The next day, I look for Krishnammal in the ashram office, and I find her in the company of a tall man, with a serious and sad face. Amma introduces him as Subramanya, leader of the Village Assembly of Kilvenmani. All together we

Krishnammal Jagannathan inside Kilvenmani Memorial, the site where 44 women and children were burned alive. (Photo taken September 1981)

get on the jeep that will take us to the village, and during the journey I hear again the story of the terrible massacre from Subramanya, who at that time was 30 years old. I asked him if the landlords responsible for the killing have ever been arrested, and he explains:

"The trial lasted for two years, and at the end all the landlords were released because there was not enough evidence. Only the two people who killed the landlord's agent were convicted and sentenced to life imprisonment. But a Naxalite from Andhra Pradesh came to the village, killed the landlord who started the fire and cut him into eighteen pieces, representing the number of the families who were destroyed in the fire. Then he left a letter saying who he was, and challenged the police to find him. Instead, the police came to the village and arrested us all. They kept us all day in the police station, without giving us anything to eat, and insisted I had to know something because I was the leader of the village. I was treated so badly, I fainted, but in the end they let us go".

The jeep crosses a landscape of green paddy fields, brightened by the colored sarees of the women who are transplanting the rice seedlings. The sky and its white clouds are reflected in the water, and here and there lines of palm trees make shade on the long, dirt road. Subramanya observes the landscape quietly and continues:

"Jagannathan and Krishnammal are for us like Lord Shiva and Parvati. At that time, we harijans were fighting for a measure of rice, and now we have eight with each harvest. We own our land, our children go to school, and we are respected. In the past, there were no contacts between us and caste people, while now we sit together in the temples and during festivals. Once, during the religious ceremonies we couldn't even be blessed, because the Brahmin could not touch our forehead. The economic changes have brought about huge social changes."

We reach the village and stop in front of a small building with a palm-leaf roof and low brick walls. We walk in to visit a

Harijan woman at home in Naivilakku Village, Nagai District. Only after helping to lead the nonviolent struggle of 1972 did she even own the land on which her hut sits. (Photo taken October 1981).

small unit for cane mat-weaving, one of the projects LAFTI is running in this area. About ten girls welcome us, happy to see Krishnammal, and they take me to see the workshop. They tell me they started working here after finishing school, and that they are very happy to be able to help their families with their salary. They ask me if I can take a picture of them with Krishnammal, and then together we walk through the small roads of the village. Behind us, a small procession of old people and children come out of their houses to greet Krishnammal, and soon we reach the area where the massacre took place. A white monument built by the Communist Party stands on the ashes of the burnt-down hut. Krishnammal talks to the village people and Subramanya breaks two coconuts for us. One of the girls from the workshop places a *bindi*[4] on my forehead. The contrast between the warmth and the jolly atmosphere of this moment and the awareness of what happened here 30 years ago is summarized in Subramanya's sad eyes.

Surrounded by the village people who keep on arriving to pay her homage, Krishnammal points at some brick houses that have been built nearby, with money from LAFTI and the Meyer Foundation. They have all been registered in the name of women. She explains,

"Many people here are still living in huts with mud walls and palm-leaf roofs. Once there were many more palm trees and it was easy to repair the roofs, which also keep the houses very cool. But now it is difficult to find the leaves, and so the roofs are full of holes and the rain comes in. When the monsoon arrives, the houses flood and the people have to live in the dankness for months. They get sick with diarrhea, and small children in particular suffer greatly. So my main objective has become to build brick houses with tiled roofs, what we call *pakka* houses. I place them in the name of the women, so if their husbands leave them, or if they fall victim to drink as many do here in the villages, the women are safe. Unfortunately the struggle against prawn farming does not allow me much time for this project, but as soon as I can I will dedicate myself only to this."

Subramanya invites us for lunch, and he is sorry to hear that we have to go back to Jagannathan, but it is time for goodbye. We drive back to Kuthur, where Jagannathan is waiting for me with another chapter of his story.

Jagannathan: Valivalam satyagraha

"At the beginning of 1972, we came to know about another problem concerning the depressed classes in a village called Valivalam. There was a rich landlord who owned 1,200 acres of land. He was very powerful, and all the officials and politicians who went to that area used to visit him. We also came to know that he was enjoying 360 acres belonging to the temple, while, according to the Temple Trust Law, temple land had to be given to the landless for tenancy. We decided to make an enquiry to see if this was true, but the landlord made our life difficult. Because he owned the tea shop and many other small shops in the village, he instructed the shops not to sell us anything, and he made it impossible for us to stay in Valivalam. We couldn't even find water to drink.

Nearby there was a village where about 65 harijan families lived, all day laborers working for the landlord. One of them, a very bold man, gave us shelter there. It was such a difficult time for us in Valivalam—for myself, Krishnammal, Natarajan, and Chris Sandler, an English friend, who was with us at that time.

We obtained proof that, in fact, the temple land was registered in the name of harijans, but in practice it was the landlord who was forcing the harijans to cultivate the land, paying them a miserable wage. People were terrified of him, so we had to encourage the young people of the village. We told them, "The temple land is in your name. Legally you are the tenants, but he is gaining all the benefits of cultivation. It is *your own land* that you are cultivating." It was difficult to give them courage. They were rightfully afraid of being killed! But we went with eight of them to the government office, and showed them that according to the law each one of them had five acres of land to cultivate, and we tried to convince them to stand up for their rights.

So those eight people started cultivating their land. The landlord simply watched, and did not do anything. But one day, while I was in another village, those young people came to me weeping, and they told me that during the night, the landlord had harvested everything in their 40 acres, and brought it to his property. He had just waited for three months, and when the harvest was ready, he called outside laborers, who came in large trucks and harvested everything in one night.

These people were desperate, and they were worried about being killed, too. So I went to the landlord, and told him that the land was under tenancy according to official records, and that those people were the legal tenants. I begged him to give the harvest back, and keep only the harvest wages, but he said he did not know anything about the harvest. So I went and told the District Collector, but he also did not know what to do because it was clear that nobody would appear against the landlord as witness.

At the end of January, I decided to fast to ask the harvest be returned. I only drank water. After eleven days, I became very weak. Finally, the District Collector decided to investigate, and found proof that the landlord had harvested the land. On the 14th day of fasting—it was the 13th of February—some of the officials were able to convince the landlord that they had witnesses and they could bring him to court, and he returned the harvest. It was the first time that something like this had happened. The paddy that was going to fill the stomach of that landlord came back after 14 days of fasting. At this point, all the other people of the village who were legally tenants had their courage renewed and wanted to start cultivating! So I wrote to the government to inform them of the situation, and after that we started organizing marches to ask that all 360 acres be distributed to the poor people. Before this, nobody even had the courage to walk in the road where the landlord was living or for their shadows to fall on his property, but Krishnammal organized the women, and invited them to march in the street singing bhajans.

Then we decided to ask for a public inquiry about the temple land and the Chief Minister of Tamil Nadu decided to find out who was really cultivating the land. Following the inquiry, the government distributed the 360 acres to 360 families! The land was actually distributed as tenancy, which meant that the people still had to give 25% of the harvest to the temple. Still, it was such a victory!

But there was still much to do in the area. As already noted, the same landlord owned 1,200 acres land in that village, a violation of Tamil Nadu's Land Ceiling Act, a law that established that a private individual could not own more than 50 acres. But the Government had foolishly made a law establishing that it was possible to create trusts, and so this man could say that 900 of his acres belonged to trusts. By law, the trust land was to be cultivated only by landless people as tenants, but again it was the landlord who was cultivating. So we started a new satyagraha to ask for the distribution of this land as well. At that time, because of our success, we had cooperation from both of the Communist parties: together we organized marches and procession. But after a while, the CPI-M Communists went to meet the landlord secretly, and they made an agreement that the land was going to be distributed only to people who were members of their party. So we had to protest against the Communists as well! We occupied the land, and were arrested, but in the end the District Collector intervened, and the land was distributed. We now had two great victories.

JP came to visit us. He stayed here for one week, and studied the temple laws, trust laws, tenancy laws, and the Land Ceiling Act. Then he met with all the political leaders of the area. In that period, this same landlord filed many false cases against the people of the Sarvodaya Movement, saying that we stole his coconuts, and other silly things like that. There were many arrests. When JP came, he met that landlord, who was a member of the ruling Congress Party, and asked him why he had filed all those false charges. But he denied they were false. Then JP went to Madras, met the Chief Minister, and explained that that landlord was so powerful that he had all and everyone in his hands, even the Collector, and that he had filed false claims. He asked the Chief Minister to help us, because we had no money for lawyers, and asked the Government to support us with public lawyers. All the false charges were finally withdrawn because the Government stepped in; otherwise that man could have crushed us.

It took us three years to win our battles in the area, but somehow we succeeded. During an All-India Meeting, a national convention with 200 workers from all over India, JP made a report on our work in Valivalam. Vinoba had not approved of our movement, because he thought we were fighting against the temple, and not against the landlords! But he was finally impressed, and from then on, he gave me the green light."

Krishnammal arrives, and Appa asks her to tell me how she organized women in those years of struggle.

Krishnammal: Valivalam satyagraha

"Surrounding Valivalam, there were seven slums where untouchables lived. They all worked for that same landlord. I wanted to organize women's marches in the village roads, and especially in front of that landlord's house, but the women were too afraid. The landlord was doing everything he could to scare people. He also had his private police marching in arms up and down his road. So I decided to begin having women's meetings to pray and sing bhajans. We used to meet in the night, so it was dark and it would have been difficult to recognize each of the women. Slowly I convinced them that if we were to march in front of that man's house singing bhajans, nothing would happen to us: they could not attack women who were marching in prayer. So for about ten days, 150 marched every night along the road they had never walked upon before, and this helped to give them courage, and prepare them for the real satyagraha ahead.

Women were involved in so many heroic actions! Jagannathan told you that when we were asking for distribution of the temple land, the farmers who had worked for the landlord refused to work for him anymore. So he called in people from outside to till the soil, people from Ramnad District. I invited women to go to the fields, untie the ploughshares from the bullocks, and take the ploughshares to the police. Women had the courage to do so, but instead of helping, the police filed a case against me.

Another time, some women came to know that that landlord had called people from outside to start harvesting, and they ran to the fields to stop them. Lila, the one you met in Gandhigram, saw the leader of these men standing by a stream with a knife in his hands. She ran and hugged him. He got so upset at being touched by a woman that he lost control and his dhoti fell off! Then the women dragged him to the police, and that was the end of it. But later on we scolded Lila because what she did was too dangerous, going to hug a man with a knife in his hands!

During the satyagraha everyone was against us. The police, who were supporting that landlord, the tillers who came from outside to work the land, and also the Communists, who were furiously angry with us of the Sarvodaya Movement because Vinoba had been opposed to the killings in Telagana.[5] They also assaulted us physically. One day they attacked us and Lila was wounded. They cut her fingers!

Then there was prison. In 1972, we were put in prison for 15 days in Thanjavur. The cells holding 14 women each were tiny: we couldn't even sit down together, and had to take turns sitting. The toilet was in the same room, so there was a terrible smell, and we could not bathe. The men's cells were very close, and we could see the police beating them as they went out for lunch. They fed us only rice and water, and we had to share one plate with entire prison. The men ate first, then the women, and we could not even wash the plate. Police were always shouting and insulting us. After protesting, we managed to get permission to bathe, but the police stood around us, so we could not take off our clothes. Then we were brought to Trichi jail, where the conditions were a little better. I had permission to get out of the cell and take a bath. I could also wash the other women's sarees. I had two with me, so I washed one, and shared the other with all the women so they could wash their sarees, too. After some time, I received permission to talk with the other prisoners. We were in Trichi jail for 53 days, a hundred women in all, some with their babies with them. It was a real hardship, but in the end the land was distributed.

Before our arrival, the situation in the Valivalam area was terrible. People did not even own the miserable houses they were living in. During Jagannathan's fasting, the Chief Minister of Tamil Nadu decided to legally recognize people as owning the huts they occupied. The night before the order was to go into effect, and government officers came to register the houses near the village of Vallivalam, some Communists, together with people sent by the landlords, came and destroyed those houses, taking away all evidences of human habitation because they wanted to show there were no houses there, only shelters for cattle. The men of the village ran away and left the women and children behind. I was sick in bed, and the doctor had told me not to move for at least ten days, but when I heard what had happened, I couldn't keep still. I waited for Jagannathan to leave—he had to go to Madras - and then, together with Chris Sandler, our English friend, I walked for three miles to reach that place. I wanted to comfort and reassure those poor women. It was dark, and they were so frightened. I explained that if the landlord's henchmen came, they were to lay down and keep quiet. After a while they did indeed arrive. They were angry and had weapons. They surrounded the women, insulting them. I told the women to lay down silently, and we spent the night like that, with the men drinking and shouting at us. Around four, I heard the birds singing and realized it was nearly dawn, so I took courage, stood up, and started shouting. "So, what do you want to do now? If you wish to kill us, it's time to do it!" Surprised by my reaction, they ran away. The same night, one of our workers saw I was not at home and came to look for me. But on the way he met the landlord's henchmen who beat him badly and locked him in a house. Fortunately he managed to escape through the roof."

Krishnammal narrates all these terrible events with her usual lightness, as if they are the stuff of dreams or fairy tales, and I can't stop being amazed by her courage and perseverance. I am deeply struck by the fact that she does not seem to be at all resentful toward the people who caused so much suffering to her and to the people she and Jagannathan helped in the course of time, and it is fascinating how she managed to gain respect and friendship from her "enemies". She tells me she is now on good terms with the famous landlord in Valivalam, who recognized the nobility of her struggle, and the purity of her ideals. Once again, I think about Gandhi's words, when he used to say that Indians should hate British rule in India, but love the British people, and I am moved by the idealism of these struggles.

I will visit Valivalam on several different occasions, the first time with Jagannathan a few days after our arrival in Kuthur. We will go to visit a school for girls that once used to be the headquarters of the campaign for the distribution of the temple land. Sitting on the table with his legs dangling, Jagannathan will greet the girls one by one. Singly, starting from the youngest, the girls will be invited by the teacher to move close to him, say their name and then sing a song or recite a poem. Jagannathan will clap his hands and laugh happily, the girls will exchange amused looks when they have to shout their name in the only working ear of this old man, whom they know to be the local hero and who will cuddle them like a grandfather, touching their small faces with his hands to distinguish their features.

Then we will go to the temple, where at the time of the struggle the meetings of the *satyagrahis* (those engaged in satyagraha) used to take place. Valivalam temple is beautiful, with tall, colorful towers in the typical South Indian style, and centuries old. Three sides of the temple are surrounded by a large water tank that is now dry, but that fills up during the monsoons, providing drinking water for animals and irrigation for the vegetable gardens. We will walk in the temple where a young Brahmin will recognize Jagannathan, greet him with respect, and show us around. We will stop in front of the *sancta sanctorum*, and the Brahmin will open the doors so that we could enjoy the sight of the image of the deity. He will light the area by moving a tray on which a piece of camphor is burning, and then will come to place some ash and tumeric powder on our foreheads in sign of blessing. The inner walls are carved with verses that ancient poets dedicated to the temple, and the Brahmin will recite them for us, filling the evening peace with his sweet voice.

Once out of the temple, Chandran will point at the wide road in front of us, noting, "This is the road where the landlord used to live. People were afraid even just to walk past, and untouchables were not even allowed to do that, not even our shadows could touch his property. Now I live here myself, and I am from a harijan family."

Other times, I will drive through Valivalam with Krishnammal, who will show me the monument built to memorialize the place where Jagannathan fasted 14 days, resulting in land distribution, and with her I will visit some of the projects started by LAFTI, including a workshop where a group of girls is learning to saw, and a school for carpenters.

The strongest memory of Valivalam I carry in my heart is that of a very, very old man, dressed in khadi, who I used to see coming slowly with his stick every time I visited the school. He is one of the brave men that 30 years ago fought alongside with Amma and Appa against prevarication, fear, prejudice, ignorance, and for the rights and the dignity of, as Gandhi was wont to say, "the last." He comes to pay homage to the couple who changed the destiny of his village. Even today, Krishnammal says she is still moved to action by the souls of the 44 women and children of Kilvenmani who, she says, now reside inside her.

Rich Monasteries and Poor Farmers

Being the seat of a movement as active as LAFTI, Kuthur Ashram is at the moment more lively than the Worker's Home in Gandhigram. Every morning, before leaving for the villages to coordinate the projects promoted by LAFTI, the workers help out in many different ways: they cut wood or help in the kitchen; take care of the children, helping them to get ready for school and assisting them with their homework; cultivate the vegetable patch or clean the grounds. The tasks are done without distinctions between men and women, and everyone is expected to do his or her bit. I remember seeing Krishnammal scolding workers who forgot to wash up after eating: she was very serious, but the scene ended with everyone laughing at her imitation of the workers walking around the ashram like lazy aristocrats, forgetting their kitchen duties.

This morning, the ashram is more animated than usual. When the cook brings us breakfast, she explains that today the kitchen will be rebuilt. Currently, the ashram cooks put their large cooking pots on top of several oil drums. These have an opening at the bottom, in which the women put wood or dried palm leaves to feed the fire. Today, this technique will be transformed with the building of a cooking area made with cement, about a meter high, with three holes for the pots on the top and three for the wood in the front.

After breakfast everyone starts working: LAFTI workers, together with some people I have never seen before, start moving around the kitchen, their *lungis*—one-meter long pieces of cloth sewn together at the ends and wrapped around the waist[1]—folded up to their knees, and pieces of cloth wrapped around their heads to protect them from the sun.

In a few hours, the new kitchen is ready, and all along the front of the building there is a new surface to sit on, and the old and broken outdoor water tap has been replaced. Everyone has been working together, laughing, joking, and singing. I think about the nostalgic stories my grandmothers used to tell me about life in the country, when works were accomplished like this, with friends, relatives, and neighbors coming to assist when they were needed. Many times I have wondered how much her memories were idealized and whether the reality was different, but spending this time in the ashram, I understand the sense of community and belonging that people who lived in my own country at the beginning of last century may have experienced. It is a feeling that I miss painfully, having grown up in the city and in a small family.

Jagannathan has finished his work in the LAFTI offices and calls me to continue our interview. Today his story will take us to a northern state of India, one of the poorest and most tormented to this day.

Jagannathan: In Bihar

"Jayaprakash Narayan greatly appreciated our work in Tamil Nadu. One day he approached us. 'Jagannathan and Krishnammal," he said, "you have done an amazing job here, but unfortunately in Bihar where I live, there is nobody who deals with these kinds of problems. Now you have a lot of experience, so I want to ask you to come with me to Bodhgaya to study the situation and prepare a report so that we can do something about the land issue there, too.' So in 1973, we both went to Bihar with the idea of staying there for a few months, but we ended up there for three years!

In Bodhgaya, where Buddha meditated for 40 days under a large banyan tree before gaining enlightenment, there is a large monastery dedicated to the spiritual master Sri Sánkara. Buddha's philosophy was in opposition to some of the basic tenets of Hinduism, which then went through a period of crises. It was this

Sri Sánkara who, in the 9th Century A.D., gave new life to Hindu doctrine. He established monasteries all over India, and one is in Bodhgaya, in front of Buddha's temple. It is a huge monastery, owning some 30,000 acres of land in about 60 villages, and the people of the villages worked for the monastery, and received a miserable wage.

When we toured these villages, we found a terrible situation. All the villagers were untouchables, and their lives were wretched. Women owned only one saree, and had nothing to wear underneath it. Their huts were made only of straw, and in that part of India it can get very cold. And what did they have to eat? Only boiled potato leaves. They boiled the leaves and drank the juice. The rice given them for their work was so poor it should have been thrown away, full of sand and stones. It was an extreme situation, much worse than what we experienced in Thanjavur District. Krishnammal could enter the huts and meet the women, but I couldn't because in that part of India *purdah* (female seclusion) is practiced.

The Sánkaracharya, chief of the *math* (temple monastery—pronounced "mutt") in Bodhgaya, behaved like a real tyrant. In the villages nearby, there were different branches of the math, each owning part of the land, and with leaders behaving in the same manner. There was a virtual system of slavery, led by a supposedly religious man, and everyone lived in terror. So we decided to stay in Bihar and do something for those poor people.

Just opposite the Bodhgaya math, there is a Vinoba ashram where we stayed for a while, but when we started our satyagrahas, we decided to move out. The director of the ashram was a slave of this Sánkaracharya like everybody else, and did not cooperate with us, so we had to leave the place and move to a nearby village.

Our first objective in organizing the land movement in Bihar was to give courage to the people, because everybody lived in such fear. They use to tell Krishnammal, "The Sánkaracharya will cut you into pieces; don't even go near the math!" Krishnammal could enter houses, and she managed to meet the women, gain their trust and give them courage. In the course of time, she decided to organize a march to the math. At first, the women refused, they were so afraid. But slowly they gained courage, and for the first time in the history of the math, they marched, singing that they wanted land, they wanted Bhoodan. We held a one-day fast, and at the end there was a meeting with about a thousand people asking for Bhoodan. At this point, the leader of the math told JP he had already given 1,000 acres as Bhoodan, and would give another 2,000 acres if we suspended the movement. So JP came to us to asked what to do. I said that if the monastery had 30,000 acres and was offering only 3,000, that was not enough. Besides, why should this people own land if they are sannyasins and have renounced all worldly possessions? They should have given all the land!" So JP refused, and we continued the movement."

Indira Gandhi's Emergency

"Everything came to a halt in June 1975, when a judge of the Allahabad Supreme Court found Indira Gandhi guilty of having used illegal means in the elections she had won four years previously. Everyone told her to resign, but she refused. So JP and a man named Morarji Desai, later Prime Minister, initiated a large protest movement. JP launched a movement for 'Total Revolution' against corruption, and thousands of students joined in. On June 26th, 1975, Indira Gandhi declared a national state of emergency, and a brutal repression began.

During the Emergency, prices of oil, sugar, food staples, and other goods skyrocketed. Shopkeepers started to hoard their merchandise to create scarcity, causing prices to grow still more. They would then sell everything on the black market. People suffered greatly. So JP told the students, "If shopkeepers do this, and the government doesn't do anything to prevent it, form your own government—people's government—and make sure the law is respected. Find the hidden goods, bring them to the market, and sell them at the normal price, and then give the money to the shopkeepers, but not more than what is right. This is the only way to control the black market."

The students carried on the movement in the cities, trying to stop corruption. At the same time we of the Sarvodaya Movement were working in the country, inviting people to create their own government, the *Janata Sarka*, or People's Government. We organized weekly markets, and people collected taxes in their own districts without paying them to the government. JP put me in charge of forming the Janata Sarka in 300 villages in three different areas, and this was my work in Bihar.

Thousands of students responded to JP's appeal, but police started arresting them and treated them harshly. They took them to police stations, put them in chains and then send them to prisons. So many people were arrested that the prisons were overflowing, and they had to create outside camps surrounded with barbed wire.

Then JP himself was arrested and the movement started to face difficulties, because there were no money. I was asked to seek funds from Tamil Nadu. So Krishnammal and I went, disguised, because otherwise we would have been arrested. At that time, our friend Kamaraj was again Chief Minister in Tamil Nadu, and we wanted to ask for his help, but in those days he was not there. So I collected some money and went back to Bihar, while Krishnammal stayed for some more time to wait for Kamaraj and more funding, and then she came back, too.

I carried on for some time, but on October 2nd, 1975 (Gandhi's birth anniversary), as I was leading a group of people protesting against the Emergency, I was badly beaten and arrested. It was worse than in the British days. We were taken to court, and then to the prison about two kilometers away. They wanted to insult us, and because I was the leader, I was tied with a rope. All the other people were chained like animals. We were treated badly because we were political prisoners, insulted and beaten all the way to the prison. They wanted to make examples out of us.

In prison, there were people who had protested against the Emergency, and also many Communists. They started making propaganda to convert our people to Communism, even bribing them with food, etc. I started organizing meetings, too, and the result was that we were separated to avoid conflict. I was transferred to another prison, a very bad one where they kept people condemned to death. There were no toilets. It was very dark, with no light all day long. I was there for six terrible months. Because I couldn't manage to sleep at all, my eyes started becoming watery all the time, but the doctor of the prison told me it was nothing. Later on, when I was back in Madras, I went to another doctor for examination, and he told me that one eye was already completely compromised, and that I should have been treated much earlier. After six months in this prison, with my father very ill, I managed to be transferred to a Madras prison, where I stayed for a year.

JP, who was already in his seventies, was treated so poorly that they severely compromised his health. They wanted to get rid of such a dangerous political rival but they could not do it openly, so they poisoned him, dispensing poison instead of a medicine he needed. When he was released, he was almost a dead man. His eyes, face, and lips were swollen. They were so sure he was going to die that they had already arranged where to cremate him, but somehow a friend took him to a good hospital in Bombay, where he was treated. By then, though, his kidneys were too severely damaged and he needed daily dialysis. Even though his health improved slightly, he lived only three years longer. Repression during the Emergency was awful. I had already experienced prison at the hands of the British during colonial days, but not in those terrible conditions, with this secret plan to compromise the health of the prisoners.

At this time, our children were both at school, and needed money for their studies, so I told Krishnammal to leave because she was under police watch and it was too dangerous. She will tell you herself how she was arrested, but somehow she managed to escape from the police van, run to the station and jump on a train. But it was such a difficult time for Krishnammal, alone with the two children. Terrible suffering we had. Each week, Bhoomi would come to the prison, bringing me some food. In prison, many people were desperate because they knew their families were in enduring great hardships, so I wrote a letter to Krishnammal asking her to find a way to help those families. So Krishnammal took charge of helping them as well. In prison, I had a bad time of it, but for Krishnammal, it was even worse.

Then, in 1977, Indira revoked the state of emergency and there were new elections. She lost, and a new government came to power. The dynasty that had ruled India since Independence was defeated, and I was released after 18 months in prison.

In the meantime, some brave young students had carried on the movement for the Bodhgaya monastery land, and they appealed to the Supreme Court. The Court ruled that 250,000 acres of the math land had to be distributed. This was one of greatest victories we've ever had."

When in the afternoon I ask Krishnammal to tell me about her experience in Bihar, I immediately realize that she remembers that period as a time of great sufferings as well.

Krishnammal: In Bihar

"When we arrived in Bihar, the student movement against corruption was already very strong, and the situation was tense. The Congress Party was in power, but there was terrible corruption. People couldn't even vote, and students had begun going to the villages to collect signatures to ask for the resignation of the local government. There was a spate of robbery, violence, and there was no law and no order, and no schools.

JP launched his 'Total Revolution' with the slogan: "Let us put an end to corruption and create a new Bihar." JP appealed for a new educational system, for decentralization of political power, and for village self-rule. His main point was to give power to the people to recall politicians who had committed wrongs, rather than forcing people to live with corruption until the next election five years hence, controlled by politicians.

We met JP in Patna, in a remote corner of the country, and then we went to visit Bodhgaya. Right there, near the Buddha temple, I saw many beggars collecting roots to eat, competing with pigs. I sat under a tree by a bangle seller, and from him I learned that the head of the *math* was a very cruel man. So I decided to go and meet him. He was on the third floor of the monastery. To reach him, there were narrow steps, and many people queuing to touch his feet. Mahant Ramji, this was the name of the Sánkaracharya, was sitting on a throne, wearing golden *chappals* (sandals). People gave him money, and everyone was frightened of him. Later I came to know that five kilometers from there, the monastery owned 30,000 acres of land, in a place called Sehuvara, and I asked to see it. I made contact with Indira Matha, who was working with village women for the local Kasturba Gandhi Trust. She asked me to stay there for some time to see with my own eyes the injustice that people had to suffer. She helped me meet the local women, but they had to come and meet me in the night so as not to be seen by the people of the math. They used to bring some food to share with us, even if they were so poor that it consisted only of garlic and potato leaves, because all the rest had to go to the head of the math. For their work, they only received powdered rice, mixed with all kind of things, and some chiles and salt.

There was in particular a group of people in that village, called the *Gargar*, who were treated like slaves. They could not even marry, because the head of the math used to take the girls from the village, and the children were left in the streets. Those women asked me to stay longer and help them. When I told this to Jagannathan, he said to me, "We are working in Valivalam. How can we leave those people like this?" But when he saw with his own eyes, he was convinced.[2]

Through the District Collector (a posted government official), who was a Tamil, I collected information about the temple land. Then I wrote a note and sent it to JP. He was enthusiastic about my plan for struggle, and so we started the satyagraha. To identify with the women and win their trust, I decided to sleep with them in their huts. I usually slept in the place normally reserved for the pig! Women owned only one saree and so they were very dirty, they had no money to buy soap, and everything in the huts smelled horribly. There were lice everywhere, and I couldn't sleep at night because they bit me constantly. But this was a very important thing to do, because nobody had ever identified with these women before. From June 1973 to the end of January 1974, I lived like that. On January 13th, I invited all the women to the Buddha temple and they came, so I was sure they were with me.

In the meantime, the news of my activity had spread, and one day I received an anonymous letter—clearly sent by the head of the *math*—saying they were going to kill me. The people from Vinoba Ashram were scared. They told me it was extremely dangerous to go against this man, and both JP and Vinoba wanted me to stop. I became very angry, shouting that I was not doing this for JP or Vinoba, but for myself only, and ran away. For three days I was away, and everybody, especially Jagannathan, feared that something had happened to me. But I was just touring around the villages, organizing a fasting program in front of the monastery for the day JP was going to come to that area.

The day of the fast, we sat in front of the temple, but people from the *math* arrived, together with some Communists, and started throwing bricks at JP and us. At that point, many students surrounded JP to protect him, and the women ran away. In the meantime the police arrived, surrounded the Communists, and started beating them. Amidst this confusion, JP told me to start speaking, even if I couldn't speak very good Hindi, so women and students came back to listen, and we managed to have our meeting anyway. After all this we went back to Vinoba Ashram. The following day I had organized a program in another place, but JP asked me to cancel it because it was too dangerous. He wanted us to go around with the jeep to tell the people the program was not going to take place, but I was too tired and decided to stop to sleep in a village. The next day I reached the place where we were supposed to have the meeting: at 6 o'clock so many women were already there! JP was enthusiastic, and that day we had no problems with the monastery people.

Because one of JP's aims was to start a form of people's government in every village, we began walking together to appeal for the creation of village assemblies, but then Indira Gandhi proclaimed the Emergency. It was very, very bad. Police, army, secret services, everyone came to Bihar. People went into hiding. So many students were killed. The police came looking for me. One day they arrived right in the room where I was, and I hid myself behind the door: they searched everywhere except there! Another time, they came while I was taking a bath. I ran away and hid in the nearby dispensary, pretending to be a patient!

In early November, JP launched a total strike in the whole of Bihar, and everything stopped. The army and police were everywhere. JP asked us to go to Patna for a meeting, even if he was sure we would be the only people there because of the presence of police and army. In fact, thousands of students managed to enter the city. Soon the police started throwing tear gas. People started to run in panic. I fell on the floor, and people trampled me. I fainted. That day, JP was arrested. We saw him entering a police van, and he told us to go back to Madras. But we couldn't do that; we had to continue the struggle.

Before JP was arrested, Jagannathan worked with him in Patna, organizing the youth, while I toured the villages with other youths, hiding in the forests. We had no food, only boiled rice and some herbs I picked in the forest. We had so many adventures.

On October 2nd, 1975, Jagannathan was arrested and beaten by the police. I was arrested, too, but I managed to escape. They came to the ashram to get me and put me in the police van, but then they thought, "This lady is not going to escape," and went for a cup of tea. So I slipped away from the van and hid in a nearby house under a bed. Jagannathan was put in a terrible prison in Bihar, while JP was in Chandigarh.

Because the police were looking for me, the only way I could go to visit Jagannathan in prison was to dress up as a Bihari woman. Then some friends advised me to appeal so that he could be moved to a Madras prison, and it worked. I moved to Madras to be close to him. I had no money at all and I started working in a hostel, but even there I was afraid I would be arrested. At that time, Bhoomi was in the Medical College, and I had no money to pay for his fees, and Sathya was in boarding school in Coimbatore. It was a difficult period for all of us."

I ask Amma and Appa to tell me about the period between their experience in Bihar and the beginning of the struggle against intensive prawn farming. This is the period during which LAFTI was founded

Krishnammal: The birth of LAFTI

"After Jagannathan was released, we went back to Valivalam Ashram, where there is now a children's hostel (yes, another one!) Some people from a nearby village told us there were 82 acres of land belonging to a Muslim trust that were cultivated by a middleman who was not paying the rent. The trust was running an orphanage, so they needed money, and they were offering to sell the land at a low price. I didn't begin with any well thought-out plan in my mind—it just seemed like a very good opportunity. So I rushed to Madras to meet the Revenue Minister—the minister in charge of collecting taxes from landowners—but he refused to help.

Then I decided to approach the banks, though I really didn't know how. I asked for a loan from the State Bank of India, but they refused. I decided not to leave it. Every day, for a whole week, I went to the bank and sat outside, waiting all day for somebody to listen to me—though I didn't know exactly what I was going to say—and watching landlords go in and come out, having their business taken care of. Finally the director decided to listen to me, but he told me that they could help me only if the regulation on loans was changed. It seems that the State Bank of India believed that it was prohibited from making loans for the purchase of land—they could only make loans for animals, improvements, and for large business ventures, all of which benefiting the large landholders. The bank was not set up to help poor people! But the director of the local branch agreed to make enquiries.

In the meantime, the middleman who was cultivating the land arranged for his relatives to buy it. I went to the director of the trust and I appealed to him saying, "Please, don't give land to that middleman who never paid you the rent. I only need three months to find the money, and in the meantime I will find something to give you in advance." I asked for 300 rupees from each landless family, to get at least one third of the price, and I also organized them to occupy the land to deter other potential purchasers. Jagannathan suggested we send a telegram to Giovanni Ermiglia in Italy to ask for assistance and I did, but I didn't get an immediate answer. So I went to Gandhigram, where I go every time I have a problem, and soon I got a message from Giovanni, saying he could provide one third of the price of the land, and I ran to the trust to give them the money. And after three months of meetings and consultations with the State Bank of India, they came to agree that loans could be made for the purpose of buying the land.

To get the money, we needed to create a proper, legally recognized organization. At the beginning I didn't want to, but there was no other way and so we registered our movement under the name of LAFTI. Slowly the banks began to trust us, and we bought 500 acres of land. Unfortunately though, many of the banks still did not consider land an asset for the poor, as they did cows or hens, so soon they stopped giving us loans. I got in trouble, because I still had to pay my debt to the landlords from whom I bought the land. Four of them went to court. I started collecting money from the people, but the situation was really critical.

I received a telegram from the National Scheduled Cast Development Corporation, inviting me to a meeting in Delhi. At the meeting, there were 153 high-grade government administration officers, and only 3 people who were not from the government. The objective was to discuss how to improve the situation of the untouchables in India. Some suggested a project to get untouchables to make shoes for the army; others proposed involving them in the production of vegetables, and so on. I kept quiet, and then I asked to speak for five minutes. I explained that I myself came from an untouchable landless family, and that I was working for the landless, and if a landless person receives a piece of land, his family can survive, and finally be free. Access to land ownership is the only thing that can really improve their situation.

After a week, I received a letter asking me if I had any project to buy land. I said there was an offering of 1,000 acres that was being sold at half price, so some people of the National Scheduled Cast Development Corporation came to Tamil Nadu, and stayed with me for eight days, during which we designed a financial project that was approved. We got 50% of the money we needed, and I managed an exemption from registration fees, which could otherwise have been quite expensive."

I realize that the passage from land-gift movement to the idea of buying land cannot have taken place without a debate within the Sarvodaya Movement, and I ask Krishnammal to tell me about this:

"When I decided to buy land, some members of the Sarvodaya Movement said they did not approve, but I told them, "I want to meet the needs of landlords, too. I have decided to change methods because the situation has changed. It is not my intention to buy land for single families." Referring back to the days of Bhoodan when so much difficult-to-cultivate land was all that was offered, she adds, "When I find land available, I will negotiate to have it all, or nothing. If the people of the Sarvodaya Movement do not approve of my methods, I don't care. I am not interested in being defined as a leader of the Sarvodaya Movement, because I don't need labels. My only concern is the well-being of the people, and we can obtain well-being only through the land."

Jagannathan adds some more details to the story of the birth of LAFTI. Whereas Krishnammal stresses her change in orientation and her commitment to gaining land for the landless, whatever the avenue, Jagannathan emphasizes the continuity with the previous epics of nonviolent struggle. Taken together, what becomes clear is the expansion of their collective repertoire, which will stand them in good stead in the prawn struggles yet to come.

Jagannathan: Back to Tamil Nadu

"After I was released, we started working in Tamil Nadu again, and in 1981 we registered LAFTI as an organization in order to get loans from banks and from the government. After Valivalam and Bihar, we organized only some minor satyagrahas. For example, in 1982, during a padayatra, the people of a village called Vadapathimangalam complained to us that they had no land to cultivate, when in the same area there were 4,000 acres of land belonging to the government that nobody was cultivating. There had been a big landlord who had converted his paddy fields into sugarcane plantations to escape the Land Ceiling Act, because for this kind of cultivation there were no limits on land ownership. When a change in government occurred in the ensuing elections, the new Chief Minister cancelled the exceptions for sugarcane plantations. The plantation became government property, and it was run as a government cooperative. But the place was managed with an extraordinary degree of bribery and corruption, so it failed very soon and was closed. From then on, the land lay in waste.

So I went to the Minister of Agriculture to explain that there were more than 300 families suffering because of this situation, and after some pressure they assured me that the land was going to be distributed to the poor people. But they were always delaying, so we spent about two months in the area organizing the people for satyagraha. Krishnammal organized a 3,000 people silent march, but it was not enough, so at the end I decided to start fasting. After seven days, I was getting really weak, and the papers started reporting I was going to die. At that point the Chief Minister woke up, and told the District Collector to start distributing the land and asked me to stop the fast. The following day the land was distributed.

In the latest history of our satyagrahas, we have collected nearly 6,000 acres of land through nonviolent people's action alone. Then we bought nearly 4,000 acres more, with the help of friends from all over the world and through bank loans. Altogether, it makes 10,000 acres of land we have distributed to the poorest families in Tamil Nadu and Bihar".

Then Krishnammal, who has received India's highest civilian award—the *Padma Sri*—in recognition of her work for the poorest of poor, is suddenly inspired, and adds:

"I was able to create opportunities for so many to express their potential. Our workers come mostly from untouchable families. I am very strict with them. Logannathan used to complain about this to me. Keithan used to call me the *maharani*, the queen, because I always want to have everything under control.

For me, a fundamental aspect of what I do is assist people's spiritual awakening. In Tamil Nadu, the period from the end of December to the end of January is considered the month of the awakening of the soul. In this period, brahmins wake up at three in the morning, clean the house, have a bath, and then pray. I wanted to introduce the same practice in the village even for the people who are not brahmins, together with singing bhajans and music. Those moments represent for women the rare opportunity to have time for themselves and to listen to that which elevates the spirit. Fighting only is not enough. The spirit must be cultivated as well.

I realize that in spite of my efforts, I have not brought revolution everywhere, but I have lit some lights in the darkness, and so I can say I am satisfied."

Maharani is a proper definition of Krishnammal. Her dignified way of walking, her proud look and her manners, which at first can appear a bit authoritarian, makes one really think of a queen. At the same time though, she is always Amma, with all the sweetness, care, and love only a mother can have. I look at her as she walks away in the direction of the LAFTI offices with her firm step, and I ask myself if in my life I will ever have the fortune to meet another woman like her.

But our story is far from over—there are more struggles ahead.

No to Prawn Farming!

The heat is almost unbearable. By six in the morning, it is already too hot to do anything. We are waiting for some rain to cool the air before our one-day tour of the prawn farm area, where the hottest episodes of the most recent struggles are taking place. We are going to meet women who possessed the courage to lay down front of bulldozers to stop them from digging more ponds, people who have gone to prison for protesting against this rape of the land by Indian and multinational corporate interests, and families whose houses have been burnt to the ground by the prawn companies' gundas.

I am excited, and a bit worried, too. LAFTI workers keep on telling me how many times they have been threatened and even physically attacked by the prawn farm owners' henchmen. I can't work out if now the situation is quiet, if we are going to visit a trouble-free area, or if I have real reasons to be concerned.

Jagannathan is just about to leave to Chengalpattu, near Madras, where his daughter Sathya lives. We are going to reach there in a couple of days, as soon as our work here is finished. Before leaving, Jagannathan decides to begin to tell me the story of their involvement in this environmental struggle, which is being played out right here and throughout the world, and which he believes could be the last of his life.

Jagannathan: The struggle against aquaculture

"We moved to Nagai-e-Millath (formerly Thanjavur) District, with its headquarters in Nagapattinam on the coast, for a year-long padayatra to promote Gram Swaraj. We walked block after block organizing village assemblies, until in December 1992, we reached an area where we were approached by people who apprised us of their desperate situation. "You speak of Gram Swaraj, but you don't know what is happening here. Our land has been taken, our water has been polluted, and fish in the sea are dying!"

They explained to me that the reason for all of this was that, all along the coast, land had been purchased or leased by local capitalists and multinational corporations to start intensive prawn farming. Much of this, we later learned, was funded by the World Bank. First of all, large areas of fertile land that had been traditionally cultivated by local people was removed from cultivation, and they lost their only source of income. The economy in that area is based almost entirely on agriculture, and there is nothing else those people can do apart from working the land. But this is not all. The prawn farms are human-constructed ponds filled with water that must be partly salty and partly sweet. So these industries started pumping sweet water from the village wells, creating severe water scarcities in a very short time. To grow larger prawns, and protect them from diseases, a massive quantity of chemicals is utilized, and the water in the ponds gets polluted quickly, and has to be changed often. Prawn industrialists have discovered that the easiest way to do this is to discharge the polluted water into the sea. As a result, along the coast the fish are dying, and the fishing communities have been severely impacted. Now fishermen have to sail far out to sea, but they don't have appropriate boats, and can't afford to buy any. The same polluted water from the ponds, salty and polluted, penetrates the soil and reaches the groundwater, and many people in the villages have started experiencing skin and eyes problems.

After a few years, the ponds become unusable and have to be abandoned, leaving a polluted and salty soil, completely unfit for agriculture. The mangrove forest that used to provide a shelter for fish when they had to lay their eggs, and was a natural barrier against cyclones and sea erosion, has been destroyed all along the coast to build prawn ponds.

All together, it is a real disaster. Because of this industry, that enriches only a few industrialists and multinational investors, and provides luxury foods sold in supermarkets in Europe and America, more and more people are losing their very basis of survival. (For a more complete description of the devastation wrought by intensive prawn farming, see Appendix B.)

When I heard all this, I decided to stop our padayatra, and to organize the people for a nonviolent satyagraha in the area. In 1994, we had the largest demonstration. All the people of the villages involved - women, children, everyone - went to the place where they were building new ponds and stood in front of the bulldozers to stop them. But the prawn farm owners bribed the police who, in turn, filed a case against LAFTI and against the people from the villages saying we had weapons—knives, stones, sticks. I was myself accused of having physically attacked the managers of the prawn company. Those poor people never used violence, and in spite of the accusations they decided to continue the struggle.

Then Jalalitha[1] won the elections as new Chief Minister, and she heard about our movement. In 1995, she passed a law called the Aquaculture Regulation Act. We thought it would help the poor people, but instead it assisted only the prawn companies. So at the end of 1995, we finally decided to appeal to the Supreme Court in Delhi. The Court nominated a commission of environmental experts and sent them to explore the coast of the seven states involved in the problem. It took them one year, and in December 1996 we had the final judgment, requiring that all the prawn farms had to be closed down by March 1997, damages paid to the people in the affected areas, and six years' severance paid to the prawn farm workers.

At the time, I had an eye operation conducted by an American doctor in Madras. I had both a cataract and glaucoma, which are usually operated upon separately, but the doctor was there only for a short time and so he operated on both conditions at the same time. The operation was successful, but I had to wear a special leather patch on my eye for six weeks to protect it from smoke, dust, and glare. I went to Gandhigram to rest, but there I got word that the multinationals had heavily bribed the Central Government, which had introduced new legislation to nullify the Supreme Court decision. The bill had been approved by *Raj Sabha* (Upper House of Parliament) without debate. So the judgment was in danger, and I decided to go to Delhi with Krishnammal to meet all the political leaders and discuss the issue, and I removed the leather protection that I had on my eye.

I even met the current Prime Minister Vajpayee, who at that time was in the opposition, and he said he would fight the bill. But the government had received money from prawn industrialists, and they were in a hurry to pass the bill in the *Lok Sabha* (Lower House of Parliament), too. So I decided to start a fast near the *Gandhi Samadhi*, a place where all the visitors go. I put a tent there and started fasting. I fasted for three days, and then government ministers came to ask me to stop, saying that they were not going to discuss the bill before sending a commission to investigate the issue. So I gave up my fast, but my eyes were so affected I could not see anymore. Slowly things have started to get better, and now I can see a little again. My sight is badly affected, but I had no choice, as somehow I had to make this sacrifice to protect the Supreme Court judgment.

Now it is 1999, and still the judgment has not been implemented. Here in Tamil Nadu, we have had protests and demonstrations, but nothing has changed. So in June, I declared I was going to start a penance. I wrote a letter to the Chief Minister asking again that the prawn farms be closed; the land returned to the people; motor boats given to the fishermen who now had to go far out to sea; protection offered to the marine fauna; and mangroves protected so that the seacoast would not be destroyed by cyclones and erosion. Tamil Nadu is deeply affected by sea erosion. Many beautiful temples have already disappeared under the sea, and many others are in danger. I sent this letter to the newspapers, and on June 9th, I started my penance, consisting of a partial fast: I was taking only one meal a day.

In August, local politicians asked me to stop or at least to postpone my penance, because elections were to start. They came in person to the place where I was fasting, and gave me a paper where they promised to start implementing the sentence as soon as possible. I also started having some pains, and had to give up my fast. Nagapattinam doctors wanted to operate me on immediately, but Sathya brought me to an expert and he only suggested that I drink a lot of water because during the fast I had become dehydrated. Now I am feeling better, and I am just waiting for the new government to be formed to see who are the people to be approached. So this is the present situation."

Jagannathan is leaving tonight. Everyone in the ashram helps him in preparing his luggage, and checking that he has got everything he needs with him: a couple of shirts and dhotis in khadi cloth, his spinning wheel, his eyeglasses, the copy of the *Bhagavad Gita* he reads every morning, and the papers he is working on. He does not seem too happy to be leaving Krishnammal, not even for a few days: "I will miss her," he tells me, making me remember once again how wonderful their relationship is.

That night I decide to go through the notes I took during the meeting with K. M. Natarajan, who has been involved in the prawn issue from the very beginning, and M. Mariappan, the advocate that helped them in their suit to the Supreme Court.

I met Natarajan in his house in Madurai, where he is chairman of the Gandhi Memorial Foundation, runs the *Gram Swaraj Weekly* and cooperates with the College of Gandhian Thought. Natarajan is now his sixties, with a great sense of humor and an abiding love for Jagannathan and Krishnammal, with whom he has been working since 1971, the year he became involved in the temple land satyagraha in Vallivalam. These are his reflections on the prawn farm issue:

"In 1992, we started a padayatra for Gram Swaraj in the Nagapattinam area, and walking from village to village we came to know about this prawn issue. People told us it was no use to distribute the land, because land was already polluted there, as was the water. So Jagannathan decided to stop the yatra and asked the co-workers to take a survey to understand what was happening. We went to all the villages to listen to the complaints, and when we realized the dimensions of the problem, Jagannathan started organizing. He was already well known in that district because LAFTI had distributed 10,000 acres of land there, and so

Women march against prawn farming, Nagapattinam, 2000.

people trusted him and were ready to give their full support. Almost every time we organized a rally, there were 20,000-25,000 people! Never less than 5,000. Once we had a large meeting on the beach in Madras, and Vandana Shiva, the famous scientist and environmentalist, joined us.

This issue has been going on for the last ten years. Jagannathan is fully occupied with this issue: prawn, prawn, prawn… Nothing else! He's a very strong man. When he takes up an issue, he won't think about anything else! Even in his dreams, he will talk about that only. He has held so many fasts, also in front of the prawn companies' headquarters. When last August he had his prayerful penance, all the magazines gave much emphasis to his fast, and journalists were writing about him as one of the main environmental leaders in India, together with Sunderlal Bahuguna and Medha Patkar. This is not something he ever intended, but something the conditions faced by the poor demanded, and came about as a result of his uncanny ability to listen to their real needs. His struggle has always been for land for the tillers, but there cannot be any land for the tillers if all the land and water is polluted by the prawn farms.

In this prawn issue, the problem is both with multinationals and with local capitalists who want to make quick money, and they can really make a lot of money in this business. Among the main promoters of prawn farming are companies from Thailand. The eastern coast of Thailand has already been completely destroyed, so now the companies have moved to the western coast. Mostly they produce prawns for export. Here in India, there are 7,000 kilometers of coastal area suitable for establishing their businesses. They come and organize conferences where they advertise immediate returns on investments, and easy export to America in exchange for dollars. It is made to seem very appealing. Little do they know about the collapse of the prawn industry on one coast of Thailand, or the diseases that killed the industry in the Philippines, or chemicals used in China that made countries unwilling to import their products.[2] So the local rich people, big industrialists, and even the tobacco companies, have started investing in this business, and the government is interested, too, because they want to encourage exports in order to gain in foreign exchange.

The Supreme Court judgment is very clear: the prawn farms are to be demolished and workers compensated, and only traditional farms can be started with permission of the authorities. Practices are to be instituted so that the principle of "the polluter pays" becomes a matter of law. But the government is not interested in implementing the judgment because it flies against its interests. The judgment was a huge success, but the company owners, the state officials, and the Agriculture Department filed a petition for review. This happened two years ago, and the case is still pending. In the meantime, the government brought forth an Aquaculture Authority Bill. At first, it seemed they were trying to confirm the Supreme Court judgment, but in practice they were just trying to invalidate it. With this bill, the principle establishing the minimum distance of a pond from the sea has been canceled, and the already existent farms could go on doing their business. The bill said a government 'aquaculture authority' should decide the destiny of the single farms, but no such authority has ever existed.

This bill was prepared by the Agriculture Department, which

is also in charge of the Fisheries Department. So Jagannathan ran to Delhi and started a fast in Gandhi Samadhi. At this point, the Agriculture Minister came to see Jagannathan. He had been a member of the Communist Party, but when people come to power they all become capitalists! When he was in the opposition, he came to one of our seminars on land problems and he spoke like fire, but after he came to power we heard him saying, "When there is development, some people have to suffer—without cutting trees we cannot dig our mines." The fact is that all political parties are interested in keeping this industry alive. When they are in the opposition, they are cooperative, they come to rallies, etc., but when they come to power, they change."

I ask if he knows of any movements against the prawn industry in Thailand.

"Not in Thailand. I know there have been protests in Bangladesh, but they were crushed. There was a team from Malaysia, members of the Third World Network[3], who attended some of our meetings. They said that after reading in the newspaper that 85-year-old Jagannathan was protesting by lying in front of tractors and bulldozers, they decided to start protests there, too. In Ecuador, there have been some street fights, but I do not know exactly what happened. But in other places, such as the Philippines and Thailand, there was no opposition. When we have our conferences in Delhi, we invite all these groups from other countries, and they usually come.

At the moment, Jagannathan is not physically very well, because of his eyes and his loss of hearing. If he was only 50-years-old and with good eyes, he would do anything! Still, there is no other young leader with his energy. Nobody. Jagannathan is fully merged in this issue, and Krishnammal has to support him! They have always been together in their struggles."

Mariappan is a lawyer, a middle-class man with a nice house in Madurai and a good practice. He has been helping Jagannathan legally for the last 38 years. He had a major role in the prawn issue as he convinced Appa to appeal to the

Supreme Court of India. I meet him in his house in Madurai on a lucky day, because during our meeting it finally starts raining, a huge storm that will flood the roads in a few minutes. Mariappan tells me:

"I became involved in the issue of prawn farming seven years ago (in 1992). This industry had a sudden eruption in India, although prawns have always been fished traditionally, especially in Kerala. Intensive farming brings in a lot of money; companies have started digging huge ponds (200 long by 100 feet wide by 10 feet deep) with no kind of permission or license. Thanjavur District is very fertile because of the water of the Cauvery River, and the land has always been used for paddy cultivation. The main occupations in the area are fishing and land tilling, and people usually managed to obtain a decent wage—almost a living wage—only from paddy.

Many of the landowners sold their land because the companies were paying ten times the market price, but most of the land there belongs to the government and to the temples, and they lease it for 20-30 years. Everything happened very quietly. Nobody really realized what was happening, and in this way people have been uprooted from their land.

The companies are mainly from Japan, Europe, and the United States. And the government is supporting this industry because it brings dollars to the country, and because working on a prawn farm brings a higher wage than agriculture. But they forget about all the people who lost their employment because of prawn farming. Almost a million people have been affected.

Jagannathan declares that he is ready to give his life for this cause. He is really able to motivate people: if he goes, people follow. His technique in leading this struggle consisted of three stages: first of all talking to the affected people. Then he contacts the government to invite them to stop this industry and sends letters to the Prime Minister explaining the issue. Then he organizes this great satyagraha, where people lay in front of the bulldozers. They have all been arrested for violation of private property, and there is still a case pending on them.

But then I thought, "This whole thing is illegal: why don't we appeal to the Supreme Court?" In the beginning, Jagannathan didn't want to do it. He thought we would have to wait 10-20 years to have a verdict, but I told him that as a nonviolent leader he should have faith in justice, and in the end he agreed. With Natarajan, we walked to all the villages of the affected area to ascertain exactly what was happening, then we prepared a document divided in different sections: ecological impact, impact on health, on economy, etc.

Than we considered the *Environmental Regulation* Act, according to which no one is permitted to start industries within 500 meters from the high water zone, and the *Coastal Zone Regulation Act*, according to which it is forbidden to start any polluting activity in coastal areas. But there is no law directly prohibiting prawn farming. In Europe, Japan, and America there is already a direct ban on this kind of intensive farming. So because of the lack of a direct ban, we had to appeal to environmental laws. Jagannathan, Natarajan, and I went to Delhi and met Bhagawati, the former Chief Justice, for a consultation, because he is a good judge and is concerned about environmental issues. He suggested we meet M. C. Mehta, who is an expert in environmental law. Mehta looked at our report, and said it was a very good case to fight, and there were good opportunities to succeed particularly because of the renown of Jagannathan. He took one month to prepare the case, and then everything began.

The Supreme Court formed a commission of scientists of the *National Engineering Environmental Research Institute* (NERI), consisting of experts in aquaculture, who visited the entire coast in Kerala and Tamil Nadu. After three months, they produced a report divided in three parts: 1. Effects of prawn industries on the environment; 2. Effects on public health; and 3. Economic losses caused by prawn industries. In the meantime, the Supreme Court ordered a halt to any new construction, or enlargement of any of the existing farms.

When the case was argued, we went to Delhi by train. The prawn companies were paying 100,000 rupees a day ($25,000) to their lawyers. There were 100 companies involved, and they had called the best 112 lawyers in India, but the judges were very objective. There were audiences for 20 days, every day from 10.30 in the morning to 4:30 in the afternoon.

Many non-governmental organizations tried to become involved in this cause, some with good motivations, others just to gain greater repute. But the judges refused to include other groups in the case, noting that, given Jagannathan's reputation, his shoulders were broad enough that he easily stand for all of them, and would be expressing their views in any case. So it was Jagannathan, Mehta, and his two legal assistants, against 112 high-powered lawyers and their assistants, backed by a hundred local and multinational corporations and interests.

It was such a historic judgment, but the problem is that even if the Court gives a judgment, the Parliament can change it with a law. The prawn industry owners continue to pressure the Government not to close the existing farms, so the Government has been trying to pass a law to cancel the sentence (the Aquaculture Authority Bill). Now there is a pending review petition against the judgment, and this is what we are fighting against right now.

Nowadays, everyone knows exactly what the effects of aquaculture really are, because of what has happened in other Asian nations. But there is a lot of fast money in it, so the companies have tried, and until they are stopped once and for all, they can continue to rake it in."

When Jagannathan is ready to leave, all the ashram members gather around the jeep that will take him to the train station to say goodbye. One of the workers tells me: "Whenever he leaves, we don't know when we are going to see him again, we never know what happens next." Krishnammal hold his hand until the jeep leaves, then she walks over to me. With her usual vagueness about time, she informs me that, "Tomorrow or the next day we can go to visit the prawn area."

Saying goodbye to Jagannathan makes me sad. I like spending time with him: I like the way he is so clear when he tells me his story, how careful he is to make sure I understand everything he says, the way he knows how to smile even when he talks about the hardest times. A year after my visit, a friend on his way back from India will tell me, “He spends a lot of time meditating, isolated from the world. Then all of a sudden he calls someone to dictate a letter to the Prime Minister or something like that. He has an amazing inner strength that helps him go on in spite of his age and health problems.”

That evening, I sit on the sand in the middle of the ashram courtyard to look at the moon. Soon, a small group of children has gathered around me, and they look at me with an expression that says, ‘Well, what can we do now to have some fun?” Language problems make it difficult to communicate, but we manage to agree on ‘sing’ and ‘dance’. The children start singing some songs, and others join in. Soon Veerasami and another of the workers arrive, the latter carrying a big pot he starts playing as if it was a tabla, singing with an incredibly beautiful voice. Veerasami convinces the children to dance. In pairs, they shyly move from the sand where we are sitting, and, after a short hesitation, they start imitating Indian film stars, jumping on their skinny legs. The effect is exhilarating, and we all laugh with gusto. Krishnammal arrives to enjoy this magic moment, perfect in its simplicity: in the open air, under the moon, dancing and singing to a voice-and-pot concerto. The only problem is that soon I am asked to perform myself!

These are the moments when my heart tightens when I think how many times at home I miss moments like this, being all together—the elderly, grown-ups, and children—moments when things happen in a simple way, and everybody enjoys together the beauty of the night or a song. I think how difficult it is for westerners to be together with each other at the end of the twentieth century, and how it is still easy and beautiful to do it here. I wish I could never leave.

The first day without Jagannathan goes slowly. Krishnammal is very busy, and when we finally manage to start working, a group of women arrives from a nearby village to check to see that Amma is okay, since she still has not visited their village since her arrival in Kuthur.

I spend some time in the kitchen trying to learn something, until Krishnammal comes to tell me that today I am going to eat at Veerasami's. She arranged for someone to buy fish for me, but they can't cook it in the ashram where the food is strictly vegetarian. Once again, Amma's sense of hospitality leaves me speechless, and I think I think about how amazing is her ability to reconcile her role as an activist and revolutionary with being a wife, a mother, and a perfect host. I follow Veerasami and climb on the back of his motorbike, where I have to fight the instinct of holding on to his waist—remembering that in India physical contact between a man and a woman who are not husband and wife is highly unusual—and that women travel on motorbikes side-saddle, holding onto the seat. Veerasami lives in a small house ten minutes from the ashram with his wife and children. After introducing me to his family, he invites me to sit under the fan and he shows me with pride the bags of rice kept under a bed and on some shelves: it is the harvest from his acre of land that he himself, before becoming a LAFTI worker, received, thanks to Jagannathan and Krishnammal's efforts. Coming from an untouchable family himself, Veerasami is now one of the main workers in LAFTI, and he is secretary of the Tamil Nadu Gram Swaraj Movement, of which Jagannathan is the President. His wife appears carrying the most delicious fish I have ever tasted, and when I finish, Veerasami drives me back to the ashram with a portion of fish for one of the cooks, who is not a vegetarian.

I spend the rest of the day going through my notes, thinking about the fish I ate for lunch, and mumbling against the heat.

Chapter Eleven

In the Arena of Struggle

The next morning, around six o'clock, Krishnammal, two other workers, and I are sitting in the jeep that will bring us to the prawn farm areas. Krishnammal starts singing bhajans, and everyone seems very relaxed. We drive through a landscape that has somehow become familiar to me: small roads cutting through green paddy fields where women are working in their colorful sarees, lean men working the land with their bullocks, water buffaloes pulling carts full of paddy piled high, lumbering slowly under the hot sun. Small villages, colorful temples, mud huts, and, as usual, children going to school in their uniforms.

Then Krishnammal begins her narration:

"I think we have already done a lot around this prawn issue, but Jagannathan wants to continue on with it and I have to follow. There's nothing I can do to stop him! I would like to get on with my housing program, but if he is so clear about this, I must help him. And then when I see people suffering so much, I feel I have to do something more.

We still have to awaken the fisherfolk community to the problem, because they are too busy to even think about this prawn issue that affects them so badly. We have much left to do.

Bringing the case to the Supreme Court was very costly and we don't have money, but we managed anyway thanks to the help of our friends. The prawn farm lawyers received a lot of money, and they are really powerful. One of them is now a spokesman for the Congress Party. Mehta will not accept any money from us. We only pay for his traveling expenses.

Now we can't stop fighting. Everybody knows we are

involved in this issue and expect help from us. So here we are."

I ask her about the hottest period of the struggle:

"It was in 1995, before the Supreme Court judgment. At that time we had invited Sarvodaya leaders from all over India to come and see the problem firsthand, and they stayed with us for ten days. Another time, we organized a seven-day meeting with 500 important workers from all over the country. My main occupation in this struggle has been to organize women.

There are so many episodes of the struggle I can tell you about! Once, in a place near Perunottam village, they were building a new prawn farm. There were many excavating machines, and men were armed with knives and sticks. The women of the area joined together and told me they wanted to protest. First, we went to the temple and prayed, and then we marched to the village. There were nearly 500 of us. I was a bit worried, but the women marched straight towards the excavators. A woman went and laid in front of one of the machines, ready to die, but fortunately the driver stopped. Police came and wanted to arrest everybody, but we were too many. So they only asked for Veerasami, but the women didn't let them take him away. At the end, the police left.

The following day Jagannathan started fasting near Nagapattinam. He soon became weak and we had to call a doctor. While Veerasami was explaining the situation to the doctor, police arrived and took him away with a van, and then took Appa to a local hospital. That hospital was terrible—no water, no toilets—even though, as a Freedom Fighter, Jagannathan has the right to go to first class hospitals. When Sathya came to visit, she cried at the sight of that place, but we could not move Appa to another hospital because he was too sick. He agreed to stop fasting only when Mariappan went to see him, and together they decided together to file a case against the District Collector and the prawn farm owners."

We have been driving for almost an hour, in a north-easterly direction, when the green paddy fields suddenly give way to something resembling a lunar landscape. The rich red soil I'm used to seeing is here a dry, white crust, baking under

Arriving for satyagraha against prawn farm, Nagai District, 2001.

the hot sun. No vegetation grows on this desert, and the only living beings are goats. "The land you are looking at," one of the workers tells me "used to be prawn farms, the first to be closed after the Supreme Court judgment. Now you can see with your eyes what happens to the land after years of salt and chemicals. The white crust on the surface is salt, and the goats are here because they love licking it."

The contrast with the previous landscape is astonishing. This land that hundreds of families had been working, and which had been worked for millennia, is now unusable, and it is certain no one will invest the funds necessary to make this land cultivable again. It will stay like this for who knows how long. In the meantime, with every heavy rain the salt and the chemicals penetrate deeper into the ground, reaching the water table that feeds the nearby village wells, rendering the water unpotable.

We drive on, silent in our thoughts, and Krishnammal points out a building that looks like a small factory in the middle of the country. It is the packing shed of a prawn farm, one of the many that is still in operation. The jeep takes a small, dusty road leading to the farm, but our visit is very brief and we don't even stop for a picture. Karti turns the car and drives back very quickly. What I manage to see is a piece of land as large as a paddy field, but dug more deeply and with higher banks, and a pump that brings water in. No one is around, no one seems to be working there at the moment. Krishnammal tells me that a pond like this provides employment to two people in a year, while if it was a paddy field, at least 120 people would be employed to cultivate and harvest. She explains that the social condition of women is still very bad in their district, and it has gotten worse now that women have lost their traditional position in the household. Because of the general worsening of economic conditions in the area, they have to leave their homes to work as daily laborers for miserable wages. Being one of the weakest sections of society, women are particularly damaged by the loss of jobs and land caused by the prawn industry.

We drive past a police station, and the policemen sitting outside seem to recognize the jeep. Krishnammal tells me this is the place where they usually end up after their protests, and not voluntarily. In this area, she notes, they managed to close five farms, but three are still working. One belongs to the (now former) Prime Minister's granddaughter! And the others belong to friends or relatives of local politicians.

Our journey goes on. We are going to Tennampattinam, a small village I can't even find on the map, but that had been theater of a terrible episode in the struggle. The car takes a very small road that leads us to the heart of the village, where some people are already waiting for us in front of a big hut. Happy to see Amma, they offer us a seat in the shade and some delicious, fresh coconut water. Krishnammal introduces me to Arumugam, Vartharajan, and Thyagarajan, leader of the Gram Sabhas of nearby villages, and to Nagarajan, a lawyer who was working on the prawn issue in the area even before Jagannathan and Krishnammal knew about it. Nagarajan offered them the most precious help, and his house was used as headquarters and refuge in the difficult times when police were trying to arrest Jagannathan and his workers.

Armanikam, one of the villagers, explains to me their perspective on the prawn issue, and what happened here in 1995:

"We oppose the prawn farms. Our drinking water became salty. These industrialists began their projects through violence and force. All the fertile land has been spoiled and we lost our employment. So we started protesting through Gandhian means. The owners answered using their gundas, who often physically assaulted the people involved in this agitation. One day they set fire to 40 of our homes, and then went to the police and filed a case against, us saying we attacked them. Nearly 75 people of the village were arrested and put into Trichi prison for about four months. In this period, Jagannathan and Krishnammal supported our families and built temporary houses, and they provided us with food, lamps, etc., because we had lost everything. They built a big hut and provided us with food and clothes. In the fire, we also lost our cattle, and whatever was not destroyed in the fire was stolen by the gundas in the nights after the fire."

Nagarajan adds:

"Here most of the people depend on land, and harijans find jobs only in the fields. With prawn culture, most of the fertile land has been purchased by millionaires both from within India and from other countries. This increased unemployment among these people, who were already poor before. Prawn industries started in the coastal area, occupying a huge expanse of land. Seven states are involved in this process. Prawn farms are workable for a maximum of five years. Then they are closed, leaving a dry, salty, and dead land. The neighboring land is also despoiled. Due to the chemicals used in the ponds, people are experiencing skin diseases and eyes problems. Drinking water has been polluted.

In the initial stage of the struggle all the village people were supporting us. But prawn farms owners have begun to bribe village leaders, and so we started losing the support of many people. But then Jagannathan and Krishnammal came, visited this area and started supporting our fight."

The entire village has come to greet Krishnammal. I look at these people, mothers with small children, elderly, men and women, owning little more than a hut and some tools, maybe a cow if they are very lucky. Land is their life here—land that fed their parents, grandparents, and great grandparents, land they broke their backs on, land they have taken care of, land that sustains them and keeps them alive. It is extraordinary to think that, within a single decade, their thin lifelines are close to being cut by an activity promoted by, among others, the United Nations Food and Agriculture Organization (FAO) as a way to create job opportunities in depressed Third World areas, and to "support people with a vitamin-enriched diet". *Not a single prawn has ever appeared on the table of these people.* Prawns reach only the tables of the rich, in India, Japan, Europe, and the United States. What surely appears on the table of these poor people is polluted water, courtesy of the World Bank that funded the initial prawn farm land purchases. This is the price of globalization and unbridled multinational capitalism run amock. But, and I now see a thread running through Krishnammal and Jagannathan's struggles, this new globalization is little different from the old colonialism in that it is ruthlessly controlled from centers of power far from the people it leaves in impoverishment, and without any say on the part of the people most affected. A difference, however, lies in the fact that it is extremely difficult to figure out within the tangled web of corporate-state relationships where those centers of power even are.

Armanikam adds, in a plea that bring this all down to earth:

"If you are going to write about Amma and Appa, please, write what is happening here. We are losing our land, our sole means of livelihood. If they take our land, there is nothing left for us. Nothing at all."

We move to Nagarajan's house to rest a bit. Nagarajan lives in a nearby village called Poompuhar. His house is not much different from the others, except that the low walls are made of brick rather than mud and straw. The house consists of two rooms. The first is entirely empty, without an outside entrance door or fan, and with walls covered by the traditional palm-leaf. In the second, smaller room I catch a glimpse of his clothes, tidily hung from a string stretched tautly between the two walls. There is no bed because Nagarajan, like most of the people here, sleeps on the floor on a straw mat.

Nagarajan is dignified and elegant. Krishnammal tells me that he never got married because he has dedicated his life to his work, and could make good money working as a lawyer for the government. But he prefers staying in the village and helping as best he can, even if this means living a very simple life. When Krishnammal talks about him, he smiles modestly. Then he adds, "I am poor because I am working for poor people, and they have no money to pay me. If they give me something, that's fine, but otherwise how can I ask them for money? You see yourself how it is around here."

Some university students from the village join us. They have also been involved in the protest, helping organizing rallies, and demonstrating, while most of the people of the village were in prison, but they are a bit shy, and don't talk much. We sit on the floor, a bit wrung out by the heat. Only Krishnammal has the strength to go on talking:

"In August 1997, we hid in this house. It was our headquarters. When we moved to this area, we didn't know where to stay, and this man, although his house is small, was kind enough to give us his own home, even though he knew it was dangerous! It was nearly the anniversary of Gandhi's "Quit India Resolution". One day, Jagannathan announced to the newspaper that on the anniversary of the Resolution—August 9th—at 9 a.m., he was going to occupy the prawn farms' land. The police mobilized, arriving from different states. Jagannathan was hiding here, and could not use the jeep to move because the police and gundas would have recognized him.

On the night of the 8th of August, the people of this village helped smuggle him in the cart of a man who was carrying fish to his village. From this village, he walked to the prawn farm land very early in the morning. Another 150 people joined him, coming from unexpected directions. When they arrived all together, the police were enjoying a nice breakfast, hosted by the prawn farm owner, so they didn't notice the people coming. At 9 o'clock sharp, Jagannathan and the others came out of hiding, singing loudly. Police arrested them all, and then proceeded to the LAFTI offices and arrested all the workers there! But the following day, another 100 people were ready to offer satyagraha and were arrested. The next day another 100 arrived, and then another, and so on for 10 days! I escaped arrest, because I had to find lawyers for the people who were in jail, and take care of their families."

Arumugam, leader of the Poompuhar Village Assembly smiles as he remembers those days. He shows me pictures of the protest, happy to underscore how he was present in every moment of the struggle, leading his village people. A picture shows his animated, if elderly, face—with an amazingly long mustache—looking proudly right at the camera, first of a line of satyagrahi the police are taking to prison.

Nagarajan adds,

"The police arrested around 50 people of our village for this satyagraha, and they were in prison for 22 days and the cases are still pending. In this area, nearly 7,000 people live. The prawn industrialists own 800 acres of land in the Poompuhar area alone; 200 acres are used for prawn farms, the other 600 are lying in waste."

It's time to leave. We eat the food we carried with us from Kuthur. Every time we spend the day somewhere, the ashram cooks wrap freshly prepared food in banana leaves, so we can taste their wonderful dosas, coconut chutney, and sambar wherever we are.

We say goodbye to the students and the village people who have joined us, and provide a lift to Nagarajan and Arumugam. On the way, we see a group of people sitting

Fertile and beautiful land in Nagai District, prior to being turned into a desert-like wasteland, 1998.

under the shadow of a big tree, and Arumugam tells me these are people who oppose the struggle. Prawn farm owners bribe them with money and big promises, and have convinced them that aquaculture is a resource for everybody, bringing jobs and development. This is their present strategy: they have seen that people had the strength to oppose them and raise their voices, so now they are trying to divide the villagers, creating conflict and animosity. In the meantime, they can continue their despoliation of the land until it is time to leave it in waste.

Before leaving the village, Krishnammal wants to show me the houses that LAFTI is building in Vellampatti. She repeats that building houses for the untouchables and having them registered as the property of the village women is one of her main objectives. We stop near an area where a group of men and women are working on the construction of several houses. Nearby is a big banyan tree, under whose shade, they tell me, Jagannathan has fasted many times. “When we go to Sathya,” Krishnammal explains “I will go to Madras and approach cement and bricks producers, and rich people such as film stars, to ask for funding for my housing projects. I want to provide shelter to 8,000 families in the next three years”.

Now it's time to say goodbye to Vellampatti, to Nagarajan, to the *Gram Sabha* leader, and to the women and children who followed us on our tour. I think how much these people have already suffered in this struggle, and I fervently hope that something will come of it. I promise everyone will tell their stories, but my heart tells me that this is not enough, and I feel a bit powerless and disheartened. All those people seem to me so powerless and vulnerable, since they have to face the brute power of multinationals and corrupted politicians, and I wonder what will happen to them if these aquaculture projects are not stopped. I think about how many farmers in Southeast Asia have already lost their only source of income when their land was taken from them to build ponds, and as we drive back to the ashram a sadness overtakes my tired thoughts.

The fish market

The next day, Krishnammal takes me to see the fish market in Nagapattinam. We leave very early in the morning to reach the market at the peak of its activity. Long before reaching the village, we meet trucks and carts full of people headed for the market, and people already returning, carrying tremendous loads of fish on their heads, on the back of bicycles and scooters, or using every other available means of transport.

We have our first view of the market from Nagapattinam Bridge. Boats line up along the pier. They appear to be in

Krishnammal preparing women for march on illegal prawn farm, 2000.

such poor condition that they seem to have just been pulled up from the bottom of the sea. Groups of men off-load the fish: deckhands pass down huge baskets of the catch that are then transferred from head to head till they are emptied on the ground, forming teeming mountains of crab, shrimp, and fish of all varieties. Thousands of people walk around this strange and boisterous landscape bargaining, buying, transporting. Several women squatting on the ground are selling dried fish. Krishnammal and I start walking around, but it is made more difficult by the fact that everyone is in a hurry, the mountains of fish are everywhere, and it is very slippery. I take some pictures and we leave, with an idea of how important this fishery is for the community.

It is time to move to the heart of the fishermen's village to meet the leader of the fisherfolk community. It is, as is often the case, terribly hot, and the smell of fish is incredibly intense. Krishnammal tells me that this smell was their major nightmare for the 56 days they spent here during Jagannathan's prayerful penance.

We reach the fisherfolk leader's home. We are invited to sit under a fan with some other people I will discover are curious neighbors. The house is very trim. The orange, green, and blue of the walls, and the cane furniture and well-swept floors remind me of the interior of fishermen's homes on the Mediterranean. On a table sits a hen, so still that at first I think it is stuffed, and wonder if this is a local tradition, until a boy notices my interested look, claps his hand laughing and the hen jumps down.

The leader arrives. He is in his fifties with a large moustache, a round belly, and sardonic, sharp eyes. He's involved in politics. With a behavior that reveals his skill at public speaking, he relates:

"Until 1957, we fished with small boats we built ourselves. In those days, we had everything we needed—housing, food, clothing. And until 1976, governmental measures were taken in the interests of our community. A group of fisheries experts from several countries, including Norway and Japan, conducted research on the fertility of the coast here. They wanted to develop the fishing industry further. The Japanese gave us free motor boats, resulting in economic improvement, and people started being able to afford three meals a day! We were also able to export fish. A bridge was built over the Cauvery River, making life easier.

But since then, the situation has deteriorated. This place, a natural harbor, has not been improved. Almost 2,000 families have been affected by the lack of trade. We caught more, but there was no way to bring it to market. In 1979, the local boat-building industry closed down, bringing new unemployment.

Fishing is our only resource. Before 1976, the coastal area was protected by a thick forest, and it used to rain twice a month. We had shade, saltwater from the sea, and sweet water from the Cauvery River—ideal breeding conditions for fish that came to lay their eggs by the coast, and there was an enormous number of fish varieties. From December to March, the tide would bring the fish back to the open sea. This would also occur during the monsoon seasons (June-July, and October).

Now, all along the coast the sand has been removed to build prawn farms. The mangrove forest and all the other trees have been cut down, depriving fish the necessary shelter to lay eggs, and depriving the coast of its natural protection. Floods have completely destroyed 14 villages.

To speed up the growth of the prawns, chemicals are used, which pollute both the land and the seawater. Along the coast, near the seashore, there are no fish left, and we have to sail far out to sea. Before, there were always fish in our nets; now we often come back empty-handed. We have to sail so far that often we get very close to Sri Lanka, and this has brought about conflict with Sri Lankan fishermen, especially after the situation between Tamils and Singhalese on the island itself worsened. They accuse us of violating their territorial waters, and sometimes our people are arrested by Sri Lankan police, and sometimes they are shot. Once, a boat with 216 fishermen from five different districts was attacked by the Sri Lankans because they thought the fisherman were volunteers going to help the Tamil rebels. Recently, nearly 300 people were wounded near Rameshwaram, and lost a large fishing boat. Fishermen families are helped economically by the government only if they can prove their relatives have died, but most of the time the bodies are not found, so there are so many women with no means of sustenance, still waiting for their husbands who are likely never to return.

Losing the natural wealth of the coast, we have lost any security. In many coastal areas, the prawn farmers have taken control, and it is not even possible to gain access, as the areas are fenced and defended with big dogs. Because of pollution and poor administration, all the coastal communities are suffering. This is the last remaining fishing community, with 20,000 people depending on fishing.

The whole country would be safe with a policy of swadeshi—self reliance—but now that we have opened ourselves to the global market, we are in danger. Our political leaders have forgotten all of Gandhi's ideas."

I ask him how he became involved in Jagannathan's prayerful penance.

"My grandfather was a nationalist. I am a Gandhian and I believe in swadeshi, so I was welcomed when I approached Jagannathan and Krishnammal to help in this struggle. I am a politician, but first of all I belong to the fisherfolk community, so I wanted to help as I could.

The Supreme Court judgment has to be implemented. Otherwise we are ready to struggle more. The struggle has been hard here. In 1992, the police shot eight people during a demonstration. The fisherfolk community feels unsafe and unprotected at the moment. We think that at the least they should close the prawn farms and give us our land back."

After this meeting we move to the place where Jagannathan undertook his Prayerful Penance. On the way Krishnammal explains:

"In those 56 days of penance, Jagannathan suffered tremendously, especially because of the terrible conditions of the place. We all got sick there. We had an intense program in Nagapattinam. The first march we had was with the youth. Then we had a 500-woman fasting program, a sit-in from 9 in the morning till 6 in the evening with prayers, discussions, etc. Then on August 27th, we held a silent march, 300 women walking with their heads covered by black cloth. In every corner of the street, there was someone with a loudspeaker explaining the reasons for the march. It went on for nearly three hours, and I think this had a great impact on public officials. Then the women submitted their case to the District Collector, who claimed he had never previously heard of the Supreme Court judgment. He told us, "You only have one problem; we have so many!" Usually when we submit a paper to the authorities, only four people enter the office. That day, 300 women sat in front of the Collector's office, saying this was their last warning before they took radical actions.

The next day, the Collector called all the Sarvodaya workers. We had a meeting with around ten public officials, and we explained the problem. During the meeting one of the officials asked us, "Why don't you go to court again?" I got so angry, and shouted, "One man is suffering. Have some respect. Do you think we have money to go to court again?" I was so upset I left, but the meeting went on and we obtained the promise that they were going to implement the judgment. We asked them to make their promise in writing. They prepared it, and went to the place where Jagannathan was fasting. They also brought him lemon juice to break the fast. After three weeks, they started closing down some farms, but only 46 acres out of perhaps 10,000, and the owners are not obligated to clean up the land they have polluted and render it cultivable again."

We drive along what looks like the poorest part of the fisherfolk's village. On one side of the road is a huge expanse of dry, dusty ground. The sun beats down without pity, and there is not even a tree around, no shade to be found. In the middle of this ground is a modern temple, the old one having been slowly eroded and then washed away by the sea. In front of this temple, Jagannathan held his prayerful penance. No shade, no water, no toilets. Only sun, dust, and the smell of rotting fish. No wonder he became so dehydrated, no wonder they all got sick, no wonder Sathya was so upset when she saw the place where her 87-year-old father was fasting, and got so angry she told him and her mother they are completely mad and irresponsible.

The people of the village must have recognized the jeep, and some people start walking in the direction of the temple to greet Amma. The first to arrive is an old woman, who carries the key to the temple. Krishnammal tells me she is in charge of the temple because the Brahmin now comes only for special ceremonies. We walk around the temple, and Krishnammal explains that this is the place where they had their meeting with the village people. Then we sit to eat something, and soon it is time to leave. All the people who have gathered in the temple warmly say goodbye to Krishnammal. We get into the jeep, and as we look at the place that only two months ago saw so much suffering and sacrifice, Krishnammal says:

"I don't know what awaits us. The Supreme Court has appointed a committee to regulate the prawn farms, and they are now supposedly required to obtain a license before opening. But the leader of this committee is a very rich and corrupt man. He won't even meet Jagannathan, and says he will speak with him only through his lawyers.

I would like to dedicate myself to my housing program, but whatever Jagannathan decides to do with this struggle, it is my duty to help him. And I know he is fighting for a just cause."

If Gandhi was Alive

We are on a train again, this time on our way to Chengalpattu, a city near Chennai where Jagannathan and Krishnammal's daughter Sathya lives. With the story of the struggle against prawn farming, I have virtually finished my interviews, but I still have so many questions to ask, so many details to clarify and, Krishnammal tells me, so many experiences yet to come.

The first of these will be a visit to the local hospital, where Sathya is a doctor in the neonatology department. Chengalpattu Hospital is visited primarily by the poorest villagers of the nearby areas. Wealthier patients will, for the most part, end up in one of the many private hospitals in Chennai.

As soon as the jeep reaches the hospital, I am astonished by the quantity of people just hanging around the front and sides of the building. Groups of people squat on the ground. They wait, sleep, eat, right in front of the entrance. There are pools of stinking water from the last rains, rubbish all over the place, dogs and pigs rummaging for something to eat. It is a typical Indian urban landscape, once one moves away from the enclaves of the wealthy or the tourists, and so different from the villages I visited with Amma and Appa. Sathya explains that these people are relatives of the patients who have come from the most distant villages. Not having money enough to pay for even the least expensive hotel, they camp around the hospital to be close to their loved one. They do it for days, even weeks, dealing with terrible discomforts, an art many Indians are required to master.

The hospital itself is a building made of cement that probably is not as old as it looks, but the humid South Indian climate has already covered it with a green patina. I follow Sathya along dark corridors that make me think of a prison, but when we arrive in her department, the scene changes. Everything is clean and well-lit, and everywhere the commitment and efforts of this young and brave woman are recognizable. Sathya shows me the rooms for mothers and infants, and explains to me:

"When I arrived here, the situation was terrible. For this entire department, where an average of 30 babies are born each day, there was a single nurse and a single doctor to cover the 24 hours of the day. The babies had no beds, but were placed on the floor. Once, a baby was bitten by a rat. The mothers would walk into the babies' room without washing their hands and removing their shoes, increasing the risk of infections. The mothers' room was extremely dirty as well, since no one was caring for it.

I had to start from the very beginning. There were practical problems, like the fact that we have running water for only a few hours each day. There is never any money for supplies. Everything was lacking: personnel, beds, lamps, instruments. I had to face discrimination, because I am a woman, young, and I had studied in America.[1] People often treated me like someone who had just arrived from abroad, and did not know anything about Indian realities. I also had difficulties with the people who were working with me. Nurses would be offended when I told them to wash their hands before touching the babies. So I decided to change strategies, and to involve all the personnel—from doctors to cleaning ladies—in the analysis of the main problems of the department, in the identification of priorities, and in the elaboration of possible solutions. To discuss all this, I invited everybody for a picnic at the seaside, where we worked and played, and since then our relationship has changed, and now everybody cooperates, and feels responsible for the success of the department."

I am struck how closely this approach follows one that would have been adopted by Krishnammal, but I don't say anything. In the course of time, Sathya has managed to gain her coworkers' respect and trust, improve hygienic standards, and even found a way to make sure that mothers keep their room clean: into the room she moved a statue of a goddess that used to be in the corridor, and the mothers started cleaning the room regularly, since it had now become a place of worship! She made beds for the babies by recovering some old metal structures, so they are not on the floor anymore. Sathya explains to me that the mortality rate among the infants is still very high, because they are brought in only if they are very sick, and at the last minute. But it has decreased noticeably since her measures were implemented.

I observe Sathya as she talks to her colleagues: she looks a lot like her father, especially when she smiles, and she is extremely strong, calm, and with great inner equilibrium. From her parents she inherited the vocation to service, and all her life is dedicated to her work, in spite of all the difficulties she has to face every day. She loves her parents very deeply, even if in her life she never got to spend much time with them. So many times I've heard Krishnammal talking about Sathya's difficult childhood, having been separated from her mother since she was eight months old because Amma had to continue her work. Once Krishnammal told me with a smile that Sathya used to tell her, "In the next life I will be born as your mother, and will put you in a boarding school, so you'll see what it's like!"

One day, as we as travelling to Chennai, I ask Sathya to tell me about her childhood:

"When I was about one year old, my mother left me with my grandmother. I was with her for one year, then with one aunt, then with another aunt, always moving from one relative to the other, and then I was for some time in Gandhigram. I went to school, but I was not regularly registered. At that time in Gandhigram, there was a hostel, not for young children as there is now, but for adolescents. So when I was around nine years old, Dr. Soundaram, who was for me like a grandmother, told Amma that it was not good for me to stay there any longer, as I was the only girl, and so they sent me to a boarding school.

At the beginning, life was very difficult for me, because moving around all the time I couldn't make any friends. In boarding school, this situation changed, so from that point of view things got easier, but of course I suffered greatly at being separated from my family. In those years I learnt that relationships are impermanent, they come and go, and this has helped me a lot in life.

When I was very young, I used to think,"Why has God made parents that can't take care of their children?" Then I began to understand that they were doing it for a high and noble cause, and I became proud of them. I used to know what my parents were doing, and, of course, when they were in prison, which was often! In the period when I was in Gandhigram, my father started a fast that went on for 13 days, and he became very sick and weak. One day during the morning prayer, the teacher invited the children to pray for Jagannathan's body and soul. That is something we usually do when somebody dies, so I didn't know if he was dead or alive, and I didn't know whom I should ask!"

When I was a child I used to ask my father: "When are you going to stay with me?" And he used to answer, "When the problems of the poor people are solved." I used to think it was a question of days, and every day I thought: "Today, the poor people's problems will be solved."

I saw Bhoomi very rarely, as he was studying in another town. Because there are nine years between us, he used to treat me like a daughter, and ordered me around. But now we are even closer than brother and sister. We have such an amazing mutual understanding at the spiritual level.

Our parents are such an extraordinary couple. I often tell my mother that I could not exist with such a man, always pushing her to work and work. But she says she likes it this way, and that if she had not met a man like him she would have probably slept all her life, while with him she has been living a worthy life. When Amma stays with me, my father never calls to tell when he is going to arrive, but all at once Krishnammal starts cooking, and so we all know he is coming. They are such a high example for us that my brother and I would never accept anything less form a partnership. Their marriage has been a love marriage, and so they never forced a partner on us, because they are people who practice what they preach!"

I tell her that it is really wonderful that she is not resentful toward her parents, and she replies:

"No, absolutely. It's true we haven't seen them much, but in the little time we have spent with them they have given us so much love."

A long time after I'm back from India I receive another precious story, sent to me from Cambodia: the memory of Bhoomikumar, first child of Jagannathan and Krishnammal.

Bhoomi remembers

"It is next to impossible for me to separate present from past and to travel down memory lane without considering the future. A future is contained in the present, and the past impinges continuously on the present. I could not just think of life with Jagannathan and Krishnammal without contemplating the 'here and now', for all their lives they have been addressing the problems of the rural poor in the present. In this sad period of wars and violence, with the destruction of the Twin Towers, American bombing of Afghanistan, and the escalation of the conflict between Israel and Palestine, the first memory that comes to my mind is the memory of a peace march…

The gentle sound of drums of Buddhist monks, the brushes of the Jain monks[2], the smell of home-baked bread and cakes, Vinoba Bhave's long silvery beard, often stained with curd… These are the images of the silent peace march toward Beijing that are still engraved on my mind. It was organised in 1962 by Gandhians and by the Sarvodaya Movement when the conflict between India and China escalated into war. It was a peace march that attempted to solve border disputes amicably between nations. If it had been successful, it would have made history, like the freedom struggle that liberated India from her colonial past through nonviolent civil disobedience. Whether the peace marchers were only naïve, simply lofty idealists, only time will tell, but it was a fact that they were not allowed to cross the Indo-China border for security reasons.

Though at that time I did not understand the significance of the march, I recollect with awe the idealism and the conviction that was the moving spirit behind that event. And how fortunate was I to be with Jagannathan and Krishnammal in the midst of that and more!

My first memories have for me almost the consistency of dreams. They are memories of the magical years of the Bhoodan marches in Tamil Nadu. Every day, I was awakened at 4 o'clock and put on a jeep with the elderly and the sick, who were exempted from the foot march. Vinoba's soldiers instead marched to the next village in an atmosphere of 'prayerful penance', armed with determination, hope, and goodwill. Theirs was a pilgrimage to the 'temple of the hearts of people', as Vinoba used to say. Live like the poor, dress like them and walk with them was his message and dictum. If I think about it now, I cannot even conceive that such a movement has happened at all, so far has the world and India galloped away from those ideals and vision. During the padayatra, Jagannathan used to carry his dinner with him: flour made out of *ragi*, the 'poor man's brown millet', that nowadays is prescribed by pediatricians as the best weaning food for babies, but ironically shunned by people who consider it below their dignity to consume. Every evening, Jagannathan used to mix the ragi flour in hot water and relish his porridge. He would say to me: "Bhoomi, come here and share this *paysam* (sweet porridge served on festive occasions), or rolled it into small round balls and place them over my palm as *laddhus* (a typical South Indian sweet, also offered to deities.)

After reaching our destination, and a light meal, we would move to the center of the village, next to a temple or under a sacred tree, where people had already assembled for the evening. Most of the villages had no electricity. There was just a kerosene or a gas lamp, with insects of all kind swirling about, attempting to illuminate the sleepy faces of the villagers, full of enthusiasm and curiosity about those people dressed in khadi who were appealing to all to donate land in the name of Vinoba and Gandhi. The evening meeting used to start with a prayer, and I had the privilege of singing songs from the *Thiruvasangam*, an ancient Tamil spiritual text. Then someone would sing 'awareness songs' highlighting the travails of the landless poor, inviting the 'haves to share their riches with the have-nots'. The songs, full of sorrow and suffering, would bring tears even to the eyes of the hard-hearted. Jagannathan and Krishnammal would talk about the vision of Gandhi and Vinoba, and how the landed gentry had voluntary surrendered their lands in the neighboring villages. We marched ceaselessly from village to village, and Krishnammal used to say, "There is not village in Tamil Nadu where I haven't placed Bhoomi's cradle during Vinoba's padayatra, and nowhere where he did not sing his prayer songs."

When then my parents worked in the Batlagundu area together with Keithan, I was left to fend for myself, occasionally going to school and spending the rest of the time in a local restaurant, yielding to the promise of crisp dosas. With the little money that was given as an incentive to go to school, I would skip out and see movies like "The Call of Tarzan", which I saw at least five times. In the meantime, Jagannathan and Krishnammal were visiting remote villages, most often by foot. Everyone in the village where the ashram was located were curious about Jagannathan and Krishnammal, the 'couple wearing khadi', and at the water well they used to ask me to which caste I belonged. Later, I was told I used to answer with no hesitation that I belonged to the 'Bhoodan caste', to the bafflement of the women of the neighbourhood. They were surprised there was such a caste (there is none of course) and what this little boy of six replied without batting an eyelid.

I never knew the caste system, as I grew up in such an atmosphere of noble idealism and humane values that it was anathema even to mention the word 'caste'. Much later, after completing school, I was standing in a queue to get the application form to join the university. The clerk sitting at the desk asked everyone which caste they belonged to so as to give them the right form, as there was a government quota for different castes. I didn't know what to do, and neither had the guts nor was so naïve to answer 'Bhoodan caste' again. So when my turn came, I mumbled to the clerk that I belonged to the same caste as the candidate before me in the queue, and got the application form.

I have been so privileged to be born amidst such heady times to very special people who dedicated their life to free India from colonial rule and vowed to marry only in free independent India. Jagannathan's wedding promise to Krishnammal is to be remembered: "Do not expect any wealth or comforts from me. We shall have no property—even the vessels we use at home shall be made of mud, so that when we move on, it shall be easy to abandon them." Hand in hand they chose a difficult path, walking along on a long and hard but unique journey.

My memories of the Workers' Home in Gandhigram are also rich and beautiful. At any given time, 30 to 40 youth lived in the ashram, learning to spin, weave, throw pots, keep bees, along with the rigorous discipline of non-possession, voluntary poverty, and self-sufficiency. We used to shuttle between Gandhigram and Kaniavapatti, the ashram started by Keithan. There were many foreigners who used to come and stay with us, I remember two Germans who brought a solar energy machine to bake bricks, a couple of Mexicans who found a way to build tables using peanut shells, and then French, Italians, Israeli, Japanese, Americans, people from all over the world would come to visit the ashrams and spend time with us.

In Gandhigram, I was darling to everyone, so much so that Jagannathan used to be called Bhoomi's father, and my sister Sathya was jealous. I had a wonderful childhood, petted by everyone and affectionately called 'Bhoomiraja-motai-paiyene"—Bhoomi the bald-headed prince—and with no obligation to go to school. I spent my time collecting flowers and fruits and climbing trees. I don't think that many children had the opportunity to grow amidst so many people guided by high ideals, and by Gandhian principles and vision.

When in 1975, my father was in prison in Bihar and I was in the second year of medical school. I went to visit him. The journey was tough, but the experience was exhilarating. In prison, there were all the youth and the leaders who had taken part in JP's movement. The atmosphere was that of a second freedom struggle, and I could guess how it could have been during the initial struggle for independence. Jagannathan was in prison so many times that a close friend used to tease Krishnammal, inquiring. "Tell me, are you so unkind to your husband that he keeps rushing off to prison?"

Sometimes my father asks, with half-seriousness, "What am I going to leave to my children? We have no house, no land, no bank account!" He has not realized, or only realizes vaguely, what immense wealth he has left to both of us.

After a few days in Chengalpattu, we go back to Gandhigram, I will see Sathya again before flying back to Italy. On October 2nd, Jagannathan tells me that in the afternoon he would like me to record a declaration—a testament—whose importance will be clear to me from the very beginning. We sit in a quiet corner, and Jagannathan, now approaching 90, starts talking with deep concentration:

"Today is Gandhi's birth anniversary, and I am glad you are here to share what I think Gandhi would do today if he was alive.

There are many urgent problems in our country, but I think that the most urgent is the polluted atmosphere between Pakistan and India, which is getting worse and worse every day. The violence between the two nations, and not only in weapons, but also in the hearts of the people, is very deplorable and unfortunate. If Gandhi were alive, he would take up this problem first, and it would occupy his mind entirely.

Three years ago Pakistani soldiers entered the Kargil region of Kashmir, and since then India and Pakistan have been fighting. So how to bring about peace? Even during the freedom struggle, the Hindu-Muslim problem was very much alive, and British used it for their own benefit. They sometimes encouraged Hindus, sometimes Muslims, using their difference as an instrument for their rule and widening the Hindu-Muslim animosities.

Aware of this, when Gandhi started his freedom movement, a key part of his "constructive program" was for Hindu-Muslim unity. Even while fighting the British,he thought this unity was fundamental to freedom. Thanks to his efforts, many Muslims joined the national freedom movement. But as you know, when in 1947 we attained freedom, the country was divided. Gandhi was dead set against partition. He cried, "We are getting freedom, but it is like my body is torn in two pieces". He hoped to attain freedom for India as a whole country, but he failed, and Pakistan became a separate nation, later divided into West and East Pakistan (present-day Bangladesh).

Partition brought an enormous mass migration. Muslims migrated to Pakistan, and Hindus migrated to India. Hundreds of thousands of people. There was killing, killing, oh, terrible killing. Hindus killed Muslims, and Muslims killed Hindus, a terrible tragedy. Gandhi went first to Bengal and then to Bihar, the places where the massacres were worst. He walked from village to village to stop the incredible wave of violence. He spent the last days of his life like this. In his old age, he walked with his stick over uneven roads, bringing his peace message. He was successful, but only partially.

On August 15th, 1947, we attained independence. Lord Mountbatten, the British Viceroy, took down the British flag and raised the Indian. It was freedom. It is an extraordinary story that Lord Mountbatten himself took down his country's flag down, and raised the Indian one: this was the result of our nonviolent struggle. That day, everybody would have liked Gandhi to be in Delhi. Lord Mounbatten sent him a message, "Please, come: you are the father of the nation; you should be here in Delhi in this day, when your flag will be raised!" But Gandhi answered: "No, I will not come to Delhi. I'll be here, at the war front, trying to stop these terrible massacres. I'm in the middle of a terrible human tragedy. I can't come to Delhi."

To Gandhi, unity between Hindu and Muslims was such an important point, and he was killed by a Hindu fundamentalist, because he considered Muslims to be his brothers. Therefore, I think that if he were still here, his main concern would be how to bring about unity between Pakistan and India, so that this terrible war can come to an end. But who is thinking about this problem now? Nobody. Many Indians think, "Oh, the Pakistani Muslims are the enemy," and many Muslims think Hindus are enemies. This kind of inimical attitude is growing day after day. If we could find a nonviolent way to bring peace, it would be such an example to the whole world, just as Gandhi demonstrated that it was possible to

S. Jagannathan spinning cotton at Gandhigram, December 1998

attain freedom in a nonviolent way.

So what can we do?

In India, there are 135 million Muslims, more than in Pakistan, many of whom are really not happy living in India. They reside in India with their hearts in Pakistan. They are Indians but they do not like feel they are, they do not have a national feeling. So many Hindus consider them enemies. I think that Gandhi would first of all try to re-establish friendship and brotherhood between Indian Muslims and Indian Hindus. He would even give his life for that. He would fast for this brotherhood.

But Gandhi is not here, so what shall we do? I think that among Gandhi's followers at the moment there are not monumental personalities like Vinoba or Jayaprakash Narayan, but there are many devoted workers. We should then think about starting a movement to create peace between the two communities. We should first of all organize conferences between Hindu and Muslim leaders at the national, state, and district level. Then we should start a large women's movement. I think that women, who unfortunately are not really present in politics, can play a significant role to reconcile, unite, and pacify. They could have a tremendous impact.

Then there are youths, the easiest victims of extremism. They are used by extremists, and they are trained in bomb-making, weapons use, and organized in small armies. How many have already died in the Kargil area! So we should organise youth groups for peace.

Than there is the question of Kashmir, in contention between India and Pakistan. In that area, there is Jammu, with a Hindu majority, Ladakh with a Buddhist majority, and Kashhmir, which is mostly Muslim. Those three states used to be a single state sheltering three religions, but somehow immediately after Independence, Hindus were chased from the Kashmiri area, where they were a third of the population. I feel that Gandhi would evolve a nonviolent strategy to solve this conflict, insisting that in that area Hindus, Muslims, and Buddhists have lived together in peace for centuries. He would try to create an ideal community that could be an example for the whole world. Hindus should go back to Kashmir, with no weapons, inviting Muslims to go back to Jammu if they wish. Imagine an army of 10,000 satyagrahi in Kashmir, saying, "We want to come back home, and if you want to shoot us, do that!" It should be a transfer of population in a brotherly, human way, loving way.

So I think that we Gandhians should start a movement like this. Because of my age and my eye problems, I can't tour all over India, but I can ask other workers to start a national movement on Gandhian lines for Hindus-Muslim unity, and I am sure I can do something here in Tamil Nadu.

Even if our main objective is Gram Swaraj, the village republic, we can't ignore these problems. Solving them also means strengthening the Gram Swaraj movement.

The other burning problem in this country is still the caste

Jagannathan (left) with Prime Minister Jawarhalal Nehru at Gandhigram, circa 1950.

issue. The caste divisions were exacerbated as well by the British in Gandhi's times. Gandhi started a movement against untouchability, but our political system is reinforcing caste divisions more and more. Politics is dominated by caste. When a caste is dominant in an area, its representatives form a political party. Of course they don't do it directly in the name of the caste, but in reality it is like that, even if all the political parties proclaim they are against the caste system. It is a terrible situation. If we want to create village republics, caste has to disappear, just as religious conflicts must.

So I am planning a Manifesto for Gram Swaraj, for village autonomy, that should involve all the different groups and parties. It should be constituted around issues that can be understood by everybody. They should be mostly economic issues, especially centered on the land problem, which is common to everyone. It is a difficult task, but it has to be tried. I know I can find support in Tamil Nadu, because all the political leaders know me and appreciate our work. They know we do not belong to any political party, and our main objective is to give land to the landless. Our work has created a huge impact, and now we can count on the trust of people and political parties.

I think I could manage to reach an agreement to elevate politics from its caste basis to a politics based on solving major economic issues, in a new political approach. I have trust in this possibility, and I hope to be able to start this new job soon.

So these are the main problems I see in India. Because of my health, I cannot do too much, but I hope I can carry on this experiment at least here in Tamil Nadu. Therefore in this day of Gandhi's birthday I pray to be able to contribute to Hindu-Moslem unity, and to the elimination of the caste system, to arrive at nonviolent society and to the birth of village republics. This is my message on this day of Gandhiji's anniversary."

If Gandhi was alive. If there were thousands of Jagannathans and Krishnammals. If we were all just a little bit better, in India and throughout the world, or if at least we decided to try a little harder. But at least there are two of them....

Since 1999

Time has flown by, and it is already four years since I was in India, during which time I got married, and have been blessed with two wonderful daughters, Maya and Jasmin. I moved with my family to a World Wildlife Fund educational center near Asti, in northern Italy, where my husband and I are working to develop environmental education and eco-tourism programs.

Waiting for Jasmin to be old enough to enjoy a trip to India, I have managed to see Amma, Sathya, and Bhoomi, as they have all come to visit Italy. I also receive a steady stream of news from them on the latest developments, mostly about the prawn issue. The overall picture in India, as in other aquaculture nations, is not encouraging. There are changes in political leadership, but the despoliation of the land continues unabated, regardless of the legal status of the prawn farms. Tens of thousands of people continue to be displaced, groundwater destroyed, fishing and agricultural communities impoverished. There is money to be made.

The local pattern is well-established. LAFTI organizes large mass protests. Jagannathan starts fasting, politicians ask him to stop, and promise to take care of the problem and close down all the farms within a few months. Jagannathan halts his fast, because one of the principles of nonviolent action is to respect one's opponents when they express good intentions. He slowly regains his strength, and two or three farms are closed down immediately, while another four or five are opened up elsewhere.

My letters and press clippings file show the following:

- In May 2000, Jagannathan and Krishnammal embark on a 40-hour train journey to New Delhi. There, they begin a ten-day "People's Freedom Foot March". One of the objectives is to attract attention to the exploitation of India's natural resources on behalf of multinational interests, as is the case of intensive prawn farming along India's coasts.

- In August 2000, the Sarvodaya Movement launches a "Quit Multinationals Movement," in memory of Gandhi's "Quit India" resolution of August 9, 1942. Some 10,000 gather in Chennai, with one of their main demands being the implementation of the Supreme Court order, and the recall of the Aquaculture Authority Bill that would essentially nullify it. Another aspect of this protest is against a new government ban on commerce in common salt, thus requiring the purchase of iodized salt produced by multinational industries. While some minor health benefit might accrue to middle-class families as a result, the ban triples the price of salt, putting an even greater burden on the poor—those least able to afford it, and those most likely to engage in subsistence salt-gathering along the coasts.
- In December 2000, Krishnammal organizes a women's march to the Nagapattinam District Collector's Office with thousands of participants, heads covered in black cloth, requesting the implementation of the Supreme Court order.
- On January 26, 2001, Jagannathan commences a "Prayerful Penance" (a partial fast), and writes to the Prime Minister and the Chief Minister of Tamil Nadu, soliciting them to implement the Supreme Court order, and to assist the farmers and fisherman who have suffered as a consequence of intensive aquaculture. Thousands of people demonstrate all around the state in support of Jagannathan's requests. The Penance ends on March 21, when Tamil Nadu government officials sign a document committing themselves to meet Jagannathan's requests.

- On October 31, 2001, Jagannathan starts another fast, this time a "fast unto death", that attracts the attention of the media, with articles appearing in the newspaper titled, "A Gandhian struggle for saving ecology." After more promises from government officials, the fast is suspended.
- On September 12, 2002, a rally of more than 10,000 people is organized in the small town of Tiruvarur. Prawn farms have now extended their operations beyond Nagai-e-Millath District, and are destroying mangroves protecting the Muthuppettai Natural Reserve, one of the world's great bird sanctuaries.
- In November 2002, LAFTI organizes a 65-kilometer march in Nagai-e-Millath District. Police deny the marchers permits for security reasons, as the prawn companies have organized their own private armies of gundas to intercept the march. When LAFTI organizers reach Tiruvarur, they are met with news that the District Collection has ordered the closing of 25 prawn farms within 15 days. The attorney M.C. Mehta, the 'green' lawyer who filed the first case against the prawn farms, visits Tamil Nadu to study the possibilities of further legal action.

And so it goes. Messages from Krishnammal and Jagannathan are filled with news regarding their housebuilding projects (see Appendix C) and the youth hostels (see Appendix D), as well as the continuing cycle of droughts and floods, which is exacerbated by the land's increasing inability to sustain and protect itself. Meanwhile, the flow of capital into multinational coffers continues unabated, and more and more people are being forced off their land, or what is left of it.

Abroad, interest is picking up. In June 2003, a British non-governmental organization, the Environmental Justice Foundation, published a report titled "Smash and Grab—Conflict, Corruption & Human Rights Abuses in the Shrimp Farming

Industry" (the report can be found at www.ejfoundation.org). Making use of data, research, and interviews, the 30-page report documents a desperate situation among coastal communities in India, Bangladesh, Ecuador, Vietnam, Indonesia, Malaysia, Mexico, Philippines, Thailand, Honduras, Brazil, and Burma, where people have been killed, violently forced off their holdings, or required to move because they have lost their source of income. I have made contact with them, and we plan to meet as soon as possible to see if there is anything that Italian and English non-governmental organizations can do at least to inform consumers of this growing worldwide tragedy.

In October, an e-mail informs me that Krishnammal is on her way to Italy. She has been invited to join the peace march from Perugia to Assisi, which takes place every year involving people from all over the world. She is going to give some lectures in local schools and at other meetings in various parts of Italy. In the meantime, our friends from Modena have organized a seminar at the University to discuss the problem of prawn farming, and have involved local NGOs and environmental organizations. I am invited to introduce the issue and talk about my experience. We join Amma in Modena. She seems in good shape, and talks with enthusiasm about the experience of the peace march. But when it comes to prawns, she does not have any good news. The last, sad development is that Jagannathan was asked to go to the Supreme Court in Delhi to be a witness once more. But after a 40-hour train journey, an embarrassed secretary informed him that his hearing was postponed. So back to Tamil Nadu, another 40 hours on the train, this for a 91-year-old man.

A few days after the seminar in Modena, Krishnammal comes to our place to spend a day with us. She tells me a few more sad stories about the arrogance and the power of the aquaculture industrialists. Recently, for example, as an act of raw intimidation they sent something like a hundred vehicles filled with armed gundas to the place where the lawyer M.C. Metha was going to give a talk during his visit to Tamil Nadu.

She also tells me that more farms are opening all along the Indian coast. She tells me that Jagannathan is doing well for his age, but obviously can't move much anymore, and that now every time he starts a fast, in a few days he gets very sick, and his life is in danger.

How much suffering, how much sacrifice? Sometimes, I feel so powerless. What can we do from here? And so I wrote this book. And I had to, since after coming back from India I have been haunted by the words of a man living in a remote village in Tamil Nadu who, after explaining what the prawn industry had done to his life, said, "If you are going to write a book about Amma and Appa, please, write about what is happening to us here. We are losing our land and our livelihood. If they take our land, there is nothing else we can do here. Nothing at all. And we have nowhere left to go."

Krishnammal leaves to return to India to celebrate Deepavali (also known as Diwali in northern India) with her family. We promise to visit soon, and for the following days Maya (age 3) walks around with a *bindi* on her forehead, telling me she wants to go to Modena again to see Krishnammal, and asking "What are shrimps? Why don't we eat them?"

Prawns
An Unnatural History

When Jagannathan and Krishnammal began their padayatra in Nagai-e-Millath in 1992, they had no idea about the buzzsaw into which they would soon run. Neither had the villagers they met along the way, whose livelihoods had been destroyed, water table undermined and water poisoned, land taken and despoiled, and, ultimately, many of them separated from their children as they traveled hundreds of miles away to find work. There was precious little in their life experiences to prepare them for what they were now to face. Certainly, neither Jagannathan, nor Krishnammal, nor the villagers had ever eaten any prawns.

This, sadly, is not an uncommon tale in the Third World. So-called "free" trades runs indiscriminately over lives, land, water, and air, with decisions made continents away in corporate offices and development 'councils', among people who will never set foot on the land they despoil, and never will.

Before bemoaning both the lack of information and lack of self-determination among people in the Third World, it should be noted that much the same can be said of First World consumers. Goods make their way into our marketplaces and our consciousness and "demand", without any real comprehension on the part of consumers of the implications either for our own lives or health, or that of millions of others on the far side of world. Prices rise and fall without any semblance of understanding on the part of those who experience them. We like tasty food, and we purchase it while its true costs are hidden from our view.

In an increasingly global and interdependent world, our need to take responsibility for our behavior increases, even at such a time as our capacity to exercise it meaningfully is seemingly dissipated. While prawns may be seen as a symbol of our ability to afford to eat 'better' (the prawns, after all, do end up in our neighborhood supermarkets and on our salad bars), we are virtually as far from the corridors of economic power as those whose land was lost in producing them.

But we need to start somewhere, and, since this is after all a book, it is no small thing to start with information. Knowledge, as alive and aware individuals such as Jagannathan and Krishnammal would surely attest, is *not* power; but without knowledge there is no basis to build alternatives to the havoc that "free trade" represents for so many—in both First and Third World communities.

* * * * *

Prawns have been harvested in ponds created by natural tidal action for centuries. Wild larvae and other species are brought by tides into ponds and grow in low densities. Some are consumed by harvesters, with surpluses sold in village marketplaces, augmenting protein intake and providing small cash incomes to be used in local trade. Some of the prawns are eaten by young fish before the latter are able to make their way back to the sea. The prawns themselves feed on low levels of human waste and manure. In short, prawn aquaculture as traditionally practiced in many places has been part of sustainable, bioregional economies for hundreds of years.

It is also a practice that for the most part has now been destroyed. Seafood is currently among the most widely traded products in the world. For developing nations, total trade in seafood, according to the United Nations Food and Agriculture Organization (FAO) is greater than that of coffee, tea, rubber, and bananas combined. Prawns are now among the leading commodities. Some 1,083,641 metric tons were produced in 2000, with a value of more than $6.8 billion.

It is not surprising then that Third World nations found themselves pursuing the international seafood market. In the

1970s and 1980s, the World Bank, the Asian Development Bank, and U.S., Japanese, and European foreign aid programs provided massive loans and grants for the development of prawn aquaculture, promising export-led growth and high rates of investment return.

The problem was that, unlike the earlier forms of prawn aquaculture, no attention was paid to sustainability, and even less to impacts upon the land where this activity was to take place, or upon the people occupying this land. And, in fact, other than the biological nature of the final product, this new, intensive aquaculture had little in common with its forerunners. Ponds must be stocked with high densities of post-larvae (fry); feed is usually in the form of protein pellets; pond additives include antibiotics, pesticides, detergents, and growth hormones. Oxygen must be pumped into the water to accommodate stocking levels. Water must be replaced constantly, and fresh water brought from rivers or pumped from available groundwater sources.

Everywhere intensive prawn agriculture has been tried, the results are the same—massive profits for the few—death and destruction in its wake. What is so compelling about the journey of Krishnammal and Jagannathan in this regard, is that they quite literally walked into an awareness of this devastation even as it was occurring.

This is what they saw:

- **Destruction of the Mangrove Forests**—Mangroves are critically important to coastal ecosystems and communities. They link terrestrial and marine ecosystems, protecting shorelines from erosion, capturing sediments protecting coral reefs, providing spawning grounds for commercial fish species. They protect coast lowland rainforests from tropical storms and tidal erosion. They are critical to local biodiversity, harboring plants and animals that are virtually unique. About half of the world's mangroves have now been lost, the majority of that in the past two decades, with prawn farming as one of the leading causes.

Krishnammal and S. Jagannathan and supporters on "Quit Multinationals Day," August 9, 2000.

- **Loss of Biodiversity and Its Negative Impacts**—As already noted, subsistence and small-market prawn agriculture is native to many tropical and subtropical coastal regions. However, in the quest for more "productive" and "marketable" species, native species may be eliminated and with it a loss of genetic diversity. As a result, pathogens and parasites may wipe out entire stocks very quickly, leaving empty, polluted ponds in their wake.
- **Destruction of Bycatch in Harvesting Wild Post-Larvae**—Prawn tanks must be seeded with prawn juveniles or "post-larvae". These are caught be dragging fine-meshed nets around shallow waters. Other fish larvae and fry are discarded on beaches as bycatch, destroying the future productivity of other species.
- **Creation of Toxic Wastes and Suffocation of Prawns**—The intensive stocking of prawns, the engine of profit, contains within it the seed of its own destruction. Food eaten by prawns (usually some kind of high-protein fishmeal) ends up as waste. As waste piles up,

great bacterial plumes are created, consuming the available oxygen, thus weakening or even killing the prawns through suffocation. Toxic products, including ammonia and nitrites are created, decimating the harvest and all other species living in the tanks.

The only way to stave off this inevitable die-off even temporarily is to replace the water in the pond extremely frequently. But there is no available wastewater treatment, and polluted water is simply pumped into coastal rivers and streams, killing everything in its path, and emptying out into shallow coastal marine waters, obliterating the breeding habitats of many major species. Since the surface water is now polluted, the water to be pumped in must come from scarce groundwater resources. This, in turn, lowers the water table, often leaving shallower drinking and irrigation wells completely dry.

- **Destruction of Coastal Aquifers and Agricultural Lands**—In coastal areas, when groundwater is pumped at a rate greater that aquifers can recharge, the result is salinization. Surface water having already been polluted, now drinking water and irrigation wells necessary for the survival of villages and farms are destroyed. The land itself subsides. Salinated wastewater discharged into rivers and waterways is drawn back into irrigation canals, devastating crops, and causing lands, even those on which there were no prawn tanks, to be abandoned as salty waste, not viable for any form of agriculture. While it is theoretically possible with high capital inputs to reclaim such land, no such reclamation has ever occurred anywhere in the Third World.
- **Impacts of the Misuse and Overuse of Antibiotics, Fungicides, Parasiticides, Algicides, and Pesticides**—Given the intensive nature of prawn farming operations, disease is a constant threat, not only to

individual ponds, but to entire operations. Farmers thus use a wide array of chemicals ranging from antibiotics, pesticides, and disinfectants, to soil and water treatment chemicals, fertilizers, and hormone-laced feed additives. This, in turn, can lead both to antibiotic resistance in areas close to the farms where water is polluted, and in human consumers.

Each of these impacts carries with it tremendous human costs. As the shorelands have been submerged or salinated, as the agricultural lands have been destroyed or can no longer be irrigated, and as drinking water has disappeared, Krishnammal's children's hostels have now been filled up with children whose families have had to travel hundreds of miles away in search of bare subsistence. And as the spawning grounds of fish are gone, and what little "bycatch" is left is ground up for fishmeal to feed the prawns, the industry has spawned epidemic levels of malnutrition. Antibiotic resistance is growing, and diseases spreading, even as the prawn entrepreneurs attempt to use a wider spectrum of chemicals to stave off the inevitable collapse of the industry, but not without leaving the lives of millions shattered.

Krishnammal and Jagannathan know where this is headed. They are in regular contact with activists from around the world. A 2003 report from the Environmental Justice Foundation, published in England, provides a sense of what they are learning:

- In Malaysia, within 2-3 years of large-scale mangrove clearance, fisherman reported a loss of five-sixths of their income; catch declines in Bangladesh and in India of between 80-90% have been reported;
- In 1999, when a huge cyclone hit India, killing at least 10,000 people and making 7.5 million homeless, areas with intact mangrove forests were largely unaffected;
- In Sri Lanka, 74% of fisherfolk in prawn farming areas no longer have ready access to drinking water; in some

areas, potable water can only be found at depths exceeding 100-200 feet. Skin rashes from polluted water have become common;

- In parts of Sri Lanka and Bangladesh, in prawn farming areas, women must now walk three to four miles a day looking for fresh drinking water. Rather than attending school, children in these communities must also join the search;
- In Bangledesh, poor quality drinking water in prawn farming areas has resulted in increased illnesses and mortality among cattle. This has reduced the availability of dung fuel, resulting in less frequent boiling of water, with associated increases in human water-borne disease.
- In Indonesia in 1999, the spread of malaria in south Sumatra was partly attributed to abandoned prawn farms, fertile mosquito breeding grounds;
- In one area of Vietnam in 2001, 125,000 hectares of rice fields were converted to export-oriented prawn farms. Rice production, much of which was used to feed the local population, fell by 460,000 tons.
- Statistics from Ecuador indicate that while a single hectare of mangrove forest provides food and livelihood for ten families, a prawn farm of 110 hectares employs just six people during preparation, and a further five during the active season.
- In Thailand, nearly 50% of land used for prawn production was formerly used for rice fields. Over 20% of prawn farms in former mangroves are abandoned after 2-4 years; as many as 50% of the ponds are now abandoned, with neither plans nor expertise to restore the environment.
- In 2001, it was reported that 70% of World Bank-financed prawn ponds in seven Indonesian provinces were abandoned.
- In Ecuador, there have been thousands of cases of illegal

coastal land seizures for the purpose of setting up prawn farms. These often involve the use of military personal, with tens of thousands of acres that had been ancestrally owned for centuries seized.

- In Bangladesh in 2002, a senior police officer led a campaign of arson, bombing, and violence to drive 350 families away from land leased from the government to make way for prawn ponds. Murder, kidnapping, bomb attacks, violent intimidation, and rapes linked to the expansion of the prawn industry have become regular occurrences.
- In no fewer than 11 countries, people protesting the expansion of prawn agriculture have been murdered. Countries include: Malaysia, Bangladesh, Burma, India, Philippines, Thailand, Guatemala, Honduras, Brazil, Indonesia, and Ecuador.
- Occupational exposures to potentially harmful chemicals, including antibiotics, pesticides, and disinfectants, are common among prawn farmers and processors.
- Child labor is often used in processing. In 2002, it was reported that 200,000 children ranging in age from 3-12 worked 12-hour overnight shifts in Indian prawn processing units, earning between 20-40 cents per night. The U.S. Department of Labor, among others, reports child labor elsewhere in the prawn industry, including Burma, Indonesia, Cambodia, and Peru. In Burma, also according to the Department of Labor, forced slave labor is often used.

Of course, to many of us in the prawn-importing world, much of this seems remote. But perhaps only one example is necessary to indicate how close we really are.

And from the other side of the world…

"Welcome to Red Lobster's Giant ShrimpFest! All You Can Eat Succulent Shrimp! Only $9.95 for a Limited Time!"

screamed the television commercials during the spring and summer of 2002.

"Gigantic Seafood Sale" banners hung above the windows at the local supermarket outlets of the big chains—Safeway, Albertson's, and a whole host of the others. Virtually every week there was another sale on prawns. Syndicated articles on new recipes for barbequing prawns, sautéing prawns, stir-frying prawns popped up weekly in the newspaper, keeping a steadily increasing drumbeat.

"How low can prices go? That's what shrimp buyers and sellers alike want to know...Look for big summer promotions to move mountains of shrimp," proclaimed the featured article in the April 2002 issue of the Quick Frozen Food International newsletter. "Likening the confluence of event's in today's chaotic marketplace to the rare occurrence of "a 100-year flood," David Light, managing director of national accounts for Ocean for Ocean Seafood, said that this summer (2002) "will afford an opportunity to promote shrimp like never before." "What we have to do is get out there and communicate the great value of shrimp to restaurants and retailers," said John Filose, Vice President of Sales and Marketing for Ocean Garden Products. "We've got to go out and sell and stop whining."

So what exactly was going on? It actually didn't take a lot of detective work to find out. In fact, the very same industry newsletter touting the "mountains of shrimp" provided background as to its creation. In January 2002, the European Union (EU) banned the importation of all prawns from China and parts of Southeast Asia because of the presence of the antibiotic chloramphenicol. Chloramphenicol is a potent, broad-spectrum antibiotic drug that has been banned for use in food-producing animals in the European Union since 1994. It is used in human medicine only as a last resort, after other antibiotics have failed. Chloramphenicol is thought to cause leukemia in one out of 20,000 exposed human beings, as well as an irreversible form of aplastic anemia. It may also pose serious risks to fetuses and newborns, as it is associated with the often-fatal "gray baby syndrome", an inability of young livers to metabolize the chemical. (Chloramphenicol has also been found universally in honey exported by China, and most often used in food products—industrially baked bagels, muffins, cookies, etc.)

Needless to say, the Chinese were not happy. They were even less happy when Patrick Deboyser, a senior official for health and consumer protection at the EU's office in Tokyo, stated that there is no one in China who can explain how the drug got into food products. Without the Chinese adopting stricter legislation on food safety, setting up laboratories, and punishing companies that violate the standards, the ban would not be lifted.

Meanwhile, in March 2002, the crisis took a new turn in England, when another suspected carcinogen began showing up. According to a statement from Britain's Food Standards Agency, "Sixteen out of the 77 samples of shrimp and prawns tested positive for illegal residues of nitrofuran drugs." These cancer-causing substances, used to kill microorganisms, are banned for use in food production throughout Europe. Prawns sold by leading food retailers in the United Kingdom—Tesco, Iceland, and Safeway—were removed from the stores. Public recalls, notices, and newspaper ads warning consumers not to eat prawns already sold were published throughout the country.

So where did all the prawns go? The U.S. Food and Drug Administration's (FDA) Director of the Office of Seafood, Division of Program and Enforcement Policy Mary Snyder was quoted as saying that in the past five years of testing, they had found only seven cases of excessive chloramphenicol residues. What she didn't say was that FDA tested only a small fraction of seafood imports relative to its European counterparts, and that FDA standards were set at a level *1,567% higher* than those of the EU and Canada (5 parts/billion as opposed to 0.3 parts/billion.) When asked if the uproar over chloramphenicol residue in Europe may cause the U.S.

to lower its tolerance levels, Snyder replied, "I hope not. It would be better to do a risk assessment." However, the FDA did note, "Due to the unpredictable effects of dose on different patient populations, it has not been possible to identify a safe level of human exposure to chloramphenicol."

And so the "mountain of shrimp" (perhaps it would have been better to call it "an avalanche of shrimp") piled up on American shores, and the same Safeway stores (not to single them out as in any way special) that had pulled the sale of the product in England now held "Giant Seafood Sales". In October, once the mountain had been reduced to a rabbit hill, and Americans had eaten their fill, the FDA, without any additional risk assessment, lowered its tolerance levels to match those of the Europeans.

Resources

The Industrial Shrimp Action Network consists of 25 organizations from 22 countries, with members from Kenya to Thailand. It is a source of news, action alerts, and reports related to shrimp aquaculture worldwide, and works to works to "halt the expansion of destructive industrial shrimp farming with such consequences as impoverishment and displacement of local communities, degradation of mangrove forests and other coastal and inland ecosystems, loss of agricultural land, pollution, and the loss of cultural and biological diversity." They have published an excellent guide to the issues *Prawns to Trade, Prawns to Consume,* which is available on their website.

Industrial Shrimp Action Network
Isabel de la Torre, International Secretary
14420 Duryea Lane
Tacoma, WA 98444 U.S.A.
phone: (253) 539-5272
e-mail: isanet@shrimpaction.org
Website: www.shrimpaction.org

The London-based Environmental Justice Foundation (EJF) "trains, equips and supports communities and organizations who are directly affected by environmental abuses. Working with our partners, we investigate, expose and combat problems, and develop solutions for the future." In June 2003, in partnership with the American organization WildAid (www.wildaid.org), EJF published a major report *Smash & Grab: Conflict, Corruption & Human Rights Abuses in the Shrimp Farming Industry*, which is available on their website.

EFJ has also been spearheading a campaign against the use of the pesticide Endosulfan in the Third World. Long banned in the United States but still exported, endosulfan is an acutely toxic, easily absorbed pesticide strongly associated with central nervous system disorders, severe neurological damage, mental retardation, and cancer. It is extremely persistent in the environment, and is used on export crops ranging from cashews to coffee. Reports are available on their website.

Environmental Justice Foundation
5 St. Peter's Street
London N1 8JD U.K.
Phone: 44 (0) 20 7359 0440
e-mail: info@ejfoundation.org
Website: www.ejfoundation.org

Roofs and Walls.... On a Solid Foundation

The watershed event that brought Krishnammal and Jagannathan to the Nagai-e-Millath (then Thanjavur) District on Christmas Day in 1968 was the burning down of a house, with 43 women and children inside. For the harijans of the area, the destruction of their homes was not an especially uncommon occurrence. The burning of harijan hutments, these usually being confined to the very edge of a landlord's or temple's property, and outside the boundaries of the main village, had been a tool used repeatedly and over centuries as a way to instill terror in an entire community. It was used to reinforce the caste system, to prevent protest against low wages, to reinforce political hegemony, and, finally in its modern twist, to silence community outrage against the proliferation of prawn farms destroying the area's agricultural lands, mangrove forests, fisheries, and water supplies. In one village in Nagai District—Thennampattinam—in early 2000, while people marched on the new and illegally operated prawn tank owned by the Swarna Matsya ("Golden Fish") Company, agents of the company came to the village and set every house ablaze.

The houses are not much to start with. Generally speaking, they are made of mud, straw, and thatch, with palm fronds for roofs, and are without doors or windows. While they remain relatively cool in the heat, ventilation for cooking is poor. The straw attracts insects. Rodents, escaping floods during the rains, live in the roofs. Children sleep next to puddles on dirt floors, and are attacked by mosquitoes. The huts are impossible to keep clean, and are muddied throughout the two monsoon seasons.

As the cycle of drought and floods related to the monsoons has been aggravated by mangrove destruction caused by aquaculture expansion, the effects on the housing of the poor have been particularly devastating. Homes are literally washed away in torrential downpours and battering winds. Roofs are blown off, and can no longer be easily replaced, as palm trees have been uprooted to make way for prawn tanks.

From the very inception of their land reform-related activities in Nagai District, and especially with the founding of LAFTI in 1981, the Jagannathans—and particularly Krishnammal—have been trying to find ways to ensure decent housing for the rural poor. "Getting the land is a means to a livelihood," notes Krishnammal, "But a real house is a symbol of having gained a living. A home is what roots one to the land."

But trying to figure out how to go about it was not easy. Various government schemes had providing "houses" in the past. These usually consisted of one ten-foot by ten-foot room, with poor ventilation, and almost always with a tin or aluminum roof. The sun baking down on the roofs often turned these "houses" into ovens. Worse, they were often erected far from the fields their intended occupants worked, and far from their traditional village sites. It used to be that in traveling through Tamil Nadu one would see these houses used as goat or cattle pens in the evenings. Now, for the most part, they are abandoned.

There is virtually no wood to be found. Women will often traverse dozens of miles gathering what little in the way they can of twigs and fallen leaves to stoke fires for cooking. Local brickmaking was out of the question, as no one could afford the fuel necessary to fire the kilns (though in several villages in the mid-1990s, in order to train villagers in masonry skills, houses have been constructed of imported brick.)

And then Krishnammal hit upon an idea: cinderblocks, or, as she calls them, "hollow bricks". They require no fires, and no specially imported materials, just sand (of which there is an abundance), fine gravel (still has to be brought to the area, but from less 100 miles away), lime (the area is coastal,

Anjammal's house, before and after, Nallur, Tamil Nadu, 2002.

so there is plenty), mortar, and lots of labor. Cinderblock also has the advantage of requiring little maintenance, and does not retain heat. Krishnammal discovered some very simple machinery (picture below) that, with the required labor, could be used to fabricate cinderblocks. The plan was to fabricate enough cinderblocks to sell into the booming local cities, especially Nagapattinam, where they are at a premium, and use the profits to purchase the necessary raw materials to make enough cinderblocks so that people—men, women, and children—could build their own homes. In the process, villagers would be trained as masons and roofers, occupations in great demand, so that they could supplement their meager agricultural incomes.

In 1999, a fundraising appeal to American homeschoolers, Quakers, and friends of LAFTI raised enough funds to

purchase two of these machines. As a practice, LAFTI has set about building entire villages at one time, enlisting entire communities to build their own homes. Each house consists of 352 square feet, with a vestibule in front (often used for bicycle storage), a living area and a kitchen, and a planned kitchen garden in the rear. The buildings are usually close together, either in a square or circle if such is the traditional local pattern, or in a row by the road, the purpose being to maintain or increase community conviviality. Other agencies, most notably those from Italy, have stepped forward to raise funds for raw materials, as they did in the case of Thennampattinam (where brick was used).

Occasionally, negotiations with local governments have sped up the process. In May 2003, in the very remote village of Ramapuram, which had been partially destroyed in the most recent monsoon, local officials agreed to provide the

Hollow brick-making machine, Nagai District, 2002.

funds for clay tile roofs, if the rest of the funds could be found elsewhere. The local villagers raised the necessary funds for building foundations among themselves. Outside agencies provided funds for building materials. Relying only on local labor from the village, using both brick and cinderblocks, 30 homes were constructed in 30 days.

Even in the middle of the struggle against national and multinational aquacultural interests, Krishnammal dreams of building 10,000 new homes. "No one would have ever dreamed we'd have the land," she says, "Now our dreams are even bigger."

Tax-deductible contributions for aiding in the house-building efforts can be send to:

In North America:
Gandhian Foundation
340 Pine Avenue
Deptford, NJ 08092

Seasoning the bricks, Nagai District, 2002.

In Europe:
Overseas
Via Caselnuovo R. 1990/2
41057 Spilamberto (MO)
e-mail: overseas@overseas1971.org

"And What About the Children?"

Among the first casualties of the ecosystem despoliation resulting from the aquaculture invasion were children. The salinization of the soil brought down land yields, and with it the need for sowing and harvest labor. Often already malnourished, families found themselves on the threshold of starvation. With sources of groundwater increasingly polluted, women, in addition to their existing burdens, had to scour the area further afield for potable water. Children still in school often had to be pulled out to aid in the search, or to care for even younger ones. Families were pushed to the breaking point.

And sometimes over the brink. Families were broken apart as fathers traveled hundreds of miles away, often as far as the neighboring state of Kerala, in search for what meager agricultural employment was to be had. Entire communities were uprooted, sometimes to make way for the prawn farms, sometimes literally washed away in floods, and still others as their ties to the soil were severed in the search for bread.

Beginning in 1994, people began to approach Krishnammal about finding ways to care for the growing number of children without any active guardians. She began by setting up a hostel in Valivalam, which now has 100 girls. Her own home ashram in Kuthur has 40 boys, and the Jagannathans' old home center in Gandhigran has 55 boys and girls.

Mostly through the aid of Italian non-profit agencies, LAFTI manages to feed, clothe, house, and educate each child at a cost of approximately $125 per year. Each ashram is organized around the leadership of an older "uncle" or "aunt", but the children mostly organize themselves to care for their own needs, making use of their own individual talents. During my last visit to the Gandhigram hostel, I watched a 10-year-old "tailor" teach other children how to repair their own school clothes. Others care for farm animals, help with rice cultivation, and replant banana, lemon, coconut, and mango trees, organize evening prayers, and help with kitchen gardens, cooking, and composting.

LAFTI works hard to ensure children remain connected to at least one family member, for, in traditional communities, loss of family connection may also involve a loss of self-identity. Students are also organized in teams to work on drought relief, collecting rice and funds from the community, and redistributing them to those who have been hardest hit. They also receive occupational training, and some the opportunity to advance to higher education.

Funds to support the hostel project may be sent to:

In North America:
Gandhian Foundation
340 Pine Avenue
Deptford, NJ 08092

In Europe:
Gruppo 1%
Via Baconi 1
41029 Sestola (MO
Italy
e-mail: gruppounopercento@overseas1971.org

Notes

Introduction

1 Through much of the world, the words "prawn" and "shrimp" are used interchangeably. "Prawn" is more commonly used in India and in Great Britain; "shrimp" in the United States, though "prawn" often denotes larger varieties. A distinction can in fact be made between coldwater shrimp, which tend to be much smaller, pink, and which are commonly harvested in the Pacific Northwest of the United States, and warm water varieties, which are often intensively farmed. "Prawn" will be used throughout the text.

2 A note on Tamil names: for men, the second name is one's given name. The first name, always abbreviated to a single letter, is one's father's given name. S. Jagannathan's son, for example, is named J. Bhoomikumar. Women adopt their father's given name as their last name, until married, when they take their husband's given name in its place. S. Jagannathan's wife is thus Krishnammal Jagannathan. Their unmarried daughter is Sathya Jeganathan. The difference in English spelling is a matter of personal choice, and would not show up in Tamil.

3 Slang for vegetarian.

4 Radiation leaks have become endemic to India's nuclear plants, with more than 300 incidents of a serious nature contaminating workers. The secrets regarding these incidents seem to leak as quickly as the plants themselves, with some scientists believing that a Chernobyl-style disaster is just a matter of time. See the *Christian Science Monitor*, October 11, 2002.

5 The work of Michael Mazgaonkur, Swati Desai, and a whole new generation of neo-Gandhian activists in this regard is a real eye-opener. Read about Michael's visit to the World Bank headquarters in Washington, DC at www.rediff.com/news/2002/oct/16ash.htm

6 Gandhi himself was to write that the three greatest influences upon his life were Ruskin, Tolstoy (with whom he had an extended correspondence), and an obscure 25-year-old Jain jeweler and poet, named Raychandbhai (also known as Rajchandra), living in his hometown. Gandhi considered him the greatest of the three influences. See Gandhi, M.K., *The Story of My Experiments with Truth,* Part II, Chapter 1. Boston, MA: Beacon Press, 1993.

7 Kumar, Satish, *Path Without Destination.* New York, NY: William Morrow and Co., 1999.

8 See Appendix C.

9 See Appendix D.

Chapter One

1 A tank is a man-made collection point for surface and rainwater. It is often used for ritual bathing, as a place for meditation, and as a community gathering place, and serves as the center of towns and villages. In many communities, untouchables were forbidden from entering or even walking anywhere near the tank, for fear on the part of higher castes Hindus that the untouchables would pollute it by their mere presence.

2 An office for the collection of taxes. District Collectors are considered important local officials, though they are often not native to the area in which they work.

3 This would be a particularly noteworthy, and a not very comfortable luxury in the south Indian climate.

4 A holiday festival of lights celebrating the reunification of Rama and Sita, and the defeat of the evil ten-head demon king Ravana. In northern India and elsewhere, it is better known as *Diwali.*

5 In Hindu systems of thought, there are generally considered to be four stages of life: the student phase, also known as *brahmacharya*, and during which there is an expectation of celibacy; householder phase; forest-dweller phase; and renunciation or *sannyasin* phase. It is not wholly uncommon, however, for someone to declare themselves a sannyasin at another, earlier time of life.

6 Toyohiko Kagawa (1888-1960) was a Japanese Christian evangelist, pacifist, and social activist, who traveled throughout the world.

Chapter Two

1 Prior to British rule, India had been wholly self-sufficient in cloth, with village spinners and weavers providing for all needs. When Gandhi first searched for a spinning wheel (as he writes in his autobiographical *The Story of My Experiments with Truth*), the domination of the British had become so complete that he couldn't find a single working wheel in the entire country.

2 Krishnammal believes they met much later, in 1945.

3 *Siddha* is an ancient Tamil system of medicine, with significant use of medicinal herbs.

Chapter Three

1 E.F. Schumacher (1911-1977), author of *Small is Beautiful: Economics As If People Mattered* (1973). Today, there is a college named after Schumacher in South Devon, England, committed to "providing a place

and space where the implications of the profound changes in world-views now surfacing in so many fields of human thought and endeavors can be studied—and lived—in some depth. It was founded by Satish Kumar, editor of *Resurgence* Magazine and a former Jain monk, who has provided a vital, ongoing link between post-Gandhian thought in India and the best of the new philosophical, economic, ecological, and spiritual thinking in the West.

Chapter Five

1 A term of endearment ("dear one"), the name was given to him by Gandhi. Interestingly, it is usually a female name.

2 A Hindu scripture, actually part of the Indian epic *Mahabharata*, the *Bhagavad Gita* is a dialogue between the hero Arjuna and his chariot driver Krishna, as they assay the field of the ultimate battle, on the nature of God and the universe, and on the duty of human beings living in the world.

Chapter Seven

1 The name "Lila" means laughter.

2 The idea of a *Shanti Sena*, or peace brigade, was first proposed by Gandhi as a trained nonviolent interventionary force that could put itself between two warring factions, communities, or even nations. Of course, Gandhi himself was a one-man *Shanti Sena*. But variations on this idea have been taken up by international pacifist organizations for the past 50 years, and have operated in Latin America, the former Yugoslavia, around the Wounded Knee Reservation in South Dakota, and in various parts of Asia. One of the most recent incarnations of the concept is the Nonviolent Peace Force, which is setting up unarmed transnational intervention teams to step between warring communities in Sri Lanka. See www.nonviolentpeaceforce.org

3 A spiritual leader of the Chipko ("Hugging Trees") ecological movement in the Himalayan regions of northern India. See http://resurgence.gn.apc.org/articles/goldsmith.htm

4 Tireless organizer of a movement to stop construction of the World Bank-financed Sardar Sarovar Dam (and 3,165 smaller dams) in western India on the Narmada that would display and destroy the livelihoods and culture of more than half a million people, many of them tribal. See www.narmada.org

5 India's best known ecological scientist and ecofeminist, founder of the Research Foundation for Science, Technology and Ecology, and author

of numerous books and publications. See www.vshiva.net

6 Acclaimed and controversial Booker Prize-winning author of *The God of Small Things*, and winner of the U.S.-based Lannan Foundation's Prize for Cultural Freedom, who has used her fame to confront "Empire" in all its forms. See www.arundhatiroy.org.uk

Chapter Eight

1 Thanjavur District is now known as Nagai-E-Millath District.

2 Guerrillas espousing Marxist ideology, particularly active in Bihar, and who often promoting armed peasant rebellions against landlords.

3 CPM—Communist Party of India, inspired by Russia, and CPI-M — Communist Party of India-Marxist, inspired by China.

4 A round mark, usually red, and made of material, set on the forehead. Originally, it was said to represent a third eye: we have two eyes to see out into the world, and one to see inside ourselves.

5 Telagana is an area of Andra Pradesh where, soon after India's Independence, a violent peasant riot, backed by the Communists, took place (some 20 years earlier!)

Chapter Nine

1 *Lungis* are always colored and often in colorful patterns, and would most often be worn by laborers, though others might wear them at home. Muslims always wear lungis in plaids and checkerboard patterns; Hindus and Christians will wear floral and other designs as well. *Dhotis*, in contrast, are virtually always white (there are rare exceptions for pilgrims and holy men), and are not sewn together.

2 Note that it was Krishnammal who, over Jagannathan's objections, moved their base of operations to Valivalam to begin with!

Chapter Ten

1 An actress turned successful politician, a common occurrence in Tamil Nadu.

2 Currently, Chinese prawns are banned in the European Community, which is why there is a glut in the U.S. market. See Appendix B

3 An independent non-profit "organization of organizations", with an international secretariat in Penang Malaysia, disseminating information and coordinating action on issues related to development, the Third World, and the North-South divide. Check it out at www.twnside.org.sg

Chapter Twelve

1 Following her medical degree earned in India, Sathya held a fellowship at the Johns Hopkins University School of Public Health.

2 Jain monks sweep the soil in front of their feet when they walk in an attempt to avoid killing any living creature, and they wear a piece of cloth on front of their mouth to avoid inhaling insect, or microbes as they are breathing, killing them in the process.

About the Author, Editor, & Mapmaker

Laura Coppo (author) is a former researcher at a peace center associated with the University of Turin, Italy, specializing in Gandhian thought and issues related to the environment and social justice in India. She currently works at a World Wildlife Fund environmental education center in the Piedmont region of Italy, when she lives with her husband and two young daughters.

Writer and lecturer **David H. Albert** (editor) has been associated with the work of S. Jagannathan and Krishnammal Jagannathan for almost 30 years. He is the author of several recent books on homeschooling and on the uses of storytelling, and was founder of New Society Publishers. He currently resides in Olympia, Washington.

Mapmaker Lauren McCann, age 9, lives in Olympia, WA.